Brazier makes this medieval Japanese text highly accessible to the modern reader – and to the student of Dōgen – by focusing on the text as a fundamental guide to Zen B[illegible]hist practice. His interpretation also locates the text wi[illegible]philosophy and teaching of Chinese Taoism, whic[illegible]meaning and also reflects the importance of [illegible]China. Throughout Brazier masterfully [illegible]aching and inspires us with its fund[illegible]

– **Ryugin Rita Cumming**[illegible]Center

This is a beautifully written b[illegible]y readable and full of precious insights. This classic te[illegible] Zen Buddhism comes to life through Brazier's translation and comments. I have added it to my shelf of spiritual classics.

– **Miguel Farias**, DPhil., co-author of *The Buddha Pill*; Director of the Brain, Belief, & Behaviour Lab

As an 'all round Buddhist' in scholarship and practice, and as a psychotherapist and philosopher, Brazier offers fascinating and new perspectives on Dōgen's personal life, vision and work. Further, by taking Dōgen as a starting point for a critical consideration of our contemporary vision of Buddhism that so easily reflects only what suits our prior expectations and preferences, he makes us reconsider our own understanding and practice. In short: enriching and definitely worth reading!

– **Willem Scheepers**, Zen teacher and Dharmaholder in the Soto lineage of Maezumi Roshi

David Brazier's remarkable book transcends the limited and stereotypical perception of Dōgen prevalent in the West. It does so by placing Dōgen squarely within the broader religious milieu of his time and capturing Dōgen's distinctive spiritual insights expressed in his *Genjō Kōan*.

– **Kenneth K. Tanaka**, Professor Emeritus, Musashino University, and Past President, International Association of Shin Buddhist Studies

The Dark Side of The Mirror

Also by David Brazier

A Guide to Psychodrama
Beyond Carl Rogers: Toward a psychotherapy for the 21st century
Zen Therapy
The Feeling Buddha
The New Buddhism
Love and Its Disappointment
Who Loves Dies Well
Never Die Alone
Her Mother's Eyes and Other Poems
Not Everything is Impermanent
Buddhism Is a Religion
Questions in the Sand: Buddhist questions & answers
The Oxford Handbook of Meditation (2019)

THE DARK SIDE OF THE MIRROR

Forgetting the Self in Dōgen's Genjō Kōan

David Brazier

Windhorse Publications
17e Sturton Street
Cambridge
CB1 2SN
UK
info@windhorsepublications.com
windhorsepublications.com

Cover design: Katarzyna Manecka
Cover image: Picasso, Pablo (1881-1973): *Girl Before a Mirror* (Boisgeloup, March 1932). New York, Museum of Modern Art (MoMA). Oil on canvas, 64 x 51 ¼" (162.3 x 130.2 cm). Gift of Mrs. Simon Guggenheim. Acc. n.: 2.1938. © 2019. Digital image, The Museum of Modern Art, New York/Scala, Florence. © Succession Picasso/DACS, London 2019.

Typesetting and layout by Ruth Rudd
Printed by Bell & Bain Ltd, Glasgow

British Library Cataloguing in Publication Data:
A catalogue record for this book is available from the British Library.

ISBN: 978 1 911407 25 6

CONTENTS

PREFACE

Life is a near-paradox: one needs to take care of it and at the same time, in view of its transiency, relinquish attachments. A young Japanese boy, Ehei Dōgen, born 1200 AD, experienced this when he became an orphan at the age of eight. He then vowed to become a Buddhist monk to find solace and ordained at the age of thirteen. Some of the teachings he received stated that all humans have Buddha nature, implying that nothing needed to be done. Other teachings stated that becoming enlightened was too difficult for ordinary humans. This confused Dōgen. He practised without solving his pain. In 1223 he went to China as a senior monk in search of more original teachings. There he experienced humiliation, not being recognized as a monk. After several years, when there was a new abbot, Ju Ching, he was admitted, but only as a layperson. After witnessing an interaction between Ju Ching and another monk, unexpectedly enlightenment happened to Dōgen. From that moment his aim in life became to teach liberation by practice and transmission.

Back in Japan, in 1233 Dōgen wrote the enigmatic *Genjō Kōan*, consisting of just seventy-seven lines, describing the near-paradox and how to live it. Enlightenment transforms grief into energy to practise. Forget the obstructing self. After enlightenment blossoms still fall and weeds do grow, but one experiences these differently. Dōgen's work is a valuable bridge between Theravada and Mahāyanā Buddhism. Posthumously

Dōgen's teachings brought forth the Soto school of Zen Buddhism, still thriving in several parts of the world.

In this wonderful book, David Brazier gives a historic background, a new translation, extensive comments and a convincing interpretation of *Genjō Kōan*, clarifying the provocative language of Dōgen. Brazier uses words that are clear like the bright moon and intimate like a subtle poem. Many remarks in this book are essential for practitioners today. Meditation intent on self-enhancement will not bring enlightenment: one needs to be humble, practise and then surrender. Then, when one forgets the self, it may happen.

Henk Barendregt
Vipassana teacher and Emeritus Professor of
Foundations of Mathematics and Computer Science
Radboud University, Nijmegen, the Netherlands

PUBLISHER'S ACKNOWLEDGEMENTS

Windhorse Publications wishes to gratefully acknowledge a grant from the Triratna European Chairs' Assembly Fund and the Future Dharma Fund towards the production of this book.

Windhorse Publications also wishes to gratefully acknowledge and thank the individual donors who gave to the book's production via the 'Sponsor-a-book' campaign.

AUTHOR'S NOTE

My purpose is to write a readable volume, accessible and useful to the general reader and the Buddhist practitioner, that, nonetheless, contains enough precision for scholarly criticism to be possible. It is unlikely that every point that I make in this book will be the final and last word on the subject. Debate will continue and I hope my book will be a useful contribution.

My numbering of lines in the text is idiosyncratic as Dōgen did not number them. My numbers are simply for ease of reference to the text within this book. Other authors may number the lines differently or not at all.

ABOUT THE AUTHOR

David Brazier, aka Dharmavidya, born in 1947 in England, now lives in a hermitage in France when not lecturing internationally. He is a founder member and chief priest of the Order of Amida Buddha. Trained in Vajrayana with Chögyam Trungpa, then in Sōtō Zen with Reverend Master Jiyu-Kennett, he became a member of the Tiếp Hiện Order of Thích Nhất Hạnh, until the founding in 1996 of Amida Trust under the patronage of Pure Land Sensei Gisho Saiko and other Japanese teachers. Brazier's published works include *The Feeling Buddha*, *The New Buddhism* and *Love and its Disappointment*.

PART ONE

INTRODUCTION

I

CONTEXT

1.1 *GENJŌ KŌAN*

Genjō Kōan is a small masterpiece of religious writing composed in medieval Japan by Eihei Dōgen (1200–53), de facto founder of Sōtō Zen, the monk who went to China. In a series of analogies and memorable figures it succinctly sets out the gist of Dōgen's personal integration of Chinese and Japanese religion and is a manifesto for a life of propriety, naturalness and liberation that is coincident with a sudden change of religious consciousness. Many modern people might not put propriety, naturalness, liberation and religious consciousness together, but to Dōgen this was the solution both to his own personal spiritual problem and to the main religious questions current in his world in his time. Also, in his own mind, the designation 'the monk who went to China' probably had a great deal more meaning to him than the notion of being founder of a sect. He felt his mission to be that of bringing back the wisdom that he had found across the sea and, as we shall see, that wisdom was not narrow or sectarian, but partook of the whole universe of Chinese religious sensitivity.

Dōgen was Buddhist. He was not eclectic, nor was he woolly in his thinking. He was not saying that all religions are the same, nor even that the three religions of China were the same. Yet he was deeply influenced by Chinese styles of thought and spiritual vision, and these had their roots as much, or more, in Daoism and Confucianism as they did in Buddhism itself.

Although Dōgen's work was not greatly acknowledged in his time, he is now widely regarded as the most important writer on Zen in Japanese history. *Genjō Kōan* can be seen as the key to all his other writings and, consequently, is one of his most translated works.[1] As Sōtō Zen has become popular in the West, his message has spread to continents that he himself did not know existed. According to De Bary, Keene, Tanabe and Varley, "Although Dōgen died in relative obscurity, in modern times his writings have achieved wide recognition as works of religious and philosophical genius."[2]

Although *Genjō Kōan* is of enduring importance, it is impossible to fully understand Dōgen's text without an appreciation of the social, cultural and religious context of the time. There follows, therefore, an introduction that provides this background. Along the way we shall encounter some of the leading Buddhist figures of the period and I provide brief tables that explain who they are, when they lived, what they did and why they are relevant here.

I.2 WORKING WITH THE TEXT

As one reads the many translations of this work one can hardly escape the feeling that there is something here of great

1 For a translation and extensive commentary, see Okumura, Shohaku 2010. *Realizing Genjokoan: The Key to Dogen's Shobogenzo*, Somerville, MA: Wisdom Books. Some notable other examples of translations are, alphabetically by author, "Genjokoan – The Problem of Everyday Life" in Kennett, Jiyu 1972. *Selling Water by the River: A Manual of Zen Training*, New York: Pantheon Books: 142–5; "The Spiritual Question as it Manifests Before Your Very Eyes (Genjo Koan)" in Nearman, Hubert and Daizui MacPhillamy 1996. *The Shōbōgenzō or The Treasure House of the Eye of the True Teaching by Great Master Dōgen*, Mount Shasta, CA: Shasta Abbey: 52–60; "Genjokoan" in Nishijima, Gudo and Choto Cross 1994. *Master Dogen's Shobogenzo*, 4 vols, Woking: Windbell: 33–8; "Actualizing the Fundamental Point" in Tanahashi, Kazuaki 2000. *Enlightenment Unfolds: The Essential Teachings of Zen Master Dōgen*, Boston, MA: Shambhala: 35–9. Several more can be found on-line.

2 De Bary, William Theodore, Donald Keene, George Tanabe, and Varley, Paul 2001. *Sources of Japanese Tradition*, New York: Columbia University Press, vol. 1: 309.

importance. The radiance of the spiritual experience of the author shines through, warms the heart and tantalizes the mind. Nonetheless, after reading many renderings of the text into English, one can still be left wondering. What is Dōgen really saying? How do the beginning, middle and end of the text fit together? Are the wonderful figures and analogies in it all saying the same thing, or are they saying a variety of different things? If the former, why the repetition? And if the latter, why such diversity?

People writing about the text tend to use it as a starting point for saying what they want to say, but sometimes these expositions can seem more to be digressions than explanations. I was often left with the impression that much of what they did say, true and interesting as it might be, was only tangentially related to Dōgen's original thought. Now all of this may simply be due to my own ignorance and misunderstanding, but I have found that I am not alone.

The text is like a code insofar as virtually everything in it is an allusion to one or another aspect of established Buddhist thinking – and not just Buddhist, as we shall see. Dōgen's style is to rework existing terms, metaphors and well-established tropes of religious discourse to suit his purpose. For modern students of the text, therefore, the amount of possible research in teasing out all the implied meanings is virtually limitless. Furthermore, as I have repeatedly found, these discoveries can substantially revolutionize one's understanding of the whole text.

Given my experience of this text to date, I would not be surprised if I go on having further new ideas about it as long as I live. I hope that you will find it as fascinating. In order to tempt you in that direction I have included many notes, comments and reflections on translation difficulties as we go along. If you want to come near to replicating my experience, unless you are already familiar with it, I suggest that you could now pause in reading this book and go and read at least two other translations of the text and see what you make of them before continuing. They can easily be found on the internet.

One of the fundamental aspects of discovering the text is that it is full of images. There is the moon reflected in a dewdrop;

there are the fish in the sea and the birds in the air; there is wood and ash. There is a tendency, natural to the Western reader – this was certainly my case – firstly, to read these as a series of separate metaphors and, secondly, to take them as telling us something about how the world is. We evaluate them to see how they 'work' as metaphors. A metaphor depends upon a parallel process, extending meaning from one process that one knows well to a new one that the author wants to elucidate. However, Dōgen's images do not always work that well when taken in this way. He says that birds never leave the sky. Is that true? He says that ash has a past and a future, but firewood is cut off from its past and future. What does that mean? At first reading, it all seems a bit strange. Then the whole text ends with a cryptic little story about a fan in which the vital point seems to be that the wind is everywhere. What does that mean?

Another problematic aspect arises from the fact that the text is called a *kōan*, which loosely means 'problem'. My own Zen teacher spoke of *genjō kōan* as 'the problem of everyday life', which seems like a very useful concept, but how does it relate to the actual text? Dōgen does mention daily life in the text a couple of times, but it does not seem to be the central concept. All these and many similar questions are challenging and at first nothing seems entirely clear.

As I worked on the kōan I gradually started to get a feel for Dōgen's distinctive manner of expression. I started to see that the material is not a series of metaphors so much as of allusions. Dōgen was evidently well-read and deeply versed not only in Zen, but in Chinese religion as a whole. The text is not so much about the nature of the world, but more specifically and precisely a description of satori, 'enlightenment', its nature and how it functions. All this, I hope, will become clear as we go on.

1.3 WHO WAS DŌGEN?

TRAGIC CHILDHOOD

Dōgen came from a well-connected family, but suffered early misfortune. This is a common pattern with many significant Buddhist figures, from Śākyamuni onward. Dōgen's father died when he was two years old and his mother when he was eight. Thus, the first stage of Dōgen's life was a sad childhood in which the truth of impermanence was borne home very strongly. It is said that he decided to become a monk as he watched the incense smoke rise over his mother's coffin. During his infancy he must have imbibed some aristocratic values of nobility and perseverance, so he would have tried to be brave when his parents died, but it cannot have been an easy childhood.

A YOUNG MONK

The second stage, mid-adolescence, he spent at the great Tendai monastery of Enryaku-ji on Mount Hiei near Kyoto, the then capital of Japan. He was ordained at the age of thirteen and spent four years in a highly institutional environment learning the teachings of Tendai Buddhism, which gave rise to a strong inner conflict for him. The Tendai teaching of 'original enlightenment' – of which more below – suggested that fundamentally all is well with the world, yet for young Dōgen all had certainly not been well. Dōgen became a monk in order to deal with his grief and he was willing to work hard and practise hard with a view to spiritual liberation. Teachings that undermined this effort caused him confusion.

While at Mount Hiei, he came under the influence of a master called Kōin who told him that he might find the answer to his problem by specializing in Zen practice and that the very best course in this respect would be, if he could, to visit China. In those days, China was the prestigious source of ideas and practices, which gradually percolated from there to Japan. If one wanted to learn the best and most up-to-date practice, it was to China that one needed to go. Perhaps Kōin saw that this young man, who had a lot of drive, needed to put his energy into strenuous training and that Zen practice could meet that need.

STUDYING WITH MYŌZEN

People grew up earlier in those days. At age seventeen, Dōgen left Mount Hiei and went to the Rinzai Zen monastery at Kennin-ji, which was at that time under the direction of a thirty-three-year-old teacher named Myōzen, successor of the founder, Eisai, who had died two years earlier. Kennin-ji had the most Chinese style of Zen then available in Japan. Dōgen got on well with Myōzen, settled in at Kennin-ji and practised there, but did not manage to resolve his pain.

In 1223, Myōzen himself decided to go to China and Dōgen jumped at the chance to go with him. Myōzen's idea was to follow in Eisai's footsteps and bring the best practice back to Japan. However, he was never to return, dying in China in 1225. It is possible that some of Dōgen's later zeal to bring teachings back to Japan was driven by a sense of needing to fulfil the mission that Myōzen had been unable to complete.

IN CHINA

When they arrived in China, the Chinese immediately recognized Myōzen as a monk and he went to Tiantong monastery, where he remained until he died. Dōgen, however, had the humiliation of being told he was not a monk because he had not taken the right precepts in Japan. He was, therefore, left in the port at a loose end. This gave him time to read and to travel and he visited several important monasteries, had some illuminating encounters with various monks, and learnt a lot about Zen practice and organization, knowledge that would later stand him in good stead. At the time, however, his experience must have been frustrating as he waited for replies to his petitions to be treated as a monk, which, after considerable delay, were turned down.

Eventually, full of disappointment, he was about to find a boat back to Japan when he heard that a new abbot, Rujing, had been appointed at Tiantong. Dōgen thought it worthwhile to try once more and returned to Tiantong. Rujing had some sympathy for the situation of the foreigner and admitted him. On ceremonial occasions, Dōgen still had to stand with visiting Daoists rather than in the monastic ranks. However, he was admitted to the abbot's quarters – a privilege that he appreciated hugely.

One day, Dōgen was sitting in meditation in the hall. The monk next to him had dozed off to sleep. The master, Rujing, appeared and chastised the monk, saying to him, how could he sleep when the purpose of sitting in *zazen* was to cast off body and mind. Hearing these words, Dōgen had a great awakening experience. This satori was in due course confirmed by Rujing. Dōgen had found what he was looking for.

Dōgen stayed a further year or so studying with Rujing before returning to Japan. We can, therefore, see the period from age seventeen to age twenty-nine as the third major phase of Dōgen's life: a period of searching, wrestling with his personal spiritual problem, and arriving at a sense of meaning and direction through the experience of the care and patronage of his Chinese master. From then on Dōgen often referred to Rujing as 'the old Buddha'.

RETURN TO JAPAN

When Dōgen returned to Japan he was full of inspiration, enthusiasm and Chinese ideas. He went back to Kennin-ji, but found that he did not have scope there to practise in the way that he now wished. In 1230 he left and, as the famous poet monk Saigyō and the great controversial saint Hōnen had both done half a century earlier, he went to practise in a small hermitage in the mountains east of Kyoto.

Here he refined his ideas on the right way to practise and he gradually drew a following. Perhaps he hoped that history would repeat itself and he would achieve the same acclaim as his famous predecessors had done. They too were erudite monks who settled for a simple way of presenting the Dharma, and both, just as he, had been orphaned at a young age and become monks at Enryaku-ji, though Saigyō had spent a period as a soldier before 'leaving the world'. Now Dōgen was establishing himself in the same area that they had done. By 1233 he was able to found a centre that was to become his own monastery, Kōshō-ji. In the autumn of that year he wrote *Genjō Kōan*. We can, therefore, see *Genjō Kōan* as something of a manifesto. It was Dōgen hoisting his colours and making a clear statement of what he stood for.

Three independent monks			
Saigyō	1118–90	Quintessential poet monk	Exemplar
Hōnen	1133–1212	Famous religious innovator	Exemplar
Dōgen	1200–53	Leading writer on Zen	Author of *Genjō Kōan*

In investigating the background to *Genjō Kōan* we shall encounter a number of the key figures of the age. From among these, I would particularly like to single out Saigyō and Hōnen as reference points and make occasional reference to their lives and works to help put Dōgen into perspective. Since Saigyō, Hōnen and Dōgen are thought of as belonging to three different schools of Buddhism, they are not generally discussed together. However, at the time that Dōgen lived, these sectarian boundaries were not as deeply distinguished. Zen was not yet a distinct school in Japan. Saigyō's affiliations were very loose, and the Jōdo Shū (Pure Land School) that Hōnen established was as yet more an amorphous movement than a distinct organization. Dōgen was a religious innovator who had a highly poetic style. Hōnen was the greatest religious innovator and Saigyō the greatest poet of the time. They belonged to a generation before Dōgen and could be considered his spiritual grandfathers. Saigyō had been dead ten years when Dōgen was born and Hōnen died when Dōgen was eleven or twelve years old. Saigyō and Hōnen both became well known in their own time and even more so in the years immediately following their deaths, so they and their works would have been significant influences in the cultural world in which Dōgen lived his formative years.

In this fourth phase, from age twenty-nine to forty-three, therefore, Dōgen was trying to establish himself at the centre of Japanese life and culture. *Genjō Kōan* was written in this context. Dōgen was reaching out to laypeople as well as to actual and potential monastics. He wrote many of his most famous essays during this period.

LIFE IN THE NORTH

Dōgen now had his own temple and a small but keen following. His euphoria, however, did not last. He did not have Saigyō's solitary nature, but he did not have the common touch that Hōnen had been gifted with either. Hōnen was popular with the people and a friend of the prime minister. Dōgen did not attract such big crowds, nor did he gain favour with those in power. In fact, he soon found that being so close to the capital was not always an advantage. The Buddhist establishment did not view new developments favourably. Furthermore, he was developing a way of training his disciples that required concentrated attention. The distractions of the nearby city, not to mention political machinations and the attractions of rival Buddhist groups, were not conducive to focus and meditation. In 1243, ten years after writing *Genjō Kōan*, Dōgen moved his community to a more remote location in Echizen province to the north.

Moving to Echizen in the north was something of an admission of defeat.[3] Dōgen may well have gone through a period of depression at this time, which must have reawakened the grief of his early years. However, as at that earlier time, Dōgen's way out of the pain was, after a period of retreat, once again to throw himself into a demanding project. He may not have achieved great public acclaim, but he had around him some truly dedicated followers. Now, therefore, Dōgen's effort went into training this core group in the most rigorous way he could, calling upon everything he had learnt in China. The monastery they established was to become Eihei-ji, which remains the national centre for the Sōtō School of Zen in Japan. At Eihei-ji Dōgen was able to continue his writing and give many lectures, resulting in a considerable corpus of literature including the essays later arranged as the book *Shōbōgenzō*,[4] now regarded as his *magnum opus*, as well as the lectures that together make up the Eihei Kōroku, another important work.

---

3 Dōgen had been advised by Rujing not to get involved in worldly life and to establish himself in a remote place, in accordance with the Chinese 'mountain monastery' tradition. Now he had to admit that Rujing had been right.

4 正法眼蔵 (*Shōbōgenzō*) is variously translated. The first three characters signify 'the right (correct) Dharma eye'. The final character, 蔵, can mean a 'treasury' or 'storehouse', but it can also signify a hidden place. The character represents guarded valuables. The title thus suggests that the text will reveal the hidden secret of how to see the Dharma correctly.

In Echizen, Dōgen wrote fewer position statements and gave more talks. It must have caused him some chagrin to let go of his earlier hopes, but his own philosophy enabled him to cope with the setback. Inexorably the ironic dialectic of fate continued. Dōgen had failed as an evangelist to the public so now concentrated on what he was actually best at, which was training a group of talented people who would be his successors. These people then started to attract the public and some years after setting up in Echizen, Dōgen found himself conducting many fine precept ceremonies for the local lay population. It was on the strength of this public support and the work of these successors that the continuance of the Sōtō School was to rest. So, in the end, a certain kind of public support did come his way at last.

FINAL YEARS

It is also possible to divide these last ten years of Dōgen's life into two periods, in the sense that as he got older he placed more and more emphasis upon the fundamentals of the Buddhist religion: having faith, taking refuge, keeping the precepts, the thirty-seven fundamental doctrines, and making offerings to the Buddhas. This may mark a phase in his literary output, but I doubt that it really marks a change in Dōgen himself. I am inclined to the view that it was simply a matter of Dōgen 'coming out' more as he got older and had less to prove. In the years at Kōshō-ji he had taught what was distinctive in his own interpretation. In later years, still in his own style, he taught the bedrock upon which his religious life rested.

In 1253, Dōgen became ill and went back to the capital in search of a cure, but died there at the age of fifty-three, his great literary work still unfinished.

One can remember the landmarks of Dōgen's life in decades. At thirteen he was ordained, at twenty-three he went to China, at thirty-three he wrote *Genjō Kōan*, at forty-three he moved to Echizen and at fifty-three he died.

The above history is based mostly on Dōgen's own account. There are some issues about whether this account is trustworthy, especially the events in China, since there is virtually no external validation and the main witness, Myōzen, never came back to give his version. In the circumstances and pressure of sectarian competition Dōgen would have had plenty of motivation to exaggerate the aspects that portrayed him in a favourable light, and some points – such as Dōgen telling his disciples that people came from all over China to the funeral of Myōzen – do stretch credulity.[5] However, these controversies need not detain us. All agree that Dōgen wrote *Genjō Kōan* and, while understanding the context will certainly help us, our main purpose is to take it on its own merits.

It is also worth reflecting upon the parallelism between the lives of spiritual leaders. If we compare Dōgen with Śākyamuni and with Hōnen, for instance, we see that all three suffered bereavement in childhood, all three in due course embarked upon a spiritual quest that cost them a lot personally, all three arrived at a personal understanding that was sufficiently compelling to lead them to risk everything in their lives to convey it to others. All three then lived saintly lives, practised an evangelical mission, and faced many vicissitudes of fortune along the way that required considerable leadership skills. All three did their utmost to bring on members of their respective communities to carry forward the work after they were gone and each has left a distinctive legacy.

1.4 SUBLIMATION

Before continuing to fill in the historical background, let us turn to the emotional reality. Since oriental studies generally take place within academies, the focus of interest tends to be on ideas and intellectual formulations. However, ideas alone would not be sufficient to have generated a work like *Genjō Kōan* and, certainly, given the hazards involved at the time, would not have sufficed to send Dōgen across the treacherous sea to China.

In the foundations of this work are present the pain and anguish of a little boy watching the incense smoke rise over his mother's coffin. Buddhism seemed to promise relief, but

5 For a full discussion of these questions, see Heine, Steven 2006. *Did Dōgen Go To China?* Oxford: Oxford University Press.

what kind of relief and how? Dōgen was certainly willing to exert himself to the uttermost, however punishing the effort might become, but the chemistry of emotions is not a simple matter. There is no magic pill to overcome pain, nor is it simply a matter of trying harder and harder.

Consider Saigyō. He had also suffered. He and Hōnen lived through a period when the social situation was degenerating into a most terrible civil war.[6] He too had had bereavements and, it seems probable, had been broken-hearted from an ill-fated love affair. As with Dōgen, such factors contributed to his decision to become a monk. At first, as mentioned above, he lived in a hermitage close to the capital, but perhaps this was still too close to his old life. He went travelling and spent much time in the mountains. Like Śākyamuni, who was exemplar to all these masters, he threw himself into asceticism. Dōgen was also given to being very strict with himself and has left a legacy of a rather ascetic style of monastic practice. Grief resides in the body and in the mind. Sometimes it seems that they deserve the severest punishment for tormenting us so. For Dōgen, perhaps, the words of Rujing – to cast off body and mind – may have given permission that enabled him to moderate extremes to which he might otherwise have gone. Rujing was like a kind parent or grandparent to him, and the idea of cultivating a 'grandmotherly mind' of tender concern was to become significant in Dōgen's teaching later on.

Saigyō was never given such release, yet had another channel. He was able to express his inner turmoil through his poetry, which is part of what makes it so appealing, the other part being his remarkable skill with words. The latter enabled him to express several layers of meaning even in a short verse. In fact, much of his poetry is, at first sight, simply descriptive of nature – mountains, grasses, streams, mist, waves on the sea, ice in winter, blossoms in spring. Many of Dōgen's later sermons also take this form.

Saigyō describes scenes of the 'forgotten' people, including astute observation of workmen and poor folk. In all this there is

6 See LaFleur, William R. 2003. *Awesome Nightfall: The Life, Times and Poetry of Saigyō*, Boston, MA: Wisdom Books.

evident great sensitivity and pathos. The quality that Japanese call *yugen* haunts much of his verse – a bitter-sweetness, celebratory of loneliness or wistful longing. It is easy to see how, for Saigyō, the pain of loss has been converted into a profound sensitivity to beauty, just as for Dōgen it became an appreciation of tenderness. Saigyō writes of how, were he not frightened of being laughed at, he could gaze upon cherry blossom all day long.

We are here, surely, talking about the process that we call sublimation, whereby emotional energy that is tormenting the body and mind becomes re-channelled toward some constructive, loving or sublime end. Love, truth and beauty are media through which such transformation occurs and release from or solace of torment is effected.

Above all subjects, Saigyō celebrates the moon and we are going to see how the moon plays a central role in *Genjō Kōan*. The moon epitomizes cool beauty. Nor was it, to medieval people, simply an astronomical body. The heavens were the home of the ancestors and the gods. The day is ruled by the sun. Its heat gives passion to life. The moon, by contrast, seems the most perfect symbol of nirvāṇa, beautiful and cool. Among other practices, Saigyō learnt a meditation in which one internalizes an image of the moon so that even when the silver disc is not visible in the sky, still it resides close to one's heart.

Lovers gaze upon the moon. Lonely souls draw solace from it. Religious hermits sing its praises. Its light entering into us works a precious alchemy. Hence, in oriental culture, the moon has long been a symbol for the Dharma.

Hōnen's life was also shaped by grief. When he was a child his father was assassinated. As he was dying the father told the son not to seek revenge, but to seek the Dharma. In due course, in early adolescence, Hōnen, like Saigyō before and Dōgen after, went to the monastery. While he was away his mother died. For many years he sought a method of practice that would ease his pain and bring similar ease to all the ordinary people of the world who were caught up in similar grief. Eventually he adopted the practice of invocation of Amitābha Buddha. He wrote a poem summarizing his message which said,

The light of the moon shines
into every hamlet in the land
but only those who turn toward it
can carry its light in their heart.

It seems that for Saigyō and for Hōnen and perhaps for many others the contemplation of the moon was more than simply a symbol, certainly more than an idea. It was a powerful element in a process of sublimation in which grief was not abolished but rather transformed into a bittersweet appreciation of beauty, stillness and peace, where everything discordant could fall away.

This experience was not a matter of abolishing feeling, but of refining it. In Buddhism there are those who interpret the teaching as a matter of leaving all passion behind. Saigyō and Hōnen, however, provide examples of saintly figures who encompassed the whole gamut of sentiments from the most joyful to the most dire, yet, most especially, those in which the sweet and sour elements are inseparably mixed. This made them highly creative people in whom the tragedies of early years later fed into works of beauty and compassion. Another established symbol for nirvāṇa is ash – the sign of the fire having faded – but is this ash dead or is it fertile? In these examples we see its fertility and Dōgen was to find a similar salvation.

When Dōgen went to China he probably thought that he did not have much to lose. However, on arrival, he met with humiliation. We can only guess at his emotional state when he entered Rujing's monastery. It cannot have been easy. That the master took pity on him must have meant a lot. Then came the unexpected death of Myōzen. How much can one take? Then he heard Rujing's words "Let body and mind fall away." Suddenly something seemed possible after all. The ice began to melt.

When Dōgen returned to Japan he wrote *Genjō Kōan* in which the principal image is that of the moon lodging within whatever surface is in a condition to receive and reflect it. The experience of satori and its accompanying transformation is described through an analysis and extension of this image. The moon lodges within when body and mind fall away. Sublimation happens when we are no longer attached to our pain. It is not that the pain vanishes, nor that we become immune. Tender sentiments continue to flow and, in fact, appreciation of beauty intensifies. When we are no longer consciously and deliberately fighting it, the pain itself is reconfigured into the very substance of compassion and sensitivity.

Thus, in the work of these three great masters, we see a pathway out of tragedy that transforms its energy into the signs of enlightenment, signs that do not designate a sterile and frigid person, but one full of feeling and tender. It is this transformation and this process that Dōgen seeks to explicate in *Genjō Kōan*.

1.5 DŌGEN, SHINRAN AND EISAI

Dōgen is nowadays seen as one of the great religious writers and, of those from medieval Japan, he is one of the foremost, second only to his older contemporary Shinran, who, nonetheless, outlived him by ten years.[7] Dōgen and Shinran were contemporary with Francis of Assisi (1182–1226) and Thomas Aquinas (1225–74) and are of similar stature. Dōgen is regarded as the founder of the larger of the two main schools of Zen in Japan, the other being Rinzai, founded by Eisai.

In Japan, Shinran is better known than Dōgen, since he was the founding figure of Shin Shū, the foremost school of Buddhism, which is considerably larger and more significant than Zen. Dōgen is, however, better known in the West, because Zen has caught on here, whereas Shin has not.

Commonly, Zen and Shin are seen somewhat as opposites. Zen is 'self-power Buddhism' and Shin is 'other-power Buddhism'. Self-power (*jiriki*) means that you become enlightened by your own effort and by the realization of your own potential. Other-power (*tariki*) is the belief that we do not have such power in ourselves, but need, and do receive, help – in the West we might say 'grace' – from the Buddhas.

The West, especially America, with its culture of self-reliance, has preferred the former, whereas East Asia has, for the most part, preferred the latter. As we shall see, however, this simple dichotomization may not be entirely justified, at least as far

---

7 For a comparison of Dōgen and Shinran see Abe, Masao 1992. *A Study of Dōgen*, New York: State University of New York Press.

as the categorization of Dōgen is concerned. Dōgen was more 'other-power' than it at first appears. It makes more sense to see Dōgen as reconciling self-power and other-power than as setting up one against the other.

There are still plenty of popular accounts of Zen in the West that assume it is non-ritualistic, non-devotional, has no priesthood or dogmas, does not use scriptures, abhors intellectual learning and lacks the other normal accoutrements of religion, all of which is completely untrue. We do not need to go into the anthropology of Zen here, but we should be open to other possibilities when we read Dōgen and not assume that he will fit into our own religious or irreligious preferences. Dōgen was an erudite monk who established a monastery and a priestly hierarchy, emphasizing ritual purity and monastic rules. While being a sensitive poet, he was also highly intellectual and scorned those who did not know their texts. He went to China to seek salvation, found what he was looking for, came back and propagated the teaching.

We find, in *Genjō Kōan*, an approach to spiritual practice that is fundamentally religious. Western people have often taken to meditation as a methodology intended to achieve various things that might be gathered together under the heading of 'personal growth'. Such people may feel drawn to Dōgen because he was a foremost advocate of zazen – sitting meditation. However, for Dōgen, zazen was certainly not a procedure with such a self-enhancement goal. As Dan Leighton writes, "Dōgen's meditative praxis is a faith expression of the beneficial gift of grace from the buddhas and ancestors, analogous to how nembutsu and shinjin are provided to the Shinshū devotee thanks to the vow of Amida.... Dōgen certainly speaks of relying on the cosmic buddhas and bodhisattvas for assistance, and even in totally entrusting [*sic*] them."[8]

However, in their own time, neither Dōgen nor Shinran was a particularly significant figure. Each had a small devoted following, each had distinctly unconventional views and each had a considerable output of writing in a very distinctive style

8 Leighton, Taigen D., "Dōgen's Zazen as Other-Power Practice" at http://www.ancientdragon.org/dharma/articles/dogens_zazen_as_other_power_practice (accessed 8 December 2017).

that then failed to attract public attention in the centuries immediately following his death. In their writings and interpretations, both were willing to take quite substantial liberties with the source materials that they drew on, recasting them into poetic and impassioned prose as expressions of their distinctive modes of operation.

Shinran was a disciple of Hōnen and Dōgen of Myōzen, the disciple of Eisai. Being, respectively, the founders of the Jōdo and Rinzai schools of Buddhism in Japan, Hōnen and Eisai were much more significant figures in their own and Dōgen's time. They were the two figures of the previous generation who had challenged the Buddhist establishment most successfully. Their ideas, writings and practices were still strongly provocative, widely followed, and discussed in the time when Dōgen and Shinran lived. They had struck out in new directions as a result of becoming disenchanted with the hypocrisy of politics and religion in their time.

Contemporaries			
Eisai	1141–1215	Brought Rinzai Zen to Japan	Founded Kennin-ji
Myōzen	1184–1225	Successor to Eisai	Took Dōgen to China
Shinran	1173–1263	Founding figure of Shin Buddhism	Comparable author
Dōgen	1200–53	Founding figure of Sōtō Zen	Author of *Genjō Kōan*

Eisai was a slightly younger contemporary of Hōnen. He too began as a Tendai monk and he travelled twice to China. On his second trip, he was on his way back to Japan when the boat was driven off course and he ended up back in China for several more years, during which he received Zen training and became a fully qualified Rinzai teacher. This method he then brought back to Japan. After various political tribulations, the Rinzai training monastery, Kennin-ji, was established in 1202 as a branch temple of Enryaku-ji.

Relations between Enryaku-ji and Kennin-ji were generally rather strained. We now think of Rinzai Zen as a distinct school of Buddhism, but at that time it was just one of the approaches incorporated within the Tendai school. However, there were different kinds of Zen and there were debates within Tendai about which kind was best.

Eisai had come back from China with what he regarded as the right and more up-to-date approach, but leading figures at Enryaku-ji resented his attempts at reform. Eisai advocated the strict application of monastic discipline, which was also not popular at Enryaku-ji, which was, according to your perspective, more easy-going, or more corrupt. It was against considerable opposition that Eisai had been able to establish Kennin-ji as a specialist centre practising the 'new' approach to Zen. However, it was by no means a purely Zen temple. Other practices also took place there.

Eisai had no intention of establishing a separate Rinzai denomination of Buddhism; he simply wanted to reform the Zen element within Tendai, but subsequent history took things in a different direction and Rinzai became a separate school. Eisai's successor was Myōzen and, as we saw earlier, when Dōgen left Mount Hiei he went to Kennin-ji to study with Myōzen.

1.6 THE SETTING OF THE TEXT

WITHIN DŌGEN'S OPUS

Genjō Kōan is one of the earliest texts written by Dōgen. If we try to follow the fluctuations of Dōgen's mood and fortunes, we can see that it was written at a high point between two periods of struggle – the troubles and humiliations he had experienced in China and the troubles and disappointments he later had trying to get his views accepted in Japan. At the time of writing, however, he was full of enthusiasm to propagate his understanding, replete with the religious consciousness that had entered and inspired him. Having been liberated by something that had turned him around, changing his whole sense of what religion was, he wanted to share it with others. This text therefore is a gospel – a text of 'religious good news'. It was originally written for a lay supporter, but Dōgen intended to use it as the first chapter of the *Shōbōgenzō*, his masterwork. At the time it was written, it was a first setting out of his essential idea.

The *Shōbōgenzō* was going to be a book of one hundred chapters comprehensively expounding Dōgen's vision, written in his inimitable style. Unfortunately the book did not get finished. Nonetheless, by the time of his death, more than three quarters of the work had been produced, if not revised. Like *Genjō Kōan*, each chapter of *Shōbōgenzō* can be read as a standalone essay. The topics are wide-ranging, covering everything from commentaries and explanations of Buddhist doctrines, texts and stories, through mystical and philosophical writings about the nature of enlightenment, to the minutiae of how to organize a monastery – right down to how to wash the rice.

Since his death various compilations of *Shōbōgenzō* have been made, not all of which include all of the chapters that he did complete. That *Genjō Kōan* was one of the first sections to be written, and was intended to be the first chapter, suggests that it is a particularly clear and central exposition of Dōgen's principal ideas, and most commentators have taken this to be the case. One can even take many of the other chapters as each having the function of expanding upon a theme that first appeared in *Genjō Kōan*, so there is a sense in which *Genjō Kōan* is a distillation of, or index to, the whole. All this makes it a particularly important text to study.

WITHIN HIS HISTORICAL PERIOD

Genjō Kōan was written in 1233, one hundred years after the birth of Hōnen. Hōnen, remember, more than anybody, had changed the face of Buddhism in Japan and, in so doing, had opened the way and provided a role model for teachers like Eisai and Dōgen to bring in other innovations also. Hōnen's Pure Land School taught the practice of *nembutsu* ('mindfulness of Amitābha Buddha' by reciting the Buddha's name). *Nembutsu* became very popular and is, to this day, the most widespread form of Buddhism in Japan.

The revolution that Hōnen ushered in made Buddhism accessible to many people who had previously been excluded. Anybody could practise and Amitābha welcomes everybody into his Pure Land paradise. I think that many Western commentators have under-estimated the importance of Hōnen for the generations that immediately followed him. This is probably in part because Pure Land has not become popular with Western Buddhists and in part because modern scholarship tends to be held within sectarian boundaries. Zen specialists and Pure Land specialists do not recognize the importance of each other's material. Hōnen's challenge to orthodox thinking was, at the time, however, something that made a considerable impact. It struck a strong chord with ordinary Japanese people. Hōnen never went to China. His approach was thoroughly Japanese. He was approachable, saintly, erudite and enthusiastic. He knew the doctrines of all the schools, but preached a message so simple a child could understand it. At the end of his life he and his disciples briefly fell out of favour with the imperial government and were exiled, but this only served to spread his message all over Japan.

My sense is that Hōnen had an influence at that time comparable with that of Freud in the twentieth-century West – many people disagreed with him, but nobody could ignore him, and the resulting disagreements provided the impetus for many innovations and developments in Buddhist practice. For instance, today only scholars have heard of a figure such as Myōe, but at the time he was more influential than Dōgen, Shinran or Myōzen. He was a Shingon-Kegon monk who wrote polemics against Hōnen. Nonetheless, he spent much of the last ten years of his life producing his own ideas about how to gain access to the Pure Land of Amitābha.

Hōnen had opened a door to innovation in Buddhist practice and Eisai, Dōgen and later Nichiren, founder of his own school, would all pass through that door. Some degree of revolution was, therefore, going on in Buddhism in Dōgen's time, a revolution that was still being strongly resisted by the more traditional establishment.[9] Dōgen, like Eisai before him and Nichiren after, would feel the sting of this disapproval. At the time of writing *Genjō Kōan*, however, he was still full of enthusiasm and hope.

---

9 For a critical assessment of what was happening in Japanese Buddhism at the time, see Payne, Richard Karl (ed.) 1998. *Re-Visioning "Kamakura" Buddhism*, Honolulu: Kuroda.

Three critics of Hōnen			
Myōe	1173–1232	Shingon Kegon monk	Traditionalist
Dōgen	1200–53	Founder of Sōtō Zen	Advocated zazen
Nichiren	1222–82	Founder of Nichiren School	Advocate of the Lotus Sūtra

Dōgen was ambivalent about *nembutsu* Buddhism. It did make a form of the Dharma available to the ordinary person, but Dōgen felt that in the form in which it was presented by many Hōnen enthusiasts of his day, it was simplistic and insufficient. He resisted the idea that complete enlightenment was impossible in the contemporary age. Dōgen believed that he had met a living Buddha in China in the person of Rujing. Hōnen had argued that although the traditional teachings of Buddhism were wonderful and marvellous, it was quite impossible to practise them fully in the current degenerate age and, therefore, rather than trying to be a Buddha oneself – a thoroughly arrogant notion – one should rely upon the compassion of the Buddhas, especially Amitābha, who would transfer merit and thus enable one to be reborn in his Pure Land of Sukhāvatī where conditions for practice were much better and one could have the benevolent attention of the Buddha all the time. If becoming a Buddha required an infinite amount of merit, how was this to be achieved? Transference of merit from existing Buddhas provided one solution to this otherwise seemingly insurmountable obstacle.

This meant that in Hōnen's scheme, much of the crucial process of Buddhism went on in a manner of which the practitioner was substantially unconscious. One simply entrusted oneself to Amitābha and the rest would follow. We shall see that the matter of unconscious practice has a place in Dōgen's thought too.

However, Dōgen wanted to demonstrate that it was possible in the present age to live the consummate Buddhist life and he set about creating a community in which it could be done. He brought to this task what he had learnt in China. To match the appeal of Hōnen he had to produce a vision of enlightenment as not unobtainable by real people and an explanation of how we can benefit from the compassion of the Buddhas here in this life as well as in the next one. Like Myōe and other religious innovators of his generation, Dōgen had to at least hint at how his approach could give people access to the Pure Land, though he frames it in his distinctively Chinese style.

Nonetheless, despite these differences, Dōgen also shared a good deal with Hōnen. Both implicitly rejected the notion of 'inherent enlightenment' that was popular at the time and both asserted that the essence of Buddhism was to be found in a unity of faith and practice.

Different teachers have different strengths. Dōgen was never going to be one to reach the masses in the way that Hōnen did so easily. However, he was able to write prose of great beauty and style and expose depths of meaning in traditional texts and ideas that nobody had dreamt of.

WITHIN JAPANESE BUDDHISM

So, Dōgen was a Buddhist monk who began his religious career in the Tendai School. We can think of Japanese Buddhism up to that time as evolving in three stages brought about by, firstly, the introduction of Buddhism into the country in the sixth century by Prince Shōtoku; secondly, the establishment of the Tendai and Shingon schools at the beginning of the ninth century; and from 1175 onward, in the Kamakura period, the establishment of new schools by Hōnen, Eisai, Shinran, Dōgen, Ippen and Nichiren.

Japanese Buddhism to the time of Dōgen		
552 onward	Buddhism introduced from Korea	Establishment of main temples at Nara
788 onward	Tendai and Shingon schools founded	Tendai at Mt Hiei in 805; Shingon at Mt Kōya in 806
1175 onward	Kamakura schools form	Jōdo, Shin, Ji, Sōtō, Rinzai, Nichiren

The First Phase: Buddhism came to Japan from Korea. In 552 AD the king of Paekche sent a Buddha statue to the emperor of Japan. In 584 AD a second mission from Korea resulted in the first ordinations – three nuns – in Japan. Subsequently, visiting Korean monks found an enthusiastic student in Prince Shōtoku, who in due course became regent for Empress Suiko and so gained supreme power. Shōtoku introduced Chinese models of culture, religion and government as part of a process of unification and pacification of Japan. He regarded the Lotus Sūtra as the pre-eminent Buddhist text and this has been sufficient to establish its great prestige within Japanese Buddhism ever since. I will say more about this sūtra below, as it had a major impact upon Dōgen. In this first stage the main centre of Buddhist activity was the old capital of Nara, north of Kyoto.

The Second Phase: This, we could say, began in 788 AD when the monk Saichō, the son of an immigrant Chinese family, built a hut on Mount Hiei near Kyoto. From this modest base, there gradually developed the greatest monastic complex in Japan. Mount Hiei became, and remains, one of the great holy mountains of Japan, with hundreds of Buddhist temples. The Tendai School that grew up there evolved an integrated vision of Mahāyāna Buddhism in which the Lotus Sūtra reigned supreme and many different forms of practice, including zazen, *nembutsu* and esoteric rituals, were united. In the same period, the Shingon School was founded by Kūkai. Shingon practised esoteric, which is to say, tantric, Buddhism. Kūkai's head temple was established on Mount Kōya where, to this day, it remains an important centre of Buddhist study and practice.

The Tendai and Shingon schools supposedly embodied the Mahāyāna principles of inclusiveness and egalitarianism according to which salvation was open to all alike, but in practice, since they depended substantially upon aristocratic patronage and increasingly became armed, land-owning feudal powers themselves, they were rather exclusive and authoritarian. This divergence between theory and practice sowed the seeds for the next phase.

The Third Phase: This arrives with Hōnen. Hōnen began as a Tendai monk, but in 1175 he 'descended from the mountain' and subsequently popularized the *nembutsu* as a sole practice. The main character of this third phase was, therefore, simplicity and devotion. All the subsequent innovators were simplifiers, including Dōgen, who advocated zazen as a sole practice.

At this time the Tendai School was searching for a unifying doctrine and found it in the adoption of a principle called 'original enlightenment' (*hongaku*). Attempts were made to link this teaching to Saichō and his teachers, but this is probably fabrication.[10] The real pedigree of the idea lies in earlier Buddhist doctrines of universal 'Buddha nature', of which it is an extreme form. Dōgen, like Hōnen, found this principle incoherent and it caused him considerable misgivings because it seemed to undermine the necessity of serious practice, which he found essential in his own life. It is possible to see some of Dōgen's work as an attempt to restore Saichō's original vision. Some people, however, lapped up the idea of *hongaku* and carried it to an even greater extreme that made Buddhist practice completely unnecessary. Most notable among these was a teacher called Nōnin.

Genjō Kōan is part of this third phase, a period in which new schools emerged, mostly having roots in Tendai. Dōgen's first experience of Zen was on Mount Hiei. Hōnen's first experience of *nembutsu* had been on Mount Hiei. Although Tendai has long since ceased to be the biggest school of Buddhism in Japan, it is, in a sense, the ancestor of most of those that now are: Jōdo (Hōnen), Rinzai (Eisai), Sōtō (Dōgen), Shin (Shinran), Ji (Ippen) and Nichiren (Nichiren).

Genjō Kōan, written in the midst of this period of new developments and competing schools, sums up Dōgen's claim to a special degree of understanding of what Buddhism is about.

I should say a little about Shingon and also mention the Daruma School. Shingon developed at Mount Kōya in the second phase, underwent considerable expansion during the third phase and continues to be important up to the present day. Myōe, already mentioned, was a Shingon monk, as well as being a follower of Kegon, one of the Nara schools. Saigyō was an independent practitioner, but he spent much time at Mount Kōya and had a great respect for Kūkai, the Shingon founder. Dōgen cannot have been unaware of Shingon principles and the prestige of Mount Kōya, and would have had some passing exposure to esoteric practices while at Enryaku-ji and Kennin-ji.

The Daruma School was founded at the end of the twelfth century by the monk Nōnin, mentioned above, who was rather

10 See Groner, Paul 2000. *Saichō: The Establishment of the Japanese Tendai School*, Honolulu: University of Hawaii Press, especially 45–6.

anarchistic and antinomian. This is not unlike many modern advocates of Zen, who take it to be completely iconoclastic. The Daruma School was criticized by the Tendai establishment and also by Eisai and was banned by the government. However, it continued as an underground movement, attracting a number of freethinkers and strong personalities, many of whom subsequently came over to Dōgen's school, including Ejo, who became Dōgen's leading disciple, and Keizan, who eventually became his successor. When Dōgen had to leave the Kyoto area, he chose to go north to an area where the Daruma School had a following. In understanding why Dōgen wrote what he did at this time, one influence we must consider is the on-going implicit dialogue between his group and the Daruma people.

The Echizen area was, however, also home to many followers of *yamabushi*. *Yamabushi* is not really a school of Buddhism, more a style. The word means 'mountain asceticism'. Practitioners spend much time in the mountains exposing themselves to a variety of hardships and getting close to nature. There has always been a strong current of nature worship in Japanese religion. After moving to the area, Dōgen would often refer to himself as 'this mountain monk', an epithet that aligned him both with the mountain tradition of Zen in China and also with the local *yamabushi*.

The Kamakura period was, therefore, a time of competing schools and Dōgen's group were very small fish in this pond. Nonetheless, he did give his people a deep and thorough training and this was to bear fruit much later. Within the many broad trends in the debates going on at the time, one of the most important was the contention between those who believed in strict practice (Eisei, Dōgen), those who believed in simpler, easier, but nonetheless vigorous practice (Hōnen, and his critic Myōe) and those who did not really believe in practice at all (Nōnin and some of Hōnen's disciples). There was also struggle over the issue of simplification and pluralism, and in this respect Dōgen was a master at having it both ways, deeply respecting the whole range of traditional Buddhist practice, yet philosophically advancing the idea that these were all encompassed within the single practice of zazen.

Japanese Buddhist schools			
6th century	9th century	12th century	
Nara schools			
	Shingon		founder, Kūkai
	Tendai		founder, Saichō
		Jōdo	founder, Hōnen, originally Tendai
		Rinzai Zen	founder, Eisai, originally Tendai
		Sōtō Zen	founder, Dōgen, originally Tendai
		Nichiren	founder, Nichiren, originally Tendai
		Ji	derived from Jōdo, founder, Ippen
		Shin	derived from Jōdo, founder, Shinran

So, it was to Mount Hiei that Dōgen went first to become a monk. There he found a religion with many dimensions, but in which the central unifying pivot was a focus upon the Lotus Sūtra. There he also encountered an emphasis upon the principle of 'original enlightenment'. This latter teaching brought Dōgen's kōan to the fore and set him looking for solutions. From Hiei he went to Kennin-ji. From Kennin-ji he went to China. When he came back he wrote *Genjō Kōan*. Later he was to retreat to the mountains in the north. We, therefore, have to try to understand *Genjō Kōan* in the context of the cross-currents in Dōgen's life, which include both Japanese and Chinese Buddhism. In both of these, the Lotus Sūtra assumes great importance.

Founding figures			
Shōtoku	574–622	Prince Regent	Established Buddhism in Japan
Saichō	767–822	Founded Tendai Shū on Mt Hiei	Dōgen first ordained in Tendai
Nōnin	d. 1196	Founded Daruma Shū	Daruma disciples joined Dōgen
Hōnen	1133–1212	Founded Jōdo Shū	Created the precedent for new schools
Eisai	1141–1215	Brought Rinzai Zen to Japan	Dōgen studied Rinzai at Kennin-ji
Dōgen	1200–53	Founder of Sōtō Zen in Japan	Author of *Genjō Kōan*

1.7 THE LOTUS SŪTRA

As we have seen, most of the Kamakura period reformers, different as they were, started off as monks in the Tendai School. Dōgen, as a Tendai monk, would have known the Lotus Sūtra by heart and he continued to regard it as the most important of all the sūtras. The Lotus Sūtra had originally been translated into Chinese by Dharmarakṣa in 286 AD in Chang'an, the capital of North China. This translation made a big impact at the time and it was further improved upon in a translation by Kumārajīva in the year 406 AD. Kumārajīva was a great translator. In order to render Buddhist texts into Chinese he had to invent a good deal of new terminology. We see the same thing happening as Buddhism comes to the West and words like Buddha, Dharma, karma, and so on enter Western languages.

Up until the time of Kumārajīva much of the vocabulary used to translate Buddhist texts was drawn directly from Daoism. Again, there is a modern parallel, as early Western translations tended to use Christian language and more recent ones have tended to use psychological language. Of course, neither of these can fully do justice to the original.

The Lotus Sūtra has not only added a richness of language to Far Eastern cultures, it has also added many images since the sūtra is full of parables and symbolic happenings that reveal aspects of the hidden meaning of the nature of Buddhas and their activity throughout the cosmos for the benefit of all sentient beings.

In 432 AD the monk Zhu Daosheng wrote a commentary on the Lotus Sūtra[11] which became highly influential. It is quite likely that Dōgen read this work while he was in China. Even if he did not read it, he will have encountered the ideas that it embodies. There has been debate among scholars about whether Daosheng was Buddhist, Daoist or Neo-Daoist. Neo-Daoism is basically a syncretism between Daoism and Confucianism. This kind of debate about classification, however, probably misses the point that Daosheng was simply a cultured Chinese person and freethinker who appreciated all three religions, drew from them all and had a preference for Neo-Daoist terminology even when

11 See: Kim, Young-ho 1990. *Tao-sheng's Commentary on the Lotus Sūtra*, Albany, NY: State University of New York Press.

writing about Buddhism. In this respect, Dōgen substantially followed in his footsteps, and presenting Dōgen in narrowly sectarian terms probably leads to a similar error.

What Dōgen will have learnt in China was not a narrow sectarian view, but a characteristically Chinese integration. Daosheng was certainly one of the key figures in establishing such an integration and has been claimed as the actual founder of Chan (or Zen) in China[12] before the arrival of Bodhidharma.

Daosheng spent time with Kumārajīva, the translator, in North China and with Huiyuan at Mount Lu in South China. At that time China was divided into two countries with rather different cultures and different styles of Buddhism. Daosheng speaks of nirvāṇa as 'mirror like voidness'[13] and he was certainly influenced by the so-called 'dark wisdom' of Daoism. We shall see the relevance of 'darkness', 'mirrors' and 'voidness' later in the commentary.

The Lotus Sūtra is full of imagery. *Genjō Kōan* also. Daosheng, writing about the Lotus and other sūtras, uses a mix of Buddhist, Daoist and Confucian terminology and Dōgen does the same. Daosheng makes particularly strong use of the Chinese concept Li (禮, in modern Chinese simplified to 礼). I shall explain this further in due course since, as we shall see, Dōgen does likewise. Without an appreciation of this Chinese way of using the conceptual structures of all three religions indiscriminately, one is likely to miss much of the significance of Dōgen's writing in general and of the present text in particular.

Lotus Sūtra translators and commentators			
Dharmarakṣa	*c*.240–*c*.300	Monk, traveller, linguist	Translated the sūtra into Chinese
Kumārajīva	344–413	Scholar, monk, translator	Translated the sūtra into Chinese
Huiyuan	334–417	Pure Land Teacher at Mount Lu	Influences Daosheng
Daosheng	*c*.360–434	Buddhist/Neo-Daoist monk, scholar	Wrote influential commentary on the sūtra, formative for Zen in China
Dōgen	1200–53	Author of *Genjō Kōan*	Scholar of the Sūtra and of Chinese Zen

12 By Hu Shih. See, e.g. "Development of Zen Buddhism in China", *Chinese Social and Political Science Review*, 15/4: January 1932.

13 In *Bianzong Lun*, by Xie Lingyun.

The Lotus Sūtra offers a transcendental view of the Buddha. While we must take it that Dōgen was in revolt against some aspects of Tendai teaching, we must also appreciate that he was saturated with the imagery and content of this sūtra. His writing is full of references and allusions to other Buddhist texts, but in the *Shōbōgenzō*, references to the Lotus Sūtra outnumber those to any other single work. In the Lotus Sūtra, Buddhas are eternal and there are many of them. The vision of the universe that it imparts is one in which sacred influence is everywhere, though often unseen and unrecognized. The Buddhas are everywhere trying to help us to attain salvation, using all manner of skilful means, but we ignorant beings are like children playing in a burning house, inattentive to the calls of those who are trying to rescue us. Such is the general tenor of the work and of the religious consciousness that it imparts. This background is taken for granted in Dōgen's writing.

This religious vision in which there are Buddhas everywhere then struck a chord in the Japanese culture, which was already based on a nature religion called Shinto. At the time when Dōgen lived, the idea of *honji suijaku* was widespread, and certainly believed in by Saigyō the poet. This was the idea that the Shinto gods are manifestations of the celestial Buddhas, the supreme goddess, Amaterasu, being a manifestation of Vairocana Buddha, the supreme Buddha in Shingon. Dōgen will also have been aware of these ideas and although he does not adopt them, his lavish use of imagery drawn from nature is similar to the practice of Saigyō and other Japanese writers of his time.

1.8 POETRY AND DREAM

Poetry has played a big part in Japanese culture. The imperial government sponsored anthologies of the best poetry. There were competitions, and both Saigyō and Dōgen participated in them. Poetry provided a fluid medium that could bridge several otherwise separate domains. These included court life, religion, romance and nature. The tradition was sufficiently venerable to have a well-established vocabulary of tropes and images with many layers of meaning. We have already touched on the importance of the moon, which figures as a feature of the night sky, the light of the Dharma, a healing balm, a symbol of love, and, with its phases, a token of impermanence all at the same time. We shall see a number of these images in *Genjō Kōan*. To some extent they provide us with a code with which to unravel the meaning.

The fluidity of the poetic mode of expression also enables Dōgen to say several things at once with the images he uses, relying as he does upon the literal meaning, the established poetic association and the reference back to the source of the idea. Many elements of Japanese and Chinese poetry owe their origins to the stories in the Lotus Sūtra. Again, the idea of *honji suijaku* – equivalence between Shinto and Buddhist figures – also enables a writer to multiply meanings in a short phrase. Saigyō was the supreme master of this art. The currency of his work in the time of Dōgen must have aided Dōgen in exploiting the potential of language to give more than one religious and worldly meaning simultaneously as he does in *Genjō Kōan* and many of his other writings.

The idea of creating a bridge between domains can also be looked at in another way. Poetry is closely associated with dreaming and dream consciousness. When people are composing poetry they are not generally in a tightly conceptual-rational mode. Poetry spans the left and right brain. It partakes at once of both word and music. Thus it is a connection also between the unconscious and conscious mind; or, in a more archaic manner of expression, it is the mode in which the gods speak to us. Ancient Chinese religion was concerned with communication with the ancestors. The ancestors speak through dreams and the imagery of dreams emerges in poetry. Poetry thus becomes both a manner of praising and worshipping the spirits and also a means by which they speak to and through us. Even today we speak of the poetic Muse.

Sometimes the imagery is personal and sometimes it is broader; we might say, archetypal. If the allusions and associations pertain specifically to one person, or a small group of people, then we are dealing with personal matters. The unconscious, or the gods, might well want to give one a message helping one to change course in life. Saigyō writes of his longings, of the things that catch his attention, of his sense sometimes of being lost, and so on, but he does so by means of images of natural scenes and objects. Sometimes, the objects are so generalized that finding the personal association is more difficult. In these cases we are talking about the general spiritual issues that affect all of humankind – impermanence and intractability in all their forms. Dōgen's work has more of this latter character. One can sometimes see the personal reference, or, at least, the source of the imagery in his life, as when he speaks of the sea and the sky, clearly echoing his sea journey, but substantially he addresses the universal existential problems of life and death, together with the possibility of the kind of spiritual awakening that connects these universals with the concrete situations of our fate.

In Dōgen's writing there are recurrent dream images, like motifs with which he then plays in different ways, exploiting different perspectives, and he often imbues them with a subtle irony. It is easy to make the mistake of finding a passage in which Dōgen writes negatively about something or somebody and to conclude that the contrary stance represents 'Dōgen's position' on the particular issue. This is by no means always a warranted step. That Dōgen makes fun of something in one place does not preclude the possibility that he might praise it somewhere else. Dōgen is not so much a position-taker, more an explorer of possibilities.

Here again, we can note how dreams, being the expression of the unconscious, often provide a counterweight to something that has become overly developed in consciousness. They do this not because the over-developed feature is fundamentally bad or wrong, but simply to provide balance. Dōgen's work is full of balancing features. Is it better to be a fish or a bird? It is best to be what you are. However, whatever you are will only be part of the whole.

Poetry, because it does not have to adhere to a binary logic, can hint at the whole even while delineating a part. It can also contain contradictions that are not necessarily disagreements.

The realm of the gods, which we might call the unconscious, can happily encompass opposites, and Dōgen's writing does so as a matter of course.

If one were to dream of a fan it would be profitable to ask what the fan symbolizes: what is the image behind the image? If one were to write a poem or tell a tale about a fan, likewise. At the end of *Genjō Kōan*, Dōgen relates a story about a fan. We can wonder what this means. Elsewhere,[14] Dōgen reports that an ancient master once raised a fan in the air and said: "Even though this has a thousand kinds of usages, after all there are not two types of wind". Dōgen goes on to say that he disagrees, that he can see ten thousand types of wind. Here 'wind' represents Dharma. We shall see this motif of fan and wind occur at the end of *Genjō Kōan*; however, my point here is that we cannot, from an utterance of this kind, conclude that Dōgen really rejects the interpretation of the earlier master, we can only conclude that on this particular day he raises further possibilities. In general, Dōgen opens up rather than closes down. There are not two kinds of 'wind' because Dharma is always Dharma, but there are innumerable kinds of wind because all real things are instances of Dharma; all teach and aid us on our path.

1.9 THE THREE RELIGIONS

China already had two religions before Buddhism arrived in the country, Daoism and Confucianism. To become accepted, Buddhism had to come to terms with the established creeds. This was a long and complicated story, but the upshot was a considerable degree of mutual borrowing and integration. When I was travelling in Vietnam, I visited a number of Chinese temples there. All were of rather similar design. There were always three altars. On one altar was a figure of Confucius, on another Laozi, and on the third a Buddha. One could tell to which religion the temple belonged by which of the three figures was on the central altar. This is a degree of accommodation between religions that we are not used to in the West. However,

---

14 Leighton, Taigen D. and Shohaku Okumura 2004. *Dōgen's Extensive Record*, Somerville, MA: Wisdom Books: 119.

when Dōgen went to China he may well have encountered something similar. Not only did he encounter it, he embraced it. When back in Japan, he was in a different world where Confucianism and Daoism had less influence and the only other religion was Shintoism, but Dōgen retained the language and conceptual structure of the three religions and drew many of his most important ideas from that integration.

As a Westerner studying Dōgen it is easy to overlook this fact. Dōgen tends to be studied by people who have a fairly exclusive interest in Japanese Zen and if they look any further than the Zen School it is into Mahāyāna Buddhism. Furthermore, when Dōgen came back, he does seem to have had a sense that he was the only person in the country who really understood the true nature of Buddhism and how it should be practised, and this can easily lead one to think of him as the purveyor of an exclusivist style and so miss the meanings of terms that have their roots and associations in other parts of the Chinese integration.

So how does this integration work? Laozi wrote a book called the *Daode Jing* – the book of Dao and De. Loosely speaking, Dao is the mysterious underlying spirit of the universe, and De is its application in the practical world – its virtue. Confucius taught respect for heaven and a balance between heaven and humanity. This was to manifest as a perfect society. He also used the concepts Dao and De with slightly different implications. Confucianism is strong on social theory, ritual, etiquette and social relations. The key concept here is Li. Li is not easy to translate, being a rather broad concept. The original meaning had to do with the correct ordering of the sacrificial rites. In traditional Chinese society the rites were all-important. For life to be meaningful and successful there had to be a correct relationship between heaven, earth and mankind, and to maintain this there were rites. These involved sacrifice to the ancestors in heaven. By extension, a correctly lived life was itself regarded as being a rite and also a sacrifice, in the sense of being filial rather than self-assertive. One's whole life could be one's way of revering heaven, earth and the ancestors. Li thus came to mean the rite of life, the perfect way to live. Life of such a kind brought naturalness and duty into perfect harmony.

Since modern people have substantially lost touch with the notion of rites, it may help to think of dance. In ancient times, dance and ritual were closely related. Rites included dance. Dance is a ritual. To say that life is a rite is also to say that it is a dance. In this analogy, we could say that Dao is the music of that dance. The music calls us to dance. It gets us going. With each type of music there is an appropriate form of dance, an appropriate rite.

So Li and Te are both words for the practical application of Dao. Te inclines more toward the implication that the Dao manifests spontaneously in naturally virtuous action, and Li more toward the implication that performing one's duty is the best way of according with what is ultimately natural, but for the ancient Chinese these two principles were much closer than they are for many modern people. We tend to think of duty and naturalness as somewhat contradictory, but for them, duty was natural and the best way to be natural was to do your duty.

The Chinese thus found it fairly easy to think of ' Dao Li' rather than ' Dao Te'. Lao Tzu had had most to say about the nature of the Dao and Confucius most to say about Li, so ' Dao Li' brought them together nicely. In due course, there arose what is called Neo-Daoism, which was an amalgam of Daoism and Confucianism. It promoted Dao Li. Daosheng, who wrote the famous Buddhist commentary on the Lotus Sūtra, used Neo-Daoist language to do so, and Dōgen, many centuries later, also does so to some extent.

The Chinese recognized that Buddha taught a philosophy that had elements of both Dao and Li – transcendence and ethics, if you like. He was the supreme sage. He also advocated 'enlightenment', so there was a need to understand what this was in terms that made sense to the Chinese. The obvious answer was that enlightenment meant perceiving the Dao – the 'Buddha Dao' – so clearly that its Li became second nature. The integration of the three religions, therefore, can be neatly expressed as 'Buddha Dao Li' and Buddhism, seen through Chinese eyes, becomes simply Buddha's Dao Li.

For clarity, let me go over this again. Dao is the flow, grain or music of the universe, which is to say of heaven and earth. For mankind to live in harmony with it we have to 'perform the rites' correctly. This performance is called Li. We can also think of it as joining the dance, in which case Li means performing the right dance steps. If life is a dance to the music of Dao, then one has to know how to dance. Buddha comes along as the dance teacher, or expert in the rites. 'Buddha Dao Li' thus signifies the integration of Buddhism, Daoism and Confucianism, with Buddha telling us how to live or perform (Li) in accordance with the fundamental nature (Dao) of heaven and earth. The Chinese for Buddha is '*Fo*', so this can be Fo Dao Li.

The three religions of China				
Buddhism	Buddha	Fo	Enlightenment	The teacher
Daoism	Laozi	Dao	The mysterious 'Way'	The music
Confucianism	Confucius	Li	Humanity, duty, ritual	The ritual or dance

It will help us to comprehend *Genjō Kōan* if we recognize that Buddha Dao Li is a significant dimension, or even summary, of Dōgen's thinking. One important aspect of *Genjō Kōan* is that it explains the Buddha Dao and its Li and explains enlightenment – satori – in terms of the Buddha Dao and Dao Li. We shall see that *Genjō Kōan* begins with an assertion of the Buddha Dao, and ends with explanation of Dao Li, so Buddha Dao Li is the alpha and omega of this work.

In most translations of *Genjō Kōan*, the importance of Dao Li is not apparent and, I suggest, something essential is lost thereby. *Genjō Kōan* delineates a Buddhist Way, but it does so using a conceptual framework that owes a great deal to the other two religions. It tells us about the nature of spiritual awakening seen especially through the prism of the Chinese integration.

We should also grasp that in this way of understanding, rightness is to be found in the nature of things all around us. In modern life there has grown up a sense that spirituality is almost entirely an inward affair. However, in the Confucian and Daoist view, the ways of nature embody the truth, and the spiritual task is just as much, if not more, that of letting those truths in, than of finding them hidden deep within oneself. This attitude is further accentuated in Japan by its Shinto background. Much of *Genjō Kōan* is concerned with imagery drawn from nature.

Ritual rightly performed, Li, was intended to maintain proper order and regulate the relations between humans and heaven, Nature and the ancestors. This view of the universe is different from the one to which we are accustomed. The modern person can be perplexed to learn that Dōgen believes that a life of complete liberation is one that is almost completely ritualized. Much modern thought has been concerned with achieving a kind of liberation that involves the deconstruction of traditional rituals, but here, liberation, which is also equated with salvation, means liberation from the kind of self-centredness that modern consumerism takes to be the ideal.

I.10 SELF-POWER AND OTHER-POWER

While Dōgen was being shaped by and immersed in the cross-currents of the three religions of China, back in Japan other issues altogether were at play. The question that was probably most discussed in Japanese Buddhist circles at that time was not the integration of the three religions, but the debate about self-power (*jiriki*) and other-power (*tariki*) and the associated matter of *mappō*, the 'dark age'. Hōnen had been in search of a form of Buddhism that could provide salvation for the masses in a time of terrible events. He observed that it seemed to be impossible for people of his age – or ours, though for different reasons, perhaps – to fulfil the stringent demands for human perfection found in Buddhist scriptures. How many people do you know who are perfectly ethical, have mastered all the meditation samadhis and are now tenth-stage bodhisattvas?

Many people in Japan were convinced by this argument and they believed that this was because they lived in *mappō*, as we do now. There were various theories to the effect that the more distant in time one was from the epoch when a Buddha had appeared in the world, the more difficult it was to practise, and that as a result the human race was in decline. Looking around one in Japan at the time, beset as it was with civil war, earthquakes, famines, fires and plagues, it was not difficult to believe that those were degenerate times. In this circumstance, Hōnen preached a message of other-power that spoke to people's condition. It seemed quite evident in those times that the 'self-power' practices of strict morality, pure-minded meditation and wisdom were beyond human capacity, especially for people who were obliged to work in professions such as soldiering or fishing that inevitably carried the bad karma of killing. People needed help and the Buddhas had made vows to be compassionate. Thus even if one inevitably fell short personally, was it not obviously the case that the Buddhas would help if one turned to them and asked? The practice that Hōnen advocated – calling the name of Amitābha Buddha (*nembutsu*) – was something that everybody could actually do, even while sailing a boat or ploughing a field. However, the new teaching was controversial, as much for its very popularity as anything, which threatened the hegemony of the established Buddhist organizations on Mount Hiei, Mount Kōya and elsewhere, that relied upon a much more complicated integration of Buddhist doctrine that most people respected, but did not understand.

Dōgen recognized the idea of *mappō*, but he thought that it was still possible for practitioners to reach the complete fulfilment of the salvation offered by Śākyamuni Buddha. His view was that even in the time of Śākyamuni there were people who did not attain enlightenment and even in this remote time and place (medieval Japan) a few still could. The adversity of the times should be a spur to action. He wanted to preserve the possibility of enlightenment in this life and sometimes criticized *nembutsu* as being lightweight. However, the idea of a polarity between Dōgen and Hōnen can be taken too far.[15] I believe, as I shall explain below, that Dōgen was not teaching self-power to the exclusion of other-power, but was teaching an integration of the two and was using what he had learnt in China as the key to doing so. In fact, Dōgen leans quite strongly in the other-power direction, as does the Lotus Sūtra. In his very clear and concrete later text *Dōshin* ('Heart of Dao'), Dōgen, just like Hōnen, advocated incessant chanting of the Buddhist refuge

15 For a similar view, see Cleary, Thomas 1992. *Rational Zen: The Mind of Dōgen Zenji*, Boston, MA: Shambhala, especially 27–32.

formula, especially at the time of death and in the *bardo* state between lives. Such devotion, he said, is profound realization of Dharma.

I suspect that one of the reasons that Dōgen is popular nowadays is because he emphasizes practice in the present life and most interpretations of his work stress this. However, this is a one-sided view. Certainly, in relation to Hōnen, he stressed that enlightenment in this life is a real possibility. However, it would be completely wrong to think of Dōgen as a wholly this-worldly philosopher. He was a religious practitioner and he produced his own conception of other-power and of the Way that the myriad Buddhas shine their grace upon us and rescue us from the fate of endless rebirth. His primary point is that for them to do so, we have to play our part, but then, Hōnen thought so too in his own way.

II

TRANSLATION PROBLEMS

II.1 A DIFFICULT TEXT

Genjō Kōan is not an easy text for us. Few of Dōgen's writings are. There have been many translations of *Genjō Kōan* into English and other European languages. They differ considerably. Different translators have taken the meaning in different ways. I have spoken to many Western people who have read one or another of these translations and by far the commonest report is that it is confusing. The matter was well summed up by a very experienced Zen practitioner and teacher who said to me, "I love Dōgen, but I don't understand it."

Nonetheless, we know that *Genjō Kōan* was originally written for a lay disciple named Yō Kōshū. This strongly suggests that it cannot have been anything like as obscure to an ordinary Japanese person of Dōgen's time as it seems to be even to great scholars today. There is a key missing. The difficulty is partly that of getting into the mind-set of a person from the thirteenth century living in the feudal culture of Japan. Just about all the things that we take for granted as modern, educated people of the twenty-first century probably did not form part of his world. What mattered to him is not necessarily what matters to us and vice versa.

Also, Dōgen's poetic style of writing is full of references

and allusions to other Buddhist texts and stories, many of which are themselves difficult for us to penetrate. He takes it for granted that we already know what he is alluding to and texts in those days did not have footnotes and references. It is a bit as though one were to make allusions to Bible stories with just a throwaway line. If a modern writer mentions the term 'Samaritan' we immediately have a whole story in our head. So, in some ways, Dōgen's text uses a code with which we are not always familiar. I think that I have picked up some references that others have missed, but I have no doubt that there are more that have escaped me, just as they have escaped other modern readers. Most would, however, have been perfectly clear to an educated person in Dōgen's own time.

I think that clarity has then, probably, been further obscured by the attitude of most of the translators and commentators, since they evidence a desire to make Dōgen fit into, or to use him as a support for, the currently popular rendering of Zen in the West, which tends to be technical, secular and reductionist, attitudes that had probably not even been invented in Dōgen's time and would have been strongly disapproved of if they had been.

Dōgen would probably have as much difficulty in reading us as we have reading him. The reasons that Zen in particular and Buddhism in general have evolved in this direction in modern times have to do with our history, our Judeo-Christian background, the secularization of industrial society, and the academicization of education, including oriental studies, topics that are worth several books in their own right, but which mean that we tend to look at the text through a different set of spectacles from those of the author and his original readers. Some of these points will become clear as we go along.

However, people are people and even though cultures change, some human fundamentals do not. These include the kinds of central spiritual problems that people face. Birth and death are still birth and death. Self-centredness may change its modes of expression, but it is perennial.

Then there is the question of spiritual development itself. I think that some of the translations that I have read suffer from the same kind of misunderstanding of the Dharma as Dōgen himself suffered from before he went to China. This misunderstanding is simply the idea that the whole purpose of practice must be to obtain something for oneself – something to satisfy body and mind. In modern times, self-development, personal growth and spiritual liberation have become confused. I suspect that much of what we consider to be the real value of meditation and similar practices Dōgen would have regarded as narcissistic distraction.

Although there is a good deal of rhetoric in Western Buddhist circles about practice for its own sake, often enough even those who make such remarks are still, in essence, practising with a view to their own enhancement. This is quite understandable and natural, but if, as is likely, Dōgen was actually, in some respects, trying to dispel that as an objective, then many of the things that we, in common discourse, take for granted are not going to apply. Whether I have completely managed to overcome this pitfall myself, I doubt. The problem is that such attitudes are deeply ingrained and, by definition, one is not generally conscious of what it is that one is taking for granted. It may seem so self-evident that one has difficulty understanding how an intelligent person could think differently.

II.2 WHAT WAS DŌGEN TRYING TO DO IN THIS TEXT?

In *Genjō Kōan*, Dōgen is telling us how satori happens, and, as this was intended to be a foundational chapter in *Shōbōgenzō*, he is here attempting a reassertion of the core of Buddhism according to his understanding. In particular, Buddhism is a transmission. It is, therefore, about interaction. Zen asserts that something happened between Śākyamuni and his disciple Kāśyapa and that, subsequently, something similar happened between Kāśyapa and Ānanda and that in this way the Dharma has come down to us. We say that what happened was an 'awakening'. It was sudden. It was surprising. As an interaction, it involved two (usually two) people, but sometimes one person and a natural phenomenon. This is what Dōgen helps us to understand.

Along the way, *Genjō Kōan* throws light upon a variety of other matters that are or have been controversial in Buddhism. For instance, *Genjō Kōan* can be seen as a commentary on the Buddha's assertion that Buddhism is neither eternalism nor nihilism. In the post-war period there has been a movement in Japan called Critical Buddhism,[1] which asserts that Buddhism has drifted away from Śākyamuni's original message in the direction of eternalism because of '*hongaku*' teachings such as those of Buddha nature and original enlightenment that seem to assert an underlying reality 'behind' phenomena. In theoretical terms, the Critical Buddhists are, therefore, the polar opposite of the Tendai people in Dōgen's time who were advancing the *hongaku* principle strongly. Where did Dōgen stand on this issue? Did he reject *hongaku* outright? Did he accept it in his earlier works and then change his mind later? Or was his real opinion to be found somewhere between these two poles, and if so, how is it to be understood? On this question, I am of the last opinion. I think that Dōgen holds a middle position, but it is a middle that, in a sense, incorporates both poles rather than rejecting them. He does not take on the notion of original enlightenment, but he does not swing to the opposite extreme either. He does not reject it, but he does not rely upon it either. He does have a sense of an unborn, uncreated, undying truth, but that truth is not static, nor is it something that will allow one to sink into any kind of complacency and it is certainly not to be identified with any kind of original nature of the person. This means that he also holds a middle position between self-power and other-power. How does he do this? Principally by deploying the notion of Buddha Dao. *Genjō Kōan* explains how this works.

In Dōgen, the ultimate is immanent in things insofar as they demonstrate or reflect ultimate truth, but such truth is the truth of impermanence. Thus nothing can be pinned down into static categories. As soon as one tries to do so the game is lost. Thus there is eternal truth and any ephemeral circumstance can demonstrate it to us, but we cannot grasp it as a concept. It can grasp us, but we can never grasp it in any final way. As soon

---

1 See Hubbard, Jamie and Paul Swanson 1997. *Pruning the Bodhi Tree: The Storm over Critical Buddhism*, Honolulu: University of Hawaii Press.

as we try to do so it slips through our fingers. Dōgen not only asserts this, he demonstrates it in his mode of discourse, and this demonstration often seems more important than the conceptual content of what he says.

Actual lived life is a series of encounters, endlessly giving way to one another. There is eternal truth in each, but it never manifests itself in a familiar way. It is like the churning of the ocean. Waves continually arrive at the shore, yet every wave is unique. It is always the same, yet always different. This is the Dao. It encompasses yin and yang and manifests as them. So Dōgen's 'middle' is ceaselessly active. Time and change are fundamental. To reverse a traditional French saying, 'plus c'est la même chose, plus ça change'. So it is not that the eternal, unborn, uncreated somehow defies time; it *is* time.

In this vision of things, the eternal truth, often represented poetically as the moon, sheds its light, but if that light enters into one it 'sends one forth', it provokes action, because it is the essence of change. We search for a static final truth in order to justify our smugness and to enable us to defy impermanence. When ultimate truth touches us it destroys our game and stirs us into action. As a consequence, we become actively passive or passively active: passive in the sense that we must allow the truth to enter us, yet active as a result of it doing so. Dōgen calls this 'playing our part'.

The Dharma life is a cooperation, which can be imagined as a ritual or a dance, between oneself and the Dharma, but it is the Dharma that leads. As soon as we try to take control we lose contact. Thus satori is a cooperation between ourselves and the Buddhas, or, we could say, with the Dharma manifest in a myriad ways all around us. We have to play our part, but the essential element comes from outside and enters into us, though not in a way that makes it into part of ourselves. Yet our 'playing our part' makes the Dharma evident to others which actually turns out to be even more important then it appearing to us. Dōgen tells us that enlightenment does not necessarily become personal knowledge for ourselves and we might not even know that it is happening. The aim of the exercise is not to gain something, but to serve the greater purpose, even unwittingly – the 'greater purpose' being the enlightenment of all sentient beings, the work of all the Buddhas.

With all this goes his fervent belief in the importance of practice. Dōgen needs to explain how, even though the light of the Dharma is already shining upon us, our duty is to practise diligently.

So, we can see that while Dōgen has a single central message to impart about satori, he has to do so by integrating a number of cross-currents.

1. *The Lotus Sūtra*: We can take Dōgen's writing, including *Genjō Kōan*, as expressing an inner conversation that Dōgen is having with the Lotus Sūtra. Dōgen will certainly have felt that his interpretation of Buddhadharma had to elucidate without being in contradiction to it. However, he will also have felt free to reinterpret it in his own way.

2. *A religious text*: This means that *Genjō Kōan* is a religious text. I think that it is important to stress that this text is about the real religious life. We live in an age in which the dominant trend in Western Buddhism seems to be toward presenting it as a non-religious philosophy or psychology, in which writers like Dōgen are taken as support for a secular, self-development approach. The text, however, makes a lot more sense if one understands it in an unabashedly religious way. Here, I mean religious both in the sense of the Mahāyāna Buddhist religion, and also, to an extent, in the sense of addressing the fundamentals of all and any conceivable true religion. If Dōgen had not had some sense of an eternal, universally present Buddha or Dharma nature – a highly metaphysical concept – his kōan would not have existed in the first place. It would certainly not have had the power to drive him to make the dangerous journey to China, risking his life for a solution. If he had, as so many modern practitioners, simply seen Buddhism as a technique of stress reduction, or even as an ethical philosophy, he would have stayed in Japan. Therefore, *Genjō Kōan* is about religious things, holy things, sacred things. Often the words that Dōgen chooses have several layers of meaning. The ordinary person can read this text and think that it contains many pretty word pictures of oceans and birds, firewood and dewdrops and completely miss the point.

3. *Not ontology*: This also means that this is not a philosophical work in the Western sense of the term. This is not about ontology, epistemology or logic; it is not an abstract theory of time or being. Philosophers might find that some parts of it stimulate ideas for them, but this is not Dōgen's purpose. His purpose is spiritual awakening and the explication of enlightenment: what it is and how it happens.

4. *Personal realization*: The work is Dōgen's attempt to express his own religious experience. That experience is his own personal solution to his own spiritual problem. However, the result is here universalized. If Dōgen is right – and in this commentary I will assume that he is – whatever form one's spiritual problem takes, the principles that Dōgen is enunciating here will have relevance.

5. *Daoism and yin-yang*: Dōgen found the solution to his problem at Tiantong monastery with Master Rujing. Rujing was Chinese. I think that the form in which Dōgen expresses his message owes a great deal to Chinese religiosity. In particular it smacks of a strong Daoist influence and is shot through with formulations that would have worked easily for somebody familiar with yin-yang thinking. This does not mean that Dōgen was a Daoist as such, but it is a strong influence. Dōgen would have rejected the idea that he was Daoist and this work, *Genjō Kōan*, is probably not a deliberate attempt to integrate Daoism and Buddhism, but, in many ways, it does so. Presumably, this influence came partly from Dōgen's general experience of being in China, and it probably owes a lot to the direct influence of Rujing. I suspect also a strong influence from the Neo-Daoist style of Daosheng. This has to remain speculative, of course. My hunch is that Dōgen was deeply steeped in Chinese ways of thinking. I imagine this as having been rather in the manner that many contemporary Western Buddhists, despite having consciously rejected Christianity or Judaism, are still steeped in a Judeo-Christian way of thinking and tend to present Buddhism in categories (such as justice and forgiveness, human rights, moral imperatives, and so on) that were not particularly relevant to Buddha and his contemporaries, nor to Dōgen's times either, but have powerful resonances in Western thought. Thus, in

Genjō Kōan, we have Dōgen's presentation of Buddhism and Buddhist enlightenment in a text that is clothed as much in Daoist as in Buddhist robes.

6. *Confucianism*: Confucianism has a strong social philosophy. It is about the rightly ordered life in the rightly ordered society. Dōgen strikes one as being something of a Confucian in his general style. A great deal of his work and writing is actually about organization and the correct relations between people according to their roles. He does not follow Confucianism in a narrow sense, but his temperament has a distinctly Confucian leaning. If Confucianism is about creating a perfect society, then Dōgen was interested in creating such a society in miniature in the monastic community that he established. One of the fundamental principles of his community was that nothing should be wasted. What one is provided with by life is one's lot and it is by deeply appreciating and conforming to one's lot that that one lives out a rightly ordered life. In *Genjō Kōan*, Dōgen is advancing the Li of Buddhism – the rite of enlightenment – as being such a correctly ordered life that will contribute to a rightly ordered community. For Dōgen, the epitome of rightly conducted ritual is zazen, but he carries this principle far beyond the meditation hall. All of life becomes a correctly ordered ritual. Confucius would have approved of the principle even if they disagreed about the detail.

7. *Self-power and other-power*: Ordinary people were concerned about salvation. Buddhism seemed to offer it, but it was impenetrably difficult for many ordinary people to understand. All the innovators of the third phase of Buddhism in Japan (see above p.25) had to explain the empowering force that effected the necessary change. Each did it in a distinctive way. Dōgen believed in personal effort, but he also believed that the change does not come from 'self'; it comes when self gets out of the way.

8. *Monastic and lay*: Much of Dōgen's effort went into creating and running a monastery dedicated to helping individuals attain satori. Yet, the work that he wanted to form the first chapter of his *magnum opus* was a letter to a layperson that contains no mention of monastic discipline. This has to be significant. It tells us at least that Dōgen was alert and sensitive to what lay

Buddhists were concerned about even if his forte was going to be training monks.

Although Dōgen is commonly presented as the founder of a sect, he seems to have had no intention of doing so, any more than Eisai. In fact, as has already been pointed out, Dōgen comes across in *Genjō Kōan* as an integrator, not a separator. On the one hand, Dōgen did seem to believe that when he came back to Japan he was perhaps the only person in the country who really understood what Buddhism was all about. On the other hand, he thought that it was about a seamless integration of Chinese wisdom within a Buddhist frame in which self-power and other-power were completely integrated as the yang and yin of the Buddha Dao and its Li.

We should not, however, take it that Dōgen's integration is an assertion that Buddhism, Daoism and Confucianism are just different ways of saying the same thing, nor that there is a kind of underlying common essence to the three. Rather, Dōgen, like Daosheng, has strong views about what is and is not true and genuine, and sees most of what passes for orthodoxy in all three religions as dubious. However, this does not lead him to reject their concepts, but rather to reappropriate, redefine and thereby redeem them. Dōgen is difficult, but not fuzzy. He believes in the Buddhist teaching of causation, in the importance of clear thinking, in faith, courage, altruism and self-effacement.[2]

In Dōgen, the Buddha Dao is not a hazy reality, dimly visible behind natural things. Rather, he elevates natural things to being instances of, rather than merely indicators of the Dao. This is, therefore, an immanentist view: a robust, action-oriented philosophy that nonetheless centres upon the self-effacement necessary for the Dharma to do its work.

The above are some of the conclusions and assumptions that have informed my translation. If they are wrong then I am probably off the mark. However, they do yield what I believe to be a translation in which the different parts of the text all

2 For the importance of 'effacement' in Buddha's teaching see the Sallekha Sutta, Majjhima Nikāya 8 in Ñāṇamoli, Bhikkhu and Bhikkhu Bodhi 1995. *The Middle Length Discourses of the Buddha*, Boston, MA: Wisdom Books: 123–31.

conspire together to offer a single vision. Many of the existing translations and Western commentaries use *Genjō Kōan* as a series of hooks upon which to hang supposedly correct Buddhist doctrines of considerable variety. Often the doctrines chosen by such commentators are ones that stress the uniqueness of Zen as a distinct school. These were also my own assumptions when I started this work. However, I gradually realized that Dōgen's essay becomes much more coherent when we see that all the figures used in it are different perspectives on a single idea. *Genjō Kōan* does not advance a string of loosely related doctrines so much as present a single argument in which the different parts of the text each support the single central thread. I have just said "conclusions *and* assumptions" and this is because most of the assumptions that I am conscious of having made are the result of working through the text reiteratively. It sometimes seems that every time I read it something new jumps out. I hope that you have the same experience.

II.3 YŌ KŌSHŪ'S KŌAN

When Dōgen had finished the first version of *Genjō Kōan*, he gave it to a layman named Yō Kōshū. This may have been simply for safekeeping, but it seems probable that the original version was a reply to a communication from Yō Kōshū and we are handicapped by not having that communication. What did Yō Kōshū ask? Did he ask Dōgen what his position was in relation to the big issue of the day, which was the self-power/other-power controversy? Did he ask about 'original enlightenment' and the ideas of Nōnin? Did he ask why Dōgen focuses so specifically upon zazen? We cannot know. None of these topics is overtly referred to in *Genjō Kōan*, but implicit answers to all three are to be found here.

The image of a mirror that we shall encounter later tells us the manner in which other-power enters a person without becoming part of that person. However, Dōgen's conceptualization of that power is rather different from that of Hōnen, being more immanent in a way that had less appeal to his contemporaries, though more to people of the twenty-first century.

Genjō Kōan implicitly refutes many of the ideas of Nōnin, but is, equally clearly, in dialogue with them and shares with them a sense of what could be called natural or spontaneous enlightenment.

Genjō Kōan does not mention zazen, yet it can tell us a good deal about Dōgen's sense of its inner meaning.

Yō Kōshū seems to have worked in the same government office as a man called Yakou who is mentioned in Dōgen's *Eihei Koroku*.[3] It seems likely that Yakou visited Dōgen in the year after *Genjō Kōan* was written. He was a Confucian who practised Buddhism. If Yō Kōshū was similar in this respect, then this might help to explain Dōgen's free use of Chinese terminology in *Genjō Kōan*. However, we cannot take it that this was purely an adaptation to the needs of the reader in this one text because of Dōgen's wish to use *Genjō Kōan* as the first chapter of *Shōbōgenzō*. It was clearly more significant than simply a letter to one person.

The central thread in *Genjō Kōan* is a description of what satori – enlightenment – actually is and how it works. This fundamental point solves Dōgen's own problem and, in principle, offers liberation to all people. So perhaps Yō Kōshū asked: what is practice and enlightenment? We shall never know, but Dōgen's reply remains a seminal essay that, like a good kōan, endlessly continues to reveal more and more shades of meaning.

II.4 DŌGEN'S KŌAN

Here I am using the word 'kōan' in the sense of 'a spiritual problem' that Dōgen would have been familiar with from his time at Kennin-ji. We shall soon see that Dōgen himself recasts and redefines this word. In the Tendai monastery, Dōgen learnt that we are all already inherently enlightened, and he asked himself: if this is so, what is the point of practising? Surely, practice is important, but if we are already inherently enlightened, why does it matter?

Practice could seem like hard work, and if all you got in return was something that you had had all along, it was difficult to

3 Leighton and Okumura 2004: 507–10.

see the point. When one thinks that practice is about getting something for oneself, this kind of objection is insurmountable. Why work hard to get what you already have? This was the question that Dōgen asked everywhere he went and nobody had a satisfactory answer. However, I think that behind this question, Dōgen already believed that practice was vital and what he wanted was an explanation of how that could be squared with the teachings that he had received that so easily led to antinomian conclusions. Nōnin had said that practice is unnecessary since enlightenment is already inherent and knowledge of it arises spontaneously. The young Dōgen could not accept this, but could not refute it either.

Furthermore, the idea of having an inherently perfect nature is – as Hōnen had also thought some decades before – a rather perilous idea for a spiritual practitioner to hold. It can readily lead to complacency, to over-self-evaluation and to arrogance, and also to carelessness of others since, if they already have what they need, there is no need to give them anything else. The whole idea of an inherent radiant nature also seems dangerously close to the idea of the *ātman* that was the central concept of the religion that Śākyamuni had rejected back in India. In fact, virtually by definition, Buddhism rejects the notion of an immortal, unchanging soul or god-element in the individual. How were all these points to be squared with one another?

By the time Dōgen came back to Japan, he had found a different way of viewing things. In this new vision, he could accept the unborn Dharma of all Dharmas, without reifying it, by realizing that while it is, was and always shall *be*, it is not something that one can *find originally located* in one's own body and mind, nor can one *appropriate it* to one's body or mind, but, yet, its functioning can, if one plays one's part, send one forth in the service of all sentient beings. This new way then informed all his work.

Genjō Kōan is autobiographical in that it is an account of what the author emerged with as the solution of his own deep spiritual problem, something precious that he then felt impelled to share.

II.5 RELIGIOUS CONSCIOUSNESS

The pioneering sociologist Émile Durkheim pointed out that the hallmark of religion is a distinction between, on the one side, the mundane or profane, and, on the other side, the sacred or holy. He was looking for a distinguishing feature that would enable him to say, in any culture, whether any given institution, practice, way, thought, custom, etc., was religious or not. Religions vary hugely in form from one society to another. Durkheim established this criterion and it has stood the test of time. When there is, in the consciousness of the people engaged in some activity, a distinction of this kind, then we can say that it is a religious activity. We can therefore distinguish religious consciousness as the consciousness that some things (objects, concepts, abstractions, people, actions, etc.) are holy and some are not.

If you have grasped the idea of what religious consciousness is you will realize that there is a connection between this and ideas about duality and non-duality. If there is religious consciousness then there is a duality between the holy and the non-holy. Dōgen was a religious Buddhist. He was not secular. He lived all his life as a monk. He believed in correct practice. He set up a monastery that had a strongly ritualistic basis. He wrote in a religious context and his writing is full of attempts to penetrate the relationship between the holy and the mundane.

Many people think that *Genjō Kōan*, and Dōgen's writings in general, are essentially about propounding a philosophy of non-duality. Translators and commentators, therefore, try to make the text fit with this assumption. However, as it stands, the actual text has a great deal of dualistic imagery. Furthermore, it tends to emphasize the sharpness of the distinctions in the dichotomies presented. We shall see this as we go through. The actual terms 'duality' and 'non-duality' do not occur. Dōgen deals with the subject through the idiom of the Dao, itself a rather esoteric Chinese religious notion.

Modern scholars might want to emphasize the non-dual aspect of Dōgen because they themselves have a secularizing bias, but Dōgen himself is, surely, in his writing, resolving his own religious issues. The philosophical issue of duality and non-duality is extremely slippery. If one talks about 'the non-dual', one is tempted to write it with a capital – the Non-dual – because in Dōgen's writing, insofar as a non-dual is implied, it signifies the *Dharmakāya*, which is a 'holy of holies' of Mahāyāna Buddhism. Furthermore, even in the writings of contemporary Western 'secular' Buddhists, 'the non-dual' often seems to occupy a rather 'holy' position, as a metaphysical concept that somehow offers a kind of intellectual salvation. Commonly, between the non-dual and duality there is clearly a distinction of the kind that Durkheim would recognize. Resorting to non-duality in order to prove that Buddhism is not a religion, therefore, commonly demonstrates exactly the converse.

The best attitude for a would-be translator is to try to suspend preconceptions and stay as close as possible to what the text actually says, but this is much easier said than done. In Dōgen, every concept – almost every word – involves some allusion to ideas and principles in other works, many of them scriptural or hallowed elements in Buddhist tradition or Chinese religions. Probably no rendering or interpretation is ever going to exhaust the implications of *Genjō Kōan*. One can only do one's best.

III

THE MEANING OF THE TITLE

Let me first introduce some of the discussion that has taken place around this issue, then I will give my own view on the matter.

III.1 THE PROBLEM OR ITS SOLUTION?

Genjō means to appear or show up, or it can mean what has appeared or been actualized, hence realized or made manifest. It thus can be taken as referring to the fact of spiritual awakening or as the object to which one awakens.

Kōan, ordinarily, means a spiritual problem. 'Problem' is really too weak a term. We are talking about the nub of the existential dilemma – the deep angst inherent in being a mortal being with a slippery mind and a time-limited body in a world of unreliable conditions. A friend of mine recently reported that, having heard of the death of an uncle, her four-year-old child, a week later, having evidently been thinking about the matter, burst into tears and declared that she did not want to grow up, get old and sick and then die, and wept inconsolably for half an hour. This seems to me to sum up the whole foundational impulse of Buddhism and the kōan that we all struggle with one way or another.

However, for people in medieval times, existence was not limited to these existential realities alone. They did not think of the world as a great machine, but as full of life, much of it unseen. Anguish was not just a matter of coping with worldly matters; it was to do with one's place in relation to the Buddhas, ancestors, gods, spirits and unseen forces as well. Furthermore, there was the fear of what might happen after death. Buddhist hells are not as everlasting as Christian ones, but just as gruesome.

Discussions of the title among scholars often revolve around whether the term genjō kōan refers to the problem or to its solution. If genjō means 'realization', does genjō koan mean the problem of everyday life and sentient existence? Or does it mean the ultimate reality that appears when one is enlightened and the problem is solved? Some translators lean one way and some the other.

III.2 WHAT IS A KŌAN?

In the word kōan, the syllable *kō* suggests something equal and universal that has to be conformed to while the syllable *an* suggests something individual and personal. The kōan, therefore, is one's personal manifestation of a universal spiritual issue that there is no getting away from. There is no getting away from it because we are here in the existential world, which Dōgen generally refers to as 'birth and death'. We could then say that this text is an essay explaining the problem of daily life, or, as this seems too weak, perhaps we should say, the anguish of living and dying. Yet, we can go still further and say that the title refers to the kōan as an eternal characteristic that transcends daily life altogether: that it is an instance of eternal truth made manifest.

At the same time, we can also understand the meaning as being the kōan realized or clarified by Dōgen himself. Taken this way, we can see this as Dōgen writing an essay to tell us what it was that he understood – what realization had come to him.

A kōan is a form religious consciousness. When we translate it as 'problem' this can give the mistaken impression that we are talking about a worldly or psychological dilemma. A kōan, however, is the problem of how to live a truly religious life in the midst of inevitably corrupt worldly circumstance. How can one be true to the eternal while here in the midst of the ephemeral? What is life all about? Why am I here? What do I need to do to make life ultimately meaningful? These basic religious questions disturb worldly self-indulgent complacency.

Humans are not machines, and these deep broodings that are the wellspring of religion are integral and fundamental to our being. Whether we got them from God, from karma, or by a process of biological evolution matters little in respect of the practical matter of having to live with them. A person who pays no attention to them lives a shallow life, but a person who attends to them, perhaps, finds him- or herself enmeshed in genjō kōan.

III.3 WORKING WITH A KŌAN

In sum, genjō kōan could be the anguish of being caught between impermanence and eternity. Such *is* the problem of every life. Now, one might think that the point, therefore, is how to solve and then eliminate the problem. The general drift of Dōgen's essay, however, does not seem to point in this direction. Perhaps, therefore, the point is that it is actually necessary to have and be working on this kōan, rather than to get rid of it. One can be working on it from the position of the deluded being, or from the position of a Buddha. From the position of the deluded being, Buddhas are a kind of goal to be attained that remains forever elusive, which is what makes the kōan into a seemingly insoluble problem. From the perspective of a Buddha, the ordinary deluded being is fully encompassed, which makes the kōan into an essential idiom through which to have engagement with the world. Either way, the substance of the religious life is such striving.

Buddhism is a middle way. One extreme is to give up religion and drift off into worldly life, burying the awkward questions under an anxious or compulsive façade. The other extreme is to fall into perfectionism or absolutism, affecting to have solved one's problem through dogmatic adherence to some simplistic creed, religious, ideological or merely worldly. Neither of these extremes constitutes a truly constructive life. The Buddha called them vain, ignoble and useless.

Thus, Dharma Master Hanshan (eighth or ninth century) would warn his disciples of the dangers both of sitting on the 'clean white ground' and also of hankering after 'attractive sidelines'. Do not rest in heaven, do not be seduced by the world. The spirit of genjō kōan, therefore, is that of living a life that is always 'in the sight of God' while being completely in the thick of the miscellaneous circumstances that arise. Is this what Dōgen is trying to explain?

Sino-Japanese Buddhists do not say 'in the sight of God,' they say 'in the Dao'. Dao, or way, is a pivotal term in Chinese religion in which there is a Way of Heaven and also the ways of the world. I am going to say a lot more about the way or Dao in due course.

We are here in the world and we are worldly beings, but if we turn to religion, then the Way of Heaven becomes more prominent in our attention. We have it in mind. It gets under our skin. This is inspiring, but it also throws up problems. The worldly life is easier in having fewer dilemmas of conscience, but it is shallow and artificial.

Kōans, then, are irritants in the soul. They can go on causing pain and trouble indefinitely, or they can be a valuable provocation: the grit that causes a pearl to be made.

III.4 BEHAVIOUR AND ETHICS

Kōans have to do with ethicality. What should one do? What should be done? It is said that the highest kōans are the religious moral precepts. As soon as one starts trying to keep such a precept one has problems. Take a precept such as: *Not to be proud of oneself, nor devalue others*. Try and keep it for a day. One will learn much from one's many failures and also from one's realization of how much one has done completely unconsciously, only realizing later, if at all.

Taking on a religious discipline is a challenge to oneself. One sets up a goal to keep such and such an injunction. One fails to keep it, but one learns in the process. So, trying to be ethical will tend to bring one's kōan to the surface. What one learns has much to do with human frailty. So, does genjō refer to this surfacing of hidden aspects of self?

Working with a kōan, however, is not essentially just about being good. Goodness may come as a by-product. The kōan has more to do with how one perceives and experiences the world. The substance of the religious life is not one's perfection in doing right, but one's recurrent learning from encountering one's human nature: one's lack of moral courage, lack of self-control, and personal blindness, not to mention the intractability of the world in which we are inevitably implicated in all manner of non-virtue, and that is just the start of it. Anybody who takes religion seriously faces endless dilemmas. Perhaps these are all aspects of genjō kōan.

Working with a kōan reveals our nature, reveals the world, reveals the Truth, destroys our ideals and delusions, and constitutes the very substance of real religious life. However, to be Buddha is to encompass all of this. From the worldly point of view the goal is to abolish our moral frailty, but from the perspective of awakening there is no such goal, just the ongoing act of loving and accepting such revealed nature just as it is – of cherishing genjō kōan.

III.5 FACING ONESELF

So, a kōan is the problem that a particular person has in approaching life when in some way inspired by a religious faith or vision. The identity of that problem is made up of three factors – the ideal, the actual and oneself. We embark upon this business because, at some level, we vaguely sense that we need to do something about ourselves, but have not the faintest idea how to do it – or, perhaps, we have many ideas, none of which work – so we seek a method or path. However, there is no technique or method that will do the trick. Indeed, the technique-based approach is generally focussed on trying to eliminate the symptoms of disturbance, disturbance that wells up from our depths, that is both troublesome and, at the same time, we are told, the actual gateway to liberation. Our search for such a technique actually proves to be an attempt to avoid responsibility, or to suppress the problem. Yet, to have responsibility for something that one seems to be incapable of doing anything about only intensifies the kōan.

In self-power mode, trainees sit with this tension until something gives. In other-power mode, the same kōan teaches one one's complete lack of self-power. In both cases the breakthrough takes the form of a deep experience of faith. However, this experience also involves (and only occurs when there is) a real facing of one's own 'spiritual materialism'. By this term, coined by Chogyam Trungpa,[1] I am referring to our tendency to import worldly attitudes into our own spiritual life. Behind our conscious motivation for entering the holy life lurk other darker impulses, for power, for personal gain, for status, for possession. These all constitute forms of magical thinking aimed at fame and gain. They are all to do with getting something to satisfy body or mind.

The term genjō also implies completeness. What shows up just is what it is. It is not anything else. The concrete situation is only avoidable by falling into delusion. So living without delusion is a matter of taking on the concrete reality of each situation. It is the situation itself that can show us the Way of Heaven, but it is only likely to do so while we have religious consciousness. Dōgen can show us what that means. The path, however, has many pitfalls. What is required is that we avoid posing and artificiality. Now worldly life is replete with such artificiality and when we come to religion we unwittingly bring all our bad habits with us. There is a strong tendency, therefore, for us to subvert the religious life itself in just the same ways as we are used to subverting life in the worldly world. The same patterns apply. It is we ourselves that are the problem.

III.6 SOLVING THE RIDDLE

Genjō Kōan was written by Dōgen soon after his return from China. Reading Dōgen's essay, it is difficult to escape the impression that it is a thoroughly dualistic text. Everything is

1 Trungpa, Chogyam 1974. *Cutting Through Spiritual Materialism*, Boston, MA: Shambhala.

in pairs and there is a good deal about the polarities in these pairs not overlapping. Too hasty an assumption that Dōgen is writing about non-duality may be a mistake, at least in the exclusive sense in which we tend to take the idea in the West. The Chinese have a different way, which is expressed in the dynamic polarities of yin and yang. Here, non-duality, if we can so call it, manifests *as* duality. This is an inclusive, not an exclusive vision. As we go on, I shall give this possibility some space in my discussion of the text. If this hypothesis is right then the interpretation of the title may be open to other possibilities.

When Dōgen wrote the word kōan he did not use the characters that are usually used. Some people ignore this difference, but nothing that Dōgen writes seems to be accidental. The character used by Dōgen for the *an* part of kōan was defined by his disciple Senne as meaning 'to keep one's lot or place'. The *kō* part refers to equality or balance. I think, therefore, that Dōgen's concept of kōan in *Genjō Kōan* is not the same as the idea of kōan with which he was familiar from his experience of Rinzai Zen at Kennin-ji. I will henceforth do my best to make it clear to the reader which concept I am using when I use the term 'kōan'. In the main body of the commentary and discussion from now on, you may take it that we are always talking about Dōgen's form of the word rather than the ordinary usage unless otherwise stated.

In the characters normally used for kōan, the etymology suggests 'a case treated on a par with other cases'. In Dōgen's characters it suggests 'keeping to one's true, original or allotted part or role'. These are not the same thing.

So here Dōgen is making a pun. He is fully aware of the usual term, but, while hinting at it, he also means something different. This way of disconcerting the reader is characteristic of Dōgen and his contemporaries. He gives terms new meanings, or explores dimensions that are often not looked at. He is always looking for more, or deeper, meanings, and does not let the reader rest in his or her comfort zone.

Kōan, in Dōgen's sense, means a state of rightness that occurs when both parties play their parts in a completely unaffected way, a way that accords completely with the duty that each has in the given situation, yet does not feel in the least unnatural. In the simplest terms, we can say it is life without fuss.

Further, here, Dōgen is using his sense of kōan in combination with genjō. The sense is that appearance (genjō) occurs when each one *is* in their allotted part and there is then a complete meeting of heart and mind. This may occur in the simplest of eventualities. It is not a matter of a complicated procedure, it is a matter of real meeting. What 'appears'? The Dharma and, hence, the Buddhas.

However, we should not think that this is necessarily a spectacular experience for the people actually involved. They are just playing their allotted parts. Genjō refers to the Dharma appearing, but not necessarily in such a way that the participants are conscious of it. The beauty may be in the eye of the beholder rather than that of the participant. When one watches a craftsman at work, one may experience wonder, but the craftsman is just getting on with the job.

So, genjō kōan is not so much something realized purely within oneself. It is a function of relationship. The vast majority of instances of enlightenment recorded in Buddhist, and especially Zen, texts, occur in situations of encounter between two people. If we include encounters with natural objects, then all of them do so and the nature of that relationship at that time is key.

The matter of relationship with natural objects is not trivial. Śākyamuni Buddha was enlightened when he saw the morning star. If I use a more mundane example from my own experience, when I am doing woodwork, there is me and the piece of wood. It is pointless for me to complain in such terms as: "Why is your grain so twisted? You really should not have had a knot exactly where I want to make my cut..." etc. The wood is doing its part. I have to do mine. The wood is an 'other-power'. It is not answerable to my personal will. I might think that I have the 'yang' role and am going to impose my will upon the wood, but, in fact, I do not have the power to make the wood be anything other than what it is. If we work together, each playing his proper part, then the job may get done and something good may result from it. Furthermore, there will be peace in my heart. This is, I suggest, Dōgen's sense of genjō kōan. In every detail of life we meet such other-powers and, for Dōgen, the other-power in the piece of wood or in the morning star is no different from that of the myriad Buddhas. They are the same, the same Dao. Laozi would probably not have disagreed.

If we read all this from a Daoist point of view, we can say that genjō refers to the appearance of the Dao, and the Dao Li is the demand that it makes upon us. In this case it is the Buddha Dao because this is Dōgen's explanation of how to truly take refuge in Buddha, Dharma and Sangha.

It is, therefore, possible that the form of Zen that Dōgen inherited from his Chinese master was distinctly Buddhist in its emphasis upon a sudden transformation, but was expressed in language that was formed by the tacit unification of the three religions that was such a hallmark of Chinese culture and had been near to the core of Zen thinking there ever since Daosheng. This language is deeply concerned with the proper relationship between yin and yang, emphasizing their separation yet complementarity. They are separate because, for the overall unity to appear, each has to play and take responsibility for its own part.

In the Chinese approach, Li can be seen as the way to achieve the correct yin-yang relationship that is apparent when each element is true to its nature and keeps to its allotted place in the scheme of things. In principle, this is also a strongly Confucian ideal. If Dao is the music and Li is the dance, then yin and yang are the steps, the two opposite feet that must move in turn to make the dance actually happen, or to make the performance of the rite effective.

It is also worth noting and, perhaps, especially important here, that Dōgen solved his own problem while in China, where he was allotted a place that was humbling. He lost all the status that he had had in Japan and was treated as of little account. It was while he was adhering to that diminished role that he had this realization. Satori sprang from his acceptance of a humiliating role. Such diminution is the very 'darkening' that defines the yin position.

III.7 MY OWN VIEW

A key term in this text is, in Chinese, 佛 道. Here 佛 is the character for 'Buddha' and 道 is the character 'Dao'. Now most people translate this as 'the Buddha Way'. In such a mode of translation the Daoist–Confucian association is completely obscured, though it must be obvious to a reader of the original. When it is translated as 'Buddha Way', it seems to imply Buddhism as distinct from any other way, such as, for instance, Daoism or Confucianism. However, if we do not translate it, but simply write 'the Buddha Dao,' it is immediately apparent that Dōgen is bringing Buddhism together with a wider swathe of Chinese thought. Furthermore, Dao implies yin and yang. This text is full of polarities and comments about the relationships between them. It is just as much an essay about yin and yang as it is about Buddhism. However, I have come to believe that in the mind of Dōgen these concepts were all completely fused, just as they were for many Chinese.

Nor should we overlook the influence of a name. Dōgen, 道 元 is ' Dao Yuan' in Chinese. So he is likely to have been thinking about the Dao ever since he received this name. *Yuan* 元 means 'head' in the sense of a leader. Dōgen came to live up to his name. As a character, 元 depicts a flat-topped mountain with a cloud upon it. This is also a powerful image in Buddhism. The mountains tend to represent enduring truth (Dharma) and the cloud indicates obscuration that comes and goes (*saṃskāra*), hence this can mean that the truth is not easily seen. Dōgen talks about 'mountains' in *Genjō Kōan* and in many other writings and about how clouds are attracted to mountains: "Although the white clouds have no mind, wherever they go they seem to be attracted to the old mountains."[2]

However, mountain can also represent the teacher (*shi*) and cloud the Buddhist practitioner or disciple (*unsui*). '*Un*' means cloud, and '*sui*' means water. The 'cloud-water' monk flows through life, but tends to remain in one place when he encounters enduring truth or a good teacher, just as clouds hang on the top of a high plateau. So here again we have apparent contradiction that actually adds richness to meaning.

2 Leighton and Okumura 2004: 121–2.

So, in this instance of dreamlike imagery, cloud and mountain make a yin-yang pair. 'Buddha Dao' is the name for the whole composed by such pairings. I suggest that 'genjō' means the appearance of the Buddha Dao. This appearance occurs when the relationship between yin and yang falls into its correct and original mode or balance. This means that, in general, it takes two for genjō to occur. This is why the master–disciple relationship is crucial, more crucial even than the particular practice employed.

When the enduring (unborn) truth appears in the midst of the ephemeral world and both play their parts, this is when genjō happens. This right performance of yin-yang roles is the meaning of 'kōan' in Dōgen's usage. The text explains in detail what he means and how it works. So, in *Genjō Kōan* we have the appearance of the Buddha Dao by means of the correct relationship between its yin and its yang. This correct relationship occurs when each keeps to his lot, as was explained by Senne. Senne should know. He was taught by Dōgen himself.

Again, we shall see that the correct relationship between yin and yang is one in which yin generally predominates, in the sense that one may be called upon to enter a yang mode by circumstance, but as soon as those conditions recede, the natural thing is to revert to a yin position. This is also a basic Daoist principle.

In Dōgen's writing, enlightenment – satori – is what happens when this correct relationship is found. Furthermore, as we shall see, this is not so much a result attained by effort or achievement as one that arrives when one lets go of affectation and reverts to a more natural way of being, which is also a thoroughly Daoist notion, and, furthermore, puts Dōgen a lot closer to Hōnen than most people realize.

When do we enter into such a truly harmonious relationship? When we are not trying to 'save our own skin' or satisfy our own mind particularly. When body and mind fall away, the peace of Heaven naturally manifests.

PART TWO

THE TEXT

GENJŌ KŌAN

1. Birth and death, practice and daily life, delusion and enlightenment, ordinary beings and all the Buddhas; such is the Buddha's Dharma of all Dharmas.
2. As the myriad Dharmas are other than self, when one is in their midst, there are no creating and destroying, no sentient beings and all Buddhas, no delusion and enlightenment.
3. Out of abundance and lack springs forth the original Dao of Buddha, and for this there is making and destroying, delusion and enlightenment, and there are living Buddhas.
4. So it is and nevertheless, blossom falls bittersweet and weeds spread amidst woeful resignation.

5. How deluded, to think oneself the teacher of myriad Dharmas! When myriad Dharmas come forth to train and enlighten the self, that is enlightenment.
6. All Buddhas are busy greatly enlightening delusion.
7. Those who are greatly deluded about enlightenment are ordinary beings.
8. So people who are enlightened are continually being enlightened within enlightenment.
9. Those in the middle of delusion get more deluded.

10. When All Buddhas really are All Buddhas the self does not need to know All Buddhas.
11. So, thus, we can say, enlightened Buddhas go on enlightening Buddhas.

12. Though one may deeply understand the forms of body and mind, though one may deeply understand what body and mind are saying, still this is not like a reflection in a mirror, nor like the moon in water, which is only realized on one side when the other side is dark.

13. To comprehend what we call the Buddha Dao means to comprehend the self.
14. To comprehend the self is to forget the self.
15. Forgetting self is confirmed by the myriad Dharmas.
16. This being confirmed by myriad Dharmas causes body-and-mind – and even the body-and-mind of others – to fall away.
17. This coming to a stop is the enlightenment-trace, the evidence of enlightenment.
18. This 'stopping', the trace of enlightenment, is what causes one to be going forth for ever and ever.

19. If, when a beginner seeks the Dharma, he positions himself as far away and nowhere near to the Dharma's edge,
20. then, when the Dharma is correctly transmitted to him, he is soon playing his part like a natural.

21. When a person goes riding in a boat, if he turns his eye toward the shore, he erroneously thinks that the shore is moving.
22. If he observes the boat closely, he will see that it is the boat that is going forward.
23. If we try to discern the myriad Dharmas from the perspective of our confused idea about body and mind, we make the error of thinking that it is our mind and our own nature that are permanent.
24. However, if we go back to studying the acts of our own daily life (*an ri*) intimately we shall see that the myriad Dharmas themselves are not therein.
25. Then the Dao 道 and its proper performance (Li 理) will become clear.

26. Firewood becomes ash.
27. It cannot become firewood again.
28. However, we should not see it as ash after and firewood before.

29. We should understand the Dharma position of firewood: it has a before and an after, the before and after exist, but it is cut off from them.
30. As for the Dharma position of ash, it has a before and an after.
31. The firewood has become ash completely and cannot become like firewood again.
32. After the person dies away, he does not come alive again.
33. So, the definitive Buddhist teaching is not to say that life becomes death, but rather to say 'no appearance' or 'no birth' (*fu shō*).
34. Death cannot become life.
35. The definitive transmission of the Dharma Wheel is to say this is 'no disappearance' (*fu metsu*).
36. Life is one position in time and death is also one position in time, just like, for example, winter and spring. Do not think that winter becomes spring. Do not say that spring becomes summer.

37. A person's satori is like the moon lodging in water: the moon does not get wet and the water is not broken, but it is like a vast light lodging in the smallest bit of water – the whole moon and firmament, even in so much as a dewdrop on a blade of grass.
38. Just as the moon does not pierce the water, so satori does not break the person.
39. Just as the sky and moon in the dewdrop is no hindrance, so a person's satori is no impediment.
40. As for the depth (of illumination), it shall measure as the height (of the Dharma/moon).
41. Whether for an hour or a moment, look closely and you will see, in great waters or in small, the full scale of the sky and the moon.

42. When Dharma is not yet in body and mind, when practice is not fully rigorous, one thinks that he is sufficiently in the Dharma already.
43. However, when the Dharma is in body and mind completely and sufficiently, a person feels a sense of lack.

44. For instance, if you are in a boat out of sight of land and look in all four directions, you just see a circle, but the fact is that you are not seeing what is really there: this great sea is not a circle, nor a square, the virtues of the ocean are inexpressible.
45. According to the scope of one's eye it is like a palace, like a necklace of jewels, or anything at all.
46. Just for now, one only sees a circle.
47. The myriad Dharmas are like that too.
48. Conditioned by the mundane world, or by ideals, we make assumptions, but we only apprehend what falls within the capacity of our eye.
49. In order to understand the myriad Dharmas on their own terms, we have to do more than just see squares and circles.
50. The merits of the ocean and the merits of the mountains are inexhaustible, not to mention those of the incomparable domains of the four directions.
51. One should know it is like this right here, even in a single drop.

52. Fish swim in the water, but however far they go there is no end to the water.
53. Birds fly in the sky, but however far they go there is no end to the sky.
54. However, fish and birds, now, as of old, never free themselves from the water or sky; they just make great or small use of it according to their need, so, there is no such thing as using up every morsel or exploring every single crevice.
55. If a bird leaves the sky it dies straight away.
56. If a fish leaves the water it dies straight away.
57. If you are a fish, investigate the water.
If you are a bird investigate the sky.
58. When you are a bird, you have to be a bird.
When you are a fish you have to be a fish.
59. Birds live the life of the sky (emptiness – *ku*).
Fish live the life of the water.
60. But then to go further beyond is enlightenment practice and is the way of the old living sage.
61. So, thoroughly investigate the water and, later, you will be investigating the sky.

62. If the fish or the bird tries to go through to the other domain it cannot do so.
63. The place is attained when the doing of daily activity (*an ri*) is genjō kōan.
When daily activity is genjō kōan, the Way is attained.

64. This Way, this place, is not a matter of greatness nor smallness, not about self (*ji*) and other (*ta*). It precedes the 'is not' in the 'is'.
65. Therefore, it is not in the now-manifest, yet, nonetheless, it *is*.
66. Here, in this way of penetrating and pervading, one cannot know some knowable edge, cannot get the ultimate knack of Buddhadharma
67. except by living the same life and practising the same practice, simply just as they are.
68. One should not expect to have intellectual knowledge of one's attainment. Although evidence of enlightenment is immediately apparent to the eye, the secrets of the heart are not necessarily known to the mind.

69. Zen Master Baoji was using a fan.
70. A passing monk came by and asked, "The nature of wind (Fū shō) is that it is always abiding (*Jō jū*). There is no place that the always abiding nature of wind does not encompass. What is the priest still holding onto, that he needs to use a fan?"
71. The teacher answered, "Even though you just know that the nature of wind is to always abide (*fū shō jō jū*) and there is nowhere that it does not reach, you do not know the performance of the Way (Dao-Li)."
72. The monk said, "How is it that [knowing that] 'there being no place it does not reach' is not the performance of the Way (Dao-Li)?"
73. The master simply carried on using the fan.
74. The monk bowed.

75. The proof of the Buddha Dharma, the living path of right transmission, is like this.
76. As for the idea of not using a fan since wind is 'always abiding', it does not comprehend 'always abiding' nor 'wind nature'.

77. 'Wind nature always abiding' (*fū shō jō jū*) means that the breeze blowing from the House of Buddha brings forth a golden age on earth and ripens the ambrosia in heaven.

PART THREE

COMMENTARY

I

LINES 1–4: DŌGEN'S DIALECTIC

1. Birth and death, practice and daily life, delusion and enlightenment, ordinary beings and all the Buddhas; such is the Buddha's Dharma of all Dharmas.
2. As the myriad Dharmas are other than self, when one is in their midst, there are no creating and destroying, no sentient beings and all Buddhas, no delusion and enlightenment.
3. Out of abundance and lack springs forth the original Dao of Buddha, and for this there is making and destroying, delusion and enlightenment, and there are living Buddhas.
4. So it is and nevertheless, blossom falls bittersweet and weeds spread amidst woeful resignation.

I.1 COMMENTARY

LINE ONE

The expression 'all Dharmas' can mean all things, all reality, or all teachings. In Buddhism, these three are more or less synonymous since true teachings point out real things. However, the manner of pointing out differs according to culture, language, circumstance, audience and the capacity and personality of the teacher and audience. Hence, there are many Buddhas and correspondingly many Dharmas. Dōgen wrote *Genjō Kōan* for Yō Kōshū. It is probable that Yō Kōshū was a Confucian and it may be that he had asked Dōgen what

Buddha had to say about Confucius and his 'Dharma'. Dōgen is answering by referring, not to Confucius, but to all Dharmas. Buddhism's message encompasses all Dharmas, all religions. It is about delusion and awakening from delusion, about ordinary life and practice, about life and death, about ordinary beings and Buddhas. This line, therefore, establishes that *Genjō Kōan* is a text about Buddhism – the Buddha Dharma – as the fundamental Dharma, and about what it has to say about all spiritual paths. The phenomena of delusion and awakening from it are, according to Buddhism, universal. In passing we could say that no religion can be universal unless it can also encompass all the other religions.

LINE TWO

However, when it comes to the actual experience of living an awakened life, the essence is freedom from selfishness, or, we can simply say, from 'self'. When we say 'self' we tend to think we are talking about something within ourselves. However, the actual experience of self lies all around us. It subsists in what psychologists call projection. We do not see things as they actually are – as Dharma – we see them as 'appearances' (Sanskrit: *rūpa*) that are saturated with our projection of self. We do not see the Dharma before us; we see our own reflection, and even that much we see in a biased way. For understandable practical reasons, when we are in the normal frame of mind of the ordinary person, we relate to everything in terms of how we want it to relate to ourselves. This, however, is a distortion and is, therefore, delusion. The things around us are, in fact, instances of Dharma – of truth – and are therefore, in themselves, independent of our own self. Insofar as they are independent of self they can teach and inform us, but insofar as we have colonized them with our own projections they can only tell us what we want to hear, much of which is fantasy. Thus they are only Dharma inasmuch as they are 'other than self' and inasmuch as they are other, they are Dharma. The awakened, enlightened or illuminated person, therefore, lives in a world of 'Dharmas that are other than self'. Then life is always fresh and revealing and there is no question of a separation between delusion and enlightenment, or between Buddhas and ordinary beings. In this state, we encounter things on their terms. When we encounter them, we encounter a truth that was there before we came into the picture. Thus it is an 'unmade' or 'unborn' truth, in the sense that we did not give birth to it and we cannot destroy it.

The deluded person is endlessly 'creating' and 'destroying' whereas the enlightened person is continually discovering and encountering. The terms *shō*, 'creating', and *metsu*, 'destroying', are important terms that Dōgen introduces here. The awakened person is not creating and destroying. Genjō is the appearance of a truth that we do not contrive and cannot destroy (*fu shō fu metsu*).

LINE THREE

Dōgen now introduces the term 'Buddha Dao'. Dao encompasses and consists of yin and yang. Everything is within the truth. Even delusion is part of the truth since it is true that beings are deluded. The Buddha Dao includes everything and lacks for nothing. Thus everything referred to in lines 1 and 2 happens and none of it is excluded from the total vision, wisdom and compassion of Buddha. Up to this point we can see a dialectical sequence in the three points that, if we wish, we can relate to established Mahāyāna Buddhist principles. Thus, for instance, Steven Heine says:

> The first three sentences appear to evoke the Tendai doctrine of 'three truths in their perfect harmony': the truth or perspective of the temporary or provisional (*ke*); the truth of the void or empty of own-being (*kū*); and the middle truth (*chū*) between and beyond the empty and provisional, absolute and relative, being and non-being, transcendental and worldly.[1]

This is rather technical and this is not the place for a lengthy explanation of the 'three truths' doctrine, which is about the

1 Heine, Steven 1981. "Multiple Dimensions of Impermanence in Dōgen's 'Genjōkōan' ", *Journal of the International Association of Buddhist Studies*, 4/2: 44.

different ways of seeing what is happening in Buddhist practice, but I will make some comments in the discussion section below.

LINE FOUR

Dōgen goes on to say, in line 4, that we nevertheless continue to have feelings about things that happen in the world and these feelings continue to have a love-hate quality. This point is enormously important. Buddhism is often presented as if once one has 'arrived', whether by the route set out in lines 1, 2 or 3, then all problems are solved and this often seems to carry a tacit implication that all emotion ceases, or remains upon a level happy plain. Not so, says Dōgen.

I.2 DISCUSSION

POLARITIES IN THE TEXT

Dōgen often starts an essay with a contrast, or a set of contrasts. This gives a basic impetus and vigour to his writing. However, this is more than a style. His whole philosophy is dialectical. It reflects, and is an instance of, the counterpoint of life. He proceeds in a dialectical fashion and the reason is that that is how he envisages reality itself. Nothing here is static or final. Nothing is unquestionable. In fact, the questioning, or critical edge, is the life of the matter. Generally he starts with something that will be familiar to his audience and then he uses it as a springboard. Often he uses things that will be familiar and that seem to contradict each other. This is the method of his Zen and it is his way of saying that that's life. This is why he uses the term Buddha Dao as the culmination of these first three sentences. Dao is dynamic. It encompasses opposites, yet springs forth beyond them. Each leap sets up a new scenario begging to be transcended. Hence, here, Dharma is dialectical. It is not just a matter of understanding what dialectic is; it is a matter of doing it. In the final story at the end of the text, Dōgen says that one only fully understands the meaning of a fan by using it.

We can note that the strategy adopted in many Dōgen studies, which is to try to determine Dōgen's position on various issues, is more contentious than it first appears because of this dialectical method. The fact that Dōgen seems to criticize or reject or make fun of something does not necessarily mean that you will not find him affirming it somewhere else or later on.

In life there is much that seems familiar. Our daily routine may follow a pattern. The people we meet are mostly those we have met before. The things we do are familiar to us. All these familiar things are good and necessary, but are they a treadmill or a springboard? We come alive when we take another step, when we venture into something new. However, without the old and well-established we could not take the new step. To use a Zen image, you cannot jump off a hundred foot pole without climbing the pole first. Or, more prosaically, every step in walking only takes place in order to be left behind. So Dōgen begins with what is familiar, though, of course, in his own way.

DHARMA IS ALWAYS GOING BEYOND

The first sentence tells us about Buddhadharma as a Dharma of all Dharmas. We could dispute what he meant by 'Dharma', but the detail hardly matters. He is telling us that the Dharma of Dharmas itself involves a string of contrasts. Any of these could be a springboard for another dialectical jump. 'Delusion and satori', for instance. Satori may be the transcendence of delusion, but what is the transcendence of satori? Or 'practice and daily life'... if you practise daily life, are you living practice? And why are you 'practising' when this is the definitive performance? And how would you know whether you were practising or not? And if you did know, would it throw you off balance? In any case, you cannot make a Buddha by practising. And so on.

Dōgen is not definable, but he is understandable in the sense of entering into him and letting him enter into you. If you can catch the music you might dance together, then apart, then together again, on and off, and then you might find you are learning steps that you did not know were possible and, like him, improvising on the same music.

On the face of it, line 1 is Buddhism as you find it in the most basic introductory book, so that is not a bad place to start. The bodhisattva starts where people are and then coaxes them on until they are running on their own. And it is not just Buddhism, it is, as it says, the Dharma of all Dharmas.

WHAT IS NOT SELF IS OTHER

Line 2 brings a complete reversal. All the treasures of the Dharma suddenly disappear and we are faced with raw experience. We are still on ground that will be familiar to some – we have plunged into the Buddhist teachings on emptiness, non-self, the unborn and undying. Presented as doctrines, these matters can be abstruse and even baffling. Dōgen, however, prefers concrete meanings. In this context, it is interesting that he uses the phrase *ware ni arazaru*, which is Japanese for 'other than self' rather than using formal Chinese characters for 'not self'. Why? Because he wants to show the reader that he is not just talking about an abstract religious doctrine. Dōgen puts it in ordinary Japanese because he wants it to be clear that 'not-self' means 'other', which is not abstruse at all. When we say that something is not oneself we mean that it is something else, something other than oneself. In the minds of many, 'non-self' seems to have become concretized as a kind of mystical 'true self'. This error has then, sometimes, been further compounded by being identified with ideas of 'Buddha nature', taken to be a personal attribute. What is not oneself is other. This cuts through a lot of unnecessary complication. It reminds us that Śākyamuni Buddha said *sarva Dharma anātma*, which means that all Dharmas are other than self. He meant that things are real inasmuch as we are not in them. When we put ourselves into things we thereby distort them. When we do not distort, then things are what they are, which is to say they are true, which means they are Dharma. The truth of them did not come into being through our intervention. We have to begin by receiving things as they are. As soon as our desire starts to change them, they are delusion and distortion. Of course, we do it all the time, but, in concept, there can be a world that is empty of our projections. Not only in concept, in fact, since that is the world that actually exists, just it is not the one that we perceive.

This move by Dōgen follows the track of the 'three truths' teaching, but does so in such a way as to make it concrete rather than abstract. One can learn about *ke, kū* and *chū* as academic concepts without it making an atom of difference to one's actual life. Dōgen's use of more homely language challenges us to think about living in a true world rather than one of our own making and destroying. It asks us to observe, listen, respond, and come alive. It also signals that even the holy concepts of Buddhism that are assembled in line 1 are things made and destroyed, not unborn from their own side, but created from our side, for our, albeit worthy, purposes. They are our crutches as we hobble along the spiritual path.

TRUE HARMONY IS NEVER STATIC

Where can one go after that? It has to be some kind of synthesis, something that will bridge the gap or mend the wound that has appeared between lines 1 and 2. This has to be a 'middle', the holy 'middle way' that was declared by Śākyamuni, and Dōgen could have called it that but he does not. Why not? Instead he chooses to call it the Buddha Dao. Why Dao? Surely because Dao is dynamic. Dao is about time. Dōgen is asserting time as the primary dimension of reality, but his purpose is not to make a philosophical point. It is to give us a working concept that can release us from static, positional thinking and attachment. Many philosophies try to assert ultimate truth as if time could be eliminated from the picture. Śākyamuni did not do so, and neither does Dōgen. Time goes on. Things happen. If time *is*, then change *is*, which means that the synthesis we are looking for cannot be something static. Dōgen chooses the term Dao because it has the necessary dynamic quality. Dao encompasses and consists of yin and yang and their interminable, never repeating churning which is the reality of life. This is Dōgen's message, but also his method. It is ritual dance.

So far we have loosely followed the three truths, and so we have recapitulated their 'perfect harmony', but by the choice of the term 'Dao' Dōgen gives notice that this harmony and perfection is not final, static, complete, or anything of the kind. It can itself only be another springboard for another step beyond. Where do you go after the Dharma of all Dharmas? Emptiness. Where do you go after 'emptiness'? The Dao. Where do you go after the Dao? As ever, back into real life.

We can summarize the contrasts and polarities that Dōgen covers in the first three lines in the following table.

<table>
<tr><td colspan="6">Three truths</td></tr>
<tr><td colspan="2">Line 1</td><td colspan="2">Line 2</td><td colspan="2">Lines 3–4</td></tr>
<tr><td colspan="2">Dharma of all Dharmas</td><td colspan="2">Myriad Dharmas other than self</td><td colspan="2">Buddha Dao</td></tr>
<tr><td colspan="2">(*ke* – provisional truth)</td><td colspan="2">(*kū* – emptiness)</td><td colspan="2">(*chū* – middle way)</td></tr>
<tr><td>birth</td><td>death</td><td rowspan="4">No making (*fu shō*)</td><td rowspan="4">No destroying (*fu metsu*)</td><td>abundance</td><td>lack</td></tr>
<tr><td>daily life</td><td>practice</td><td>making</td><td>destroying</td></tr>
<tr><td>delusion</td><td>satori</td><td>delusion</td><td>enlightenment</td></tr>
<tr><td>ordinary beings</td><td>all Buddhas</td><td>blossoms fall</td><td>weeds spring up</td></tr>
</table>

EMOTIONAL TRUTH

The schema set out in the table has a satisfying appearance of completeness about it. Furthermore, it does broadly fit with established doctrine. Dōgen has brought the doctrine to life, but it is still the familiar set of ideas. One could feel some satisfaction and perhaps stop at this point. In the Dao, however, while progress leads to completion, completion leads to new disturbance. He goes on... "So it is and nevertheless, blossom falls bittersweet and weeds spread amidst woeful resignation."

This is like pouring a bucket of cold water over our satisfaction. Each time we rise into the satisfying stratosphere of fine theory he brings us down again to the reality of life, and when we get our feet on the ground he coaxes us up into the 'ascended state'. However wise or enlightened one may be, one still comes face to face with the vicissitudes of real life, and with them come real feelings. Only on the basis of such reality can we look up and see the shining moon of the Dharma of all Dharmas.

Saigyō, Hōnen and Dōgen all sought to banish their grief. They plunged into the Dharma. They exerted themselves to the limit. They did not arrive at a place of endless tranquillity.

They arrived at a refined sensitivity to beauty and compassion. In the end, they had more feelings than before, and it was on the basis of those feelings that they were able to reach others.

This observation by Dōgen, therefore, is to bring the reader down to earth. It is fine to have high-flown theories about perfect harmony, but it is no good if they lead one to deny or hide from real emotional life.

THE FEELINGFUL BUDDHA

Some years ago I wrote a book called *The Feeling Buddha*, in which I challenged the common interpretation of the so-called 'four noble truths'. This common interpretation is based on two millennia of commentarial tradition, so it felt like a rather risky thing to do at the time. However, the book was better received than I expected. The four noble truths, as you probably know, is the teaching set out by Śākyamuni Buddha immediately after his enlightenment. It is, therefore, one of the foundation stones of Buddhism. How can one dare to challenge that?

The four truths are *duḥkha, samudaya, nirodha* and *mārga*. *Duḥkha* is affliction – 'blossom falling' and 'weeds spreading'. *Mārga* is the 'eightfold path' of right view, right thought, right speech, right action, right livelihood, right effort, right mindfulness and right concentration. The question is how these are linked and what is the overall meaning. The common interpretation is that suffering (*duḥkha*) is caused by craving (*samudaya*) and can be eliminated (*nirodha*) by following the eightfold path (*mārga*). This initially seems fairly sensible. One might have doubts about whether suffering or affliction really can be eliminated in this life, but it seems like a nice ideal. It conjures a picture in which enlightened Buddhas are always tranquil and happy and the job is done.

I had a number of qualms about this interpretation. Some were technical and linguistic, but some quite substantive. Firstly, it is evident that Buddha did not become enlightened by following the eightfold path: he found the path by becoming enlightened. Furthermore, the 'path' is really a description of an ideal life. If one really treads such a path, surely one is enlightened already. I proposed an alternative interpretation. Later, I learned from colleagues who had studied the nuances of the original text very closely that 'four noble truths' is not a very good rendering of the name. Better would be 'four truths for noble ones'. This information substantially confirmed my proposed interpretation, which is as follows.

Duḥkha is not something that is eliminated. Birth, disease, old age and death, separation from what is loved, confinement with what it unlovely, failure and loss are all inevitable whether one is enlightened or not. The first truth, therefore, is a truth for everybody. The second truth is not just the cause of suffering, but also the result of affliction. It literally means 'what comes up with *duḥkha*'. What comes up is a bittersweet mixture of emotions, and sometimes even woeful resignation. The way in which an ordinary person handles this eventuality does commonly lead to more *duḥkha*, as when one drowns one's sorrow in alcohol, for example. The enlightened person, however, has a broader perspective within which to contain (*nirodha*) the arising energy. This is based on faith, vision and practice. When the arising energies are sublimated in this way, the person may well be found to be on the eightfold path. The path, therefore, is not a way *to* but a way *from* enlightenment, as it certainly was for Śākyamuni. This interpretation has stood the test of time and many people have found it valuable. My reason for summarizing it here is that it seems to me that Dōgen is saying much the same thing. He says that the Buddha Dao springs forth from abundance and lack, in other words, from *duḥkha*. It manifests as Li, which, in Buddhist terms, is the eightfold path.

By adding line 4, he is saying, do not think that *duḥkha* is going to be swept away. *Duḥkha* is a truth for noble ones just as it is for everybody else. What is different about the noble ones is not their immunity to pain, but their way of responding to it. Dōgen is going to tell us how this change from one mode of response to another happens. In particular he is going to undermine the idea that it is a result of following any kind of syllabus or step-wise path.

Saigyō, Hōnen and Dōgen were all sensitive, emotional men who channelled their feelings into creative and compassionate action, eloquent writing and guidance of others. They all, at times, experienced loneliness, disappointment, love, regret, dismay, enthusiasm and many more sentiments. If we can take them as examples of enlightened people, then it seems clear enough that *duḥkha* is indeed a truth for noble ones and so is *samudaya* – to have a normal and spontaneous emotional reactions to *duḥkha* is also normal to such awakened beings. If we cannot take these men as examples of awakened beings, then I am not sure who might qualify as such, in which case the whole proposition of Buddhism would become an impractical one of merely theoretical import.

THE IMPORTANCE OF SEPARATION

Dialectic involves separating and coming together by turns. Each coming together becomes a basis for the next separation. Philosophically, therefore, Dōgen has similarities to Hegel. It is just as important to separate and analyze as it is to unify and harmonize. The two movements need each other.

As this text goes on we are going to see Dōgen's tendency to separate again and again. In a certain way, line 3 unites lines 1–2, but it does so in a way that does not deny them their separateness from one another. This works easily in the idiom of yin and yang. The Dao incorporates the two, but they remain distinct. Non-duality implies and manifests as duality; it does not deny or reject duality. An overarching wholeness there may be, but within it there is division and the divisions are what make up real life. Flowers do fall. Dōgen's dialectic goes beyond a one-sided view, but it does not encourage a complacent notion of over-easy oneness. Buddhas do not just soothe, they also disrupt. Life is lived as point and counterpoint, satori occurs in encounter, and encounter needs at least two separate participants. It is only inasmuch as they are 'other than self' that Dharmas really are Dharma, and only they can enlighten.

Dōgen says that the 'pivotal essence' of every Buddha is to see Buddha! Buddha! in every moment.[2] This 'seeing Buddha'

2 In *Zazenshin*. See Nishijima, Gudo and Choto Cross 1994. *Master Dogen's Shobogenzo*, 4 vols, Woking: Windbell, vol. 1 (Book 1): 102.

is genjō. Buddhism is to take refuge in Buddha. Dōgen says, "what Buddhist patriarchs have authentically transmitted is reverence for Buddha, Dharma and Sangha. If we do not take refuge in them, we do not revere them; and, if we do not revere them, we cannot take refuge in them."[3]

If we cannot even see Buddha, how can we take refuge? If we do see Buddha, how do we see him? Where do we see him? There is a tendency these days to assert that one must find Buddha 'in oneself'. In the normal sense of this expression, there is no trace of this idea in this text. Rather, here, we find the Dharma in what is 'other than self'. Later we shall see how such Dharma enters into one, but never as a personal quality. One finds the Buddha in the Dao of things, which, *inter alia*, means in the way that they function without regard to oneself. Buddhism is abandonment of narcissism.

Dōgen implies that we can find Buddha in a subtle appreciation of things and circumstances, which is a wondrous and mysterious intimacy, but which also involves a separation. This is bittersweet. It requires a complete acceptance of our own distinct, allotted position in relation to the Dharmas. We may take 'non-self' to be an abstruse doctrine, but the fact is that all around us are Dharmas that are not self and every encounter evokes and provokes something in us, some *samudaya*, and we can flee from it into escapism, or use it as the launchpad for the next leap beyond.

Commonly, these days, in Buddhist teaching in the West there is a good deal of emphasis upon the idea that everything is interrelated, interdependent, even that it 'interexists'. Separation is minimized. However, in *Genjō Kōan*, in several important figures, Dōgen is going to emphasize separation. At this point it is worth acknowledging that there is a value in separation and in seeing what is 'other than self'. This is an important aspect of spiritual maturity.

By way of example, we can think of our relationship with our parents. Do we see them as people in their own right with lives and motives separate from ourselves, or do we tend to see them simply in terms of their function in our own life?

3 In *Kie-Sanbo* in Nishijima and Cross 1994, vol. 4 (Book 4): 175.

One's mother may have lived the most important years of her life before one was even conceived, yet one may tend to think of her not as an independent person with special qualities of her own, but rather to always see and judge her in relation to one's own needs and wants. To realize that the other truly is 'other' and to allow them to be so is a basis for real respect and an essential step in growing up. Unless we separate from our parents, we never become mature.

If we accept that much of the thrust of Buddhist teaching is toward reducing the importance that we attach to 'myself', 'my needs', 'my opinions', and so on, then the simple fact of truly recognizing the otherness of other people and of the things in the world around us will itself already be a Dharma instruction. Accepting that the world is not answerable to my personal will helps to put me in my true place, which is what *Genjō Kōan* is all about.

IS DAO A *DHATU* AND DOES IT MATTER?

Here, Dōgen's chosen word for the 'unborn' is the Buddha Dao. In the Daoist conception, the Dao is 'prior to heaven and earth'. It gives rise to them and to the myriad Dharmas. Thus, Daoism can be seen as a '*dhātuvāda*' in the sense spoken of by Matsumoto and the 'Critical Buddhists'. Remember, the Critical Buddhists are scholars who think that Japanese Buddhism has strayed into 'eternalism' by asserting a '*dhātu*', an eternal reality behind manifest things.

Does this mean that Dōgen's message in *Genjō Kōan* is also a '*dhātuvāda*' in this sense? I do not think so. Dōgen does not use the term Buddha Dao in the sense of 'originator' or 'creator', merely as a designation of the Dharma of all Dharmas actually functioning. One can have faith in the Buddha Dao in the sense that it is the urgency that the Buddhas impart to our being. It is eternal life with the emphasis placed on the word life, the ever-renewing grace. 'Eternal' does not have to mean static and unchanging; it can also mean always happening.

Dōgen does not fall into either extreme. In one, the mystical vision of the unborn becomes detached from real experience and thus becomes a form of escapism. In the other extreme, which is more common these days, over-emphasis upon concrete experience reduces everything to a dead mechanism with no spiritual or Dharmic content or meaning. Rather, Dōgen is concerned to raise our experience of 'Dharmas that are other than self' into the 'ascended state' of being holy Dharma.

In another essay, *Kuyō-Shobutsu*,[4] Dōgen tells us to keep clearly in mind that throughout eternity, unfailingly, Buddhas exist. We should not think of them as being transitory phenomena. However, we should not think of them as static either. Dōgen says that those who make offerings to them, who leave family life behind, and follow and serve them, inevitably become Buddhas themselves. Making offerings to Buddhas is the cause of enlightenment and enlightenment cannot be arrived at in any other way. The mechanism here is that to be Buddha one needs infinite merit. How is such vast merit to be obtained? One might think that it means offering vast amounts of jewels, palaces, countries, lives and so on. Dōgen does assert this and quotes the Buddhist texts that speak of past Buddhas having made such immense offerings over long periods of time. However, if we think of merit in mathematical terms as a fraction, the numerator of the fraction is the size of the offering and the denominator is the degree of self-investment. In other words, if I give a gift in a completely unselfish way, this carries more merit than a bigger gift given with a (hidden) selfish motive. It is easy to see, therefore, that the only way to have genuinely infinite merit is for the selfish element to fall to zero. When this happens, merit is infinite, however large or small the gift may be. Dōgen's religion, therefore, is one of becoming totally unselfish.

To give a gift or offering, there has to be a separation. Something passes from one to another. If it is a pure offering there is no expectation of any return. To give because one believes that by giving to another is giving to oneself can never yield the kind of complete unselfishness that Dōgen advocates.

4 *Kuyō-Shobutsu*, one of the twelve essays that Dogen chose toward the end of his life as being particularly important. See Nishijima and Cross 1994, vol. 4: 155 et seq.

INSIDE VIEW AND OUTSIDE VIEW

Line 1 tells us about the matter of learning to become enlightened. It is as if we are studying it from the outside, like a student. We learn about a process of conversion from delusion to illumination that takes place over time. The line refers to impermanence: things are born and die; ordinary beings eventually become Buddhas. It is Buddhism from the perspective of the ordinary person, the beginner, or the person with an academic interest: Buddhism as theory and doctrine, and, therefore, Buddhism as actually taught. The challenge in all religion is to cross the gap between theory and practice. There is nothing that cannot teach us. The person who embarks upon this path can find instruction everywhere in all the circumstances that arise. It is one thing to know this theoretically and another to experience it.

Line 2, therefore, tells us about enlightenment from the inside, what it feels like, being amidst myriad Dharmas that are not appropriated as extensions of self. Then one is in receipt of influence from the unconditioned, the not-impermanent. It is Buddhism from the perspective of the genuine practitioner, and, therefore, Buddhism as experienced by the awakened. The ordinary person sees everything through the lens of self, but for the awakened person, all the real Dharmas that teach endlessly are able to do so precisely because they are not self. The basic thing that they are teaching us is that self is not that important.

SO DO FEELINGS MATTER?

Line 4 tells us that even with all three truths in supposedly perfect harmony, things still happen and we still have feelings about them. Feelings cannot be denied, but that does not make them holy either. Simply, they happen. There is, in this kind of Buddhism, a plaintive sense of solitude that is painfully beautiful. This makes it unlike some other more puritanical forms of Buddhism, in which artistic expression might be dismissed as mere self-indulgence. Here, passion is sublimated, not abandoned. It finds a more sublime expression. The sublime is both wonderful and terrible.

Feelings are both the expression of singularity and the medium of human contact, intimacy, and loneliness. They thus also partake of dialectical process. When we are together, we react to one another. When one is alone, one's sentiments evolve naturally. Dōgen is not advocating that we take them as guides, but rather that we appreciate them as the point and counterpoint of our symphony.

Observing the flow of our moods keeps us human and modest. We soon see how little control we actually have over them. The blossoms that fall are 'other than self'. They do not ask our permission. Nor do the spreading weeds. We may think ourselves very clever to have fathomed the doctrine of three truths, but we are helpless against the allure of beauty, the fright of danger, or the impact of unexpected events. Such *samudaya* is a truth even for noble ones, except that they allow it to enter into the dialectic of life. They can say thank you for the reminder it brings of our shared humanity. In them, it can evoke humility, and that lowering of the self can be the very thing that permits an influx of grace.

YIN AND YANG

Yin is the female, receptive principle and yang is the male creative principle. Together they constitute the Dao. Yin and yang are intimately interweaving. Each is continually giving way to the other, yet they need each other. However, from the yang position it is relatively easy to overlook one's dependence upon yin, whereas from the yin position, yang is always in view. If we think of yang as a bright light and yin as a dark place, we can see how this works. If you are standing in the light and I am standing in a shadow, it is much easier for me to see you than for you to see me. However, since yang needs yin just as much as yin needs yang, this oversight can be dangerous. It is much easier to overreach oneself when one is in the grip of some creative (yang) endeavour. One becomes blinded by one's own light. Dōgen realizes that Buddha's teaching, although using a different vocabulary, is very similar, which is why he, like many previous Chinese masters, feels justified calling it the Buddha

Dao. One of the Buddha's main targets is the harm and delusion that is generated by conceit, by being blinded by one's own light. The yin-yang philosophy implied by the use of the word 'Dao' provides an excellent and elegant way of explaining this that will speak clearly to his (oriental) audience.

The functioning of yin and yang is unceasing. Perhaps, reading the first two lines of *Genjō Kōan*, one conceives a determination to be in the position of line 2 – to be among the myriad Dharmas that are other than self, where there are no 'delusions', no 'satori', no 'all Buddhas', no 'sentient beings'. This might seem like the ideal or accomplished state. Then one would not have to be searching for the Dharma of all Dharmas, for all would be already achieved. However, the sheer fact that one has adopted such an intention, reinforced by the subtle conceit behind the decision, will have already thrust one back into the situation described in line 1. By setting up line 2 as the ideal and seeking it, one has re-established a distinction between 'delusion and satori', 'practice and daily life'. This is like the conundrum that if it is desire that prevents enlightenment, then the desire to be enlightened will prevent it happening. After a time one may despair of the attempt, yet in that very despair one naturally and unwittingly falls into the line 2 position, so awakening may happen just when one does not expect it – in fact, when one had given up expecting anything. Yet genuine despair is not something that one can plan. It is the very fact that it occurs without planning that makes it yin rather than yang. So here, Dōgen is highlighting one of the most fundamental internal contradictions of the idea of Buddhism being a 'path to enlightenment'.

In the yin position, one may feel bereft. This is not so much a balance of yin and yang, as the mercurial nature of actual experience. Here lies the quality called *yugen* that could lead Saigyō to write such poems as:

> With blooms of pampas grass
> for markers
> I push my way along,
> no trace of the trail
> I vaguely remembered.[5]

---

5 Watson, Burton 1991. *Saigyō: Poems of a Mountain Home*, New York: Columbia University Press: 69.

Here, purpose and pointlessness, confidence and despair, unpredictability and the sense of how things are all wrestle for the soul of the verse. In a few words, the master poet captures self and non-self, eternity and impermanence. Dōgen's own prose attempts something similar, often, as in *Genjō Kōan*, with captivating success that nonetheless still leaves one hovering, wavering, on the brink of boundlessness. The goal of such writers is not to resolve such tenuous disquiet, but to reveal it as the substance of nirvāṇa.

NOT EVERYTHING IS IMPERMANENT

Buddha's teaching emphasizes that all ordinary things – abstract as well as concrete – are dependent upon conditions and therefore subject to change, decay and death. Many people in the West take that part of his teaching as the whole of it. However, the other half of his teaching is that there is a possibility of liberation; a liberation that is a matter of identifying with what is not conditional and not impermanent. He called this by a variety of terms, but the best known is 'nirvāṇa'. In this sense, we could say that most Western Buddhism is philosophy rather than religion. It is Buddhism without the salvation. That, of course, also means that the whole of Buddha's fundamental intent is ignored. Presumably this is because we live in an ultra-materialist age.

A difficulty in understanding Dōgen is that we moderns are approaching him from the opposite side compared to most of his contemporaries. For them, the priority was salvation, and the transcendental view was paramount, but it could easily lead to quietism or to antinomianism of the 'everything is already perfect so there is nothing to be done' variety. Dōgen, therefore, emphasized concrete reality and the necessity to do something about our lives. This, however, means that the modern reader can easily take him as saying that mundane reality is all there is, and the transcendent can be ignored. Nothing could be further from the truth. Dōgen would have seen our modern secularist views as just as lamentable as he saw those of adherents to the Daruma School, who thought that because all people have Buddha nature they need not practise. To members of the

Daruma School, he is saying that faith in the unborn and nirvāṇa do not get one off the hook when it comes to dealing with real life. To modern people he would be saying that belief in real life does not get you off the hook when it comes to finding the meaning of life and salvation from its transiency.

SELF-POWER AND OTHER-POWER

Line 1 represents the self-power (yang) position, of having a journey to make from delusion to enlightenment. From the self-power perspective, one creates one's own enlightenment. However, in Buddhist thinking, whatever is created must sooner or later be destroyed.

Line 2 represents the other-power (yin) perspective in which one does not create (*shō*) nor destroy (*metsu*), but discovers the Dharma through the encounters one has. What one learns is something that one did not create. Since it was not created, it will neither end nor be destroyed.

The essence of Buddhism is to be beyond conditions and, therefore, beyond birth and death. Therefore, no enlightenment generated by the self can possibly be ultimate or lasting. Equally, whatever real enlightenment one discovers must, in principle, have no beginning. The intention or attempt to create enlightenment for oneself is, therefore, futile. However, if one encounters the unborn enlightenment, it will empower one and make a demand upon one's life. Other-power demands response, not passive resignation or complacency.

The unborn is other than self. It may enter into one and that may happen at a point in time – hence satori – but that does not mean that what has 'entered' was self-made, or, indeed, 'made' in any sense at all.

When one approaches Buddhism with the attitude of achieving something by one's own effort one needs to have a plan with a starting point and a target. One thus becomes involved in the contrasts between delusion and satori, Buddhas and sentient beings, practice and ordinary life. There is a lot to do in order to achieve enlightenment. One is concerned about one's practice and worried about birth and death. This is the framework within which many people understand, appreciate and practise Buddhism. In the West today, most books on Buddhism take it to be a path *toward* enlightenment of this kind.

Line 2 represents a path *from* or *within* enlightenment. This might be enlightenment in the 'inherent enlightenment' sense, as understood by the Tendai School and carried to an extreme by Nōnin, or it might be the 'awakening of faith' (*shinjin*) in the sense meant by Hōnen. Either way, this is the time when one is floating on the ocean of Dharma and everything is 'truly assured'. When one meets Buddha! Buddha! everywhere, one has no need of all these concepts and categories that guide one's self-power effort to attain awakening. One is not concerned with them because one is not trying to get somewhere, one is playing one's part wherever one happens to be at the time. In this mode, the Buddhas come to us.[6] Another way of thinking about this is to ask: is one trying to become a Buddha? or, is one trying to further the work of the Buddhas? In the latter, servant, role there is always something to do wherever one is, but it need not involve personal ambition.

In the third line, the Buddha Dao appears as the unifier of the first two, suggesting that there is a mysterious rightness about everything, yet there is still a need to practise. Dōgen here provokes some of the followers of Hōnen, by saying that living Buddhas do exist, and the followers of Nōnin, by asserting the necessity of practice.

Then comes line 4 with a smack of realism. He is saying that while many of these ideas about inherent perfection are beautiful and true, nonetheless, if you think thereby to arrive at a state where your feelings are always under control and clement you are mistaken. This, therefore, is Dōgen's version of the 'middle way' of Buddhism – dynamic, unpredictable and passionate.

ALL DHARMAS AND MYRIAD DHARMAS

In the Japanese syntax, the first two sentences start with "all Dharmas" (*sho hō*) and "myriad Dharmas" (*maṇ pō*) respectively.

6 The term 'Tathāgata', an epithet of Buddhas, is rendered in Japanese as 'Nyorai', which has the implication of 'coming to us'. 'Rai' means 'come' in Japanese.

This, therefore, is a first contrast. Some translators take these two terms as synonymous. This may be right, but it seems more likely, given everything we have observed about Dōgen's dialectical method, that a contrast is intended. What is it?

Many translators take 'all Dharmas' to mean everything. This, however, gives the text a very mundane feel and discards all of the sacred associations that go with the word 'Dharma'. Dharma is, after all, one of the most sacred words in Buddhism. I therefore propose to not translate the word, and, furthermore, to spell it with an initial capital, so that we do not lose these associations. The religious idiom in which we find ourselves here is one in which ordinary things are quite capable of taking on a sacred role, or of reflecting the sacred in a variety of ways, and this notion of 'reflecting the sacred' I take to be an essential part of Dōgen's meaning, which he explores from different angles as the text goes on.

All Dharmas can mean everything, but it implies the Dharmas of all Buddhas. The Mahāyāna sense, as represented in the Lotus Sūtra, is of there being innumerable Buddhas in all of the ten directions. Each Buddha has a Dharma – an expedient way of teaching. Among Dharmas, there are all the concepts and categories of religion, including those mentioned in line 1. These are the things that Buddhas teach.

However, these concepts and categories are human things – manufactured things. They are in the nature of useful illusions. They are *upāya*, 'useful means', and *saṃskāras*, 'mental confections'. Buddhism is unusual among religions in being one in which even its own concepts are regarded as open to deconstruction. This was particularly the contribution of the great first- or second-century philosopher Nāgārjuna, but it is implicit in teachings going back to Śākyamuni himself.

What about 'myriad Dharmas'? I do not know if Dōgen was aware of this or not, but, in Sanskrit and cognate Indian languages, there is a double meaning implicit in the term myriad Dharmas. The term that we translate as 'myriad' actually means 100,000. It is reasonable to translate it as myriad because no numerical precision is intended in Buddhist texts that use this term. It simply means a great many. However, the term *lak*, which means 100,000, is also the root of the term *lakṣaṇa*, which means 'an indicator', and this term has significance in Buddhism. A *lakṣaṇa* is something that points toward something else. Thus a symbol adverts to what it symbolizes, but this feature is not limited to symbols. There is no smoke without fire. A large part of our ordinary psychology is composed of things adverting to other things. The smell of coffee adverts to the drink and, by association, all the experiences that one has had of sitting in cafes, perhaps with friends. People decorate their houses with the things they like, things that have personal significance. In fact, for the ordinary person, almost everything that is significant to them points back to the self-identity one way or another, either directly or indirectly. So the smell of coffee points to the drink and the drink to various experiences and all of this to oneself as a 'coffee drinker'. This element then forms part of one's identity and one is attached to it. If somebody then says that coffee drinkers are intelligent people, one feels flattered and if they say that coffee drinkers are stupid, one feels affronted. These feelings arise because one's identity has been touched. Thus, the ordinary person lives in a world of *lakṣaṇas* that endlessly support and reinforce the sense of self.

Now, with this double meaning, myriad Dharmas can also be *lakṣaṇa Dharma*. However a reference to *lakṣaṇa* Dharmas that are 'other than self' means something different from *lakṣaṇas* in the ordinary sense. *Lakṣaṇas* in the ordinary sense are self-reinforcers, but here Dōgen is talking about *lakṣaṇas* that have nothing to do with self, but instead all those things that indicate something other than self. If they do not indicate self, what do they indicate? They indicate what is real, and what is real is Dharma – the eternal Buddha, the holy, the sacred, or, as Śākyamuni said, the Unborn, Undying, Not-Made, Unconditioned, without which there is no liberation from this world of artifice and conditioning.[7] The Dharmas of myriad Buddhas advert to those Buddhas and to their saving power. In Dōgen's usage, we can say that they advert to the Buddha Dao. So where 'all Dharmas' hints at what Buddhas tell us about

7 *Udāna* 8. See Ireland, John (trsl.) 1990. *The Udāna: Inspired Utterances of the Buddha*, Kandy, Sri Lanka: Buddhist Publication Society: 108 et seq.

things, 'myriad Dharmas' hints at what things tell us about Buddhas.

Furthermore, they do so not just as symbols, but as instances. Dōgen is often insistent on this point. An instance is different from a symbol. A symbol adverts to something that it is not whereas an instance adverts to something that it is. Thus one cat adverts to 'cats' or 'all cats'. It is not a symbol. A badge is a symbol. A policeman's badge is not a policeman, but it adverts to policemen. The myriad Dharmas are instances of the Dao – of eternal truth – not symbols for it.

What is the real difference between self-indicators and non-self-Dharmas? On the one hand, we can say that it lies in the attitude of the observer. The same physical object can be a self-indicator or a non-self-Dharma depending upon how our mind uses it. One of these attitudes is true and the other is delusion. The things around us actually are 'other than self'. They have their own reasons for being as they are. They do not exist from their own side, as it were, in order to serve our self-building agenda. I may think of that object over there as 'my table' but there is nothing inherent to the table that makes it mine. The spiritual question, therefore, is: what will tip us from seeing the world (deludedly) through the eyes of self to seeing the world (realistically) as adverting endlessly and universally to the Buddha realm, to really experiencing everything that occurs as an instance of the Buddha Dao, whether in its yin or yang mode, inviting us to play the complementary part?

Dōgen's use of the expression "Dharmas other than self" puts me in mind of the passage in the novel *The Unicorn*, written by the Platonist philosopher Iris Murdoch. The character Effingham has wandered into a bog in the night and is sinking and contemplating death.

> If one realized [that death mattered] one could have lived all one's life in the light. Yet why in the light, and why did it seem now that the dark ball at which he was staring was full of light? Something had been withdrawn, had slipped away from him in the moment of his attention and that something was simply himself. Perhaps he was dead already, the darkening image of the self forever removed. Yet what was left, for something

> was surely left, something existed still? It came to him with the simplicity of a simple sum. What was left was everything else, all that was not himself, that object which he had never before seen and upon which he now gazed with the passion of a lover. And indeed he could always have known this for the fact of death stretches the length of life. Since he was mortal he was nothing and since he was nothing all that was not himself was filled to the brim with being and it was from this that the light streamed. This then was love, to look and look until one existed no more, *this* was the love which was the same as death. He looked, and knew with a clarity which was one with the increasing light, that with the death of the self the world becomes quite automatically the object of a perfect love.[8]

Murdoch's ability to fathom the inner workings of the mind and to use that insight to bring philosophy to light is remarkable. The Dharma is about facing life and death and seeing them as the same. While we cling to one and flee the other we blind ourselves to light that is ever available.

BEYOND 'TOO MUCH' AND 'TOO LITTLE'

It bears repetition to say that Buddha Dao – its yin and its yang together – is a key concept in all this, bringing together the moment by moment transformations of life with eternal, unborn, undying truth. Dao encompasses and consists of yin and yang.

It is possible to paraphrase the first four lines thus:

1. When in yang mode, full and bright, one can see the Buddha Dharma in all Dharmas.
2. When in yin mode, empty and dark, one is surrounded by myriad Dharma, all other than self.
3. When yin and yang perform their allotted parts, the Buddha Dao springs forth naturally.
4. This Dao is not simply to be known about; it needs to be experienced in the midst of the emotional vicissitudes of life.

---

8 Murdoch, Iris 1963. *The Unicorn*, Harmondsworth: Penguin Books: 167.

Enlightenment is to wake up to the Eternal, but this is not separate from the incessant change. Later in the essay, in a rather splendid metaphor, Dōgen will tell us how this awakening happens.

So the Buddha Dao encompasses all the contrasts of delusion and satori, etc., but also the state in which they are absent. This means, *inter alia*, that we sometimes find ourselves in one position and sometimes in the other, but that none of this indicates that the Buddha Dao is not functioning as it should, whether we see it or not.

Further, if we take myriad Dharmas to mean *lakṣaṇa* Dharmas, in the sense of being Dharmas that advert to the Ultimate, then for fully enlightened people, but only for them, 'myriad Dharmas' and 'all Dharmas' coincide, because for such people even the Dharmas that do relate to self, arising from past karma, would still be experienced as adverting to Ultimate Truth – including the truth that self is illusory yet karma inexorable.

As for concepts like delusion and satori, these are Dharmas. Buddhas teach them, after all. Yet these concepts are part of us. Outside of us such ideas are not being created and destroyed. There is no need. We create these ideas because we have a sense that there is sometimes too much and sometimes too little. We have a sense of neediness. This is just as true in our religious endeavours as in our worldly ones. We have concepts like delusion and enlightenment because we want to get from one state to the other. We think that there is too much delusion and too little enlightenment. However, the Buddha Dao is not really concerned about such abundance or deficiency. The Buddha Dao is unconditional. Buddhas love us just as we already are. Nonetheless, we go on manufacturing ideas about delusion and enlightenment and these are the flowers of our religious work. However, flowers fade. And, of course, not all of our ideas are flowers – many are weeds.

The Buddha Dao does not fade. It is like an ever-turning wheel or an ever-churning ocean. The love, compassion and wisdom of the Buddhas are inexhaustible. They are inexhaustible because they do not contend. We all contend with delusion, and in the process make more delusion and exhaust ourselves. There are beautiful spin-offs from this process, but none that last forever.

SARVA DHARMA ANĀTMA

Śākyamuni said, '*sarva Dharma anātma*' – all Dharmas are non-self. This statement is one of the hallmark teachings of Buddhism. When Śākyamuni says '*sarva Dharma anātma*' he is making a contrast with two other statements, *sarva saṃskāra anitya* and *sarva saṃskāra duḥkha*. These mean, respectively, 'all *saṃskāra*s are impermanent' and 'all *saṃskāra*s are afflictive'. *Saṃskāra*, as we saw above, means 'mental formation' or 'mental confection'. Again, there are disputes about translation, to which I shall return shortly. Śākyamuni contrasts '*saṃskāra*s' and 'Dharmas'. He is saying that *saṃskāra*s are impermanent (*anitya*) and afflictive (*duḥkha*) and Dharmas are not-self (*anātma*). By saying that Dharmas are not-self, he is saying that they are not *saṃskāra*s. This is an instance of dualism and religious consciousness. Here Dharma is sacred and the *saṃskāra*s of self are mundane.

However, Dōgen also seems to be saying that *saṃskāra*s such as 'delusion' and 'enlightenment' are Dharmas. Are Dōgen and Śākyamuni contradicting each other? Not really. Śākyamuni is saying that our internal confections (*saṃskāra*s) are impermanent and cause us trouble. Dōgen is saying the same thing. Śākyamuni is emphasizing the difference between delusion (*saṃskāra*s) and Dharma, while Dōgen is emphasizing that Buddha Dharma lives in the midst of delusion and springs forth from it, while ordinary people remain enmeshed. The way Dōgen builds upon Śākyamuni here is dialectical. The superficial appearance of contradiction actually deepens the meaning.

There are many Buddhist writers who take *sarva saṃskāra anitya, sarva saṃskāra duḥkha, sarva Dharma anātma* to mean 'everything is impermanent, everything is suffering, everything is without self'. This, however, overlooks the dialectical shift from *saṃskāra* in the first two phrases to Dharma in the last phrase. Sometimes commentators reason this away by saying that *saṃskāra* means only 'conditioned things' and Dharma means 'everything', the difference being that nirvāṇa is the only thing that is not conditioned and nirvāṇa is not included in the first two phrases. I think this is too technical an idea. Buddha was not talking to doctoral scholars, but to ordinary folk. Nor was he making statements about ontology; he was giving practical spiritual advice. *Samskaras* are not things out in the world; they are the notions that we concoct in our own heads. The intended contrast is that Dharmas are not such concoctions. Buddha is not an academic ontologist. He is not talking about a mysterious quality of non-self-ness of things-in-the-world. I think he is using language in an ordinary way. What is not self is other, as Dōgen says. Dharmas are not self in the simple sense that they are not one's personal mental concoctions. They exist in their own right and it is by dint of their independence of self that they have the capacity to teach us and thereby be Dharma.

'*Sarva saṃskāra anitya, sarva saṃskāra duḥkha, sarva Dharma anātma*', therefore, is an example of Śākyamuni's use of dialectic. He is saying that our mental confections are ephemeral and that they are therefore tragic, yet there is a way beyond. When the Buddha Dao is working in us we are always springing forth.

BUDDHA DAO AS DIALECTICAL METHOD

To recap, in the first two lines, Dōgen speaks of Buddha Dharma in two contrasting ways – the Dharma of all Dharmas and Dharma other than self. In the third line, he uses the term Buddha Dao. Most translators do not see a contrast here. They translate Dao as 'way' and assume that Buddha Dharma and the Buddha Way are more or less the same thing. Such an assumption is not totally unwarranted, but if Dōgen makes such a change of terminology, it is for a reason.

Dōgen makes three statements. In the first two he talks about two aspects of Buddha Dharma. In the third he shifts to talking about Buddha Dao. 'Dao' has a somewhat more active feel than 'Dharma'. With the word Dharma we get a sense of principles that remain unchanging, whereas Dao implies ceaseless functioning: yin and yang, endlessly turning. This can fit easily with the Buddhist idea of the wheel. In his first sermon,

Śākyamuni set the Dharma Wheel turning, we say. Dōgen went to China where for many people – and Rujing may well have been one of them – the turning yin-yang disc and the turning Dharma Wheel were much the same thing.

Dao springs forth. Dōgen, following Śākyamuni, means that its principal characteristic is its dialectical nature. When Dōgen taught his disciples, one of the key things he taught them was this dialectical way of thinking, acting and interacting. He often told a story of what an ancient master said and then added, "That's what he said, and now I say..." For example, in a talk once, he related the following dialogue:

Monk: I wonder whose delusion is Buddha?
Master Zhao: It's the delusion of everybody.
Monk: How can we escape it?
Master Zhao: What is the use of escaping it?

Dōgen then goes on, "I also have a bit to say... If you ask me whose delusion it is, I would say 'One stalk of grass is the delusion of one stalk of grass; the sixteen foot golden body is the delusion of the sixteen foot golden body.' And if you ask how to escape it, I would say, 'Just escape!'"[9]

This is typical of Dōgen's dialectic. He is not so much refuting Zhao as using him as a springboard. This is not just a rhetorical device. It is part of Dōgen's idea of how Dao functions. By speaking in this way he is not just talking *about* the Dharma, he is manifesting or embodying the action of Dao, and his purpose is to induce such a way of thinking and seeing, one that always goes beyond, in the people he is teaching. One is not asked to understand a doctrine; one is invited to join in the game. There is an implicit – sometimes explicit – question: 'What will you say now?' For Dōgen, this was the meaning of Dao and also of the Buddhist principle of *prajña paramita*. We can translate this as 'wisdom of the other shore', but for Dōgen it is more a matter of always finding another shore beyond, always going beyond, and, therefore, always encountering Buddha and both going beyond together.

9 This story and many others illustrating the same point can be found in the *Eihei Kōroku*. See: Leighton and Okumura 2004: 305–6 and elsewhere.

Following on from the dialogue just reported and Dōgen's comments, one could say that the delusion of Jōdoshin-shū is Jōdoshin-shū[10] and the delusion of Sōtō Zen is Sōtō Zen (or substitute whichever other religions you like). And if asked how to get beyond them, with Zhao, one can say, 'Why would you want to? Just keep going on.' And if then asked, 'So what is the use of that?', one might say that there are many different saints sitting under the same Bodhi Tree, but each must improvise his or her own part.

Most translators think that there is more of Dōgen himself in the third statement than in the first and second, but the real spirit of Dōgen is in the dialectical counterpoint through which the Buddha Dao is always springing forth out of whatever has gone before.

The Dao is all about circulation, but a circulation like that of the ocean, in which nothing ever repeats exactly and everything produces an undercurrent that provokes the next move. The Buddha Dao starts with compassion for ordinary beings. When the ordinary person comes to practise they do so because they think that something is wrong. There is too much of something and too little of something else: too much evil and too little goodness, perhaps, or too little beauty and too much ugliness, or too much for others and not enough for me, and so on. It is natural for the ordinary person to approach practice in this way. The practitioner wants what Buddha has got that she or he believes him- or herself to be deficient in, or else wants to be free of what he or she believes to be obstacles to experiencing whatever it is that Buddhas experience. So the Buddhas' teaching has to start from that point. However, it goes beyond it.

When the ordinary person hears about delusion and enlightenment, he or she conceives an ambition and this provides the motive for a kind of practice. Such practice is not the practice of Buddhas, but it is something. Nonetheless, in this form of practice, based on wanting more or wanting less, there is much delusion. Dissimulation continues. Many believe that when they have got what Buddha has got, the distress that

10 Jōdoshin-shū is the school that takes Shinran to be its founder as Sōtō Zen takes Dōgen.

they feel will end. This is only half true. Half of their distress is natural and half is artificial. The natural part is the suffering and affliction inherent in sentient life. The artificial part is generated by their own sense of lacking what they believe Buddha has got. The Buddha hopes to take them beyond this to a place where the natural part is a continually renewing springboard for a real spiritual satisfaction.

CONCLUSION: LINES ONE TO FOUR

Lines 1–2 offer different contrasting perspectives on Buddhism. The third verse resolves the apparent contradiction of the first two. This resolution is achieved by the introduction of the idea of Buddha Dao. Buddha Dao accommodates an idea of fundamental truth in a way that also encompasses endless functioning. Thus the contrast of lines 1 and 2 manifests as two different modes of appearing – two positions in time – of the Buddha Dao.

The implication is that illumination, or spiritual awakening – satori – is a matter of playing one's part in the Buddha Dao. It is not a matter of holding to one or another of the modes alluded to in the first two lines. They are the yang and yin. Dōgen is going to go on to give us several other yang-yin contrasts in this text.

The 'appearing' of the Buddha Dao is what Dōgen means by genjō. However, that it should simply appear is not enough. One has to experience and act. There is a rite that celebrates the Buddha Dao and that rite is the correct ordering of daily life – right view, right thought, right speech, right action, right livelihood, right effort, and right mindfulness, not just right satori.[11] This right action involves self-effacement, playing one's part, and it is called, in Dōgen's way of writing the term, kōan. When a person's life accords with kōan, genjō occurs naturally and vice versa.

Without kōan there is no genjō, and without genjō there is no kōan. This is why Dōgen's approach is a matter of sudden awakening. Since you cannot have one without the other, they

11 These are the eight elements of the 'eightfold path', a fundamental Buddhist doctrine.

are not a cause–effect sequence. However, when one's life is genjō kōan, one may, as in a dance, at any given moment, be more on one foot than the other. Or, to use another metaphor, as in jazz, life is a jamming session. Each player has his part but nothing is predetermined, and nothing ever exactly repeats. Each move depends upon the last, but never mechanically.

Thus genjō and kōan are also an instance of the yin and yang of the Buddha Dao. In *Genjō Kōan*, therefore, much that would otherwise seem contradictory starts to appear as a wholeness, and the spiritual life becomes not so much a resolution of the contradictions as a living out of that wholeness through an endless dialectical 'dance' (Li).

II

LINES 5–9: DO NOT PUT ON AIRS

5. How deluded, to think oneself the teacher of myriad Dharmas! When myriad Dharmas come forth to train and enlighten the self, that is enlightenment.
6. All Buddhas are busy greatly enlightening delusion.
7. Those who are greatly deluded about enlightenment are ordinary beings.
8. So people who are enlightened are continually being enlightened within enlightenment.
9. Those in the middle of delusion get more deluded.

II.1 COMMENTARY

The main themes of this section are:

- the sharp difference between delusion and enlightenment
- the danger of self-aggrandizement
- accomplishment through self-effacement
- humility: the importance of responding
- the transforming effect of taking the yin position

Line 5 comes on the heels of line 4 and so implies a rebuff of the kind of person who affects to be beyond all passion. However, Dōgen goes on starkly to sharpen the contrast and separation between delusion and enlightenment. Not merely enlightenment, but enlightenment within enlightenment. Not merely delusion, but delusion within delusion. Out of the synthesis of line 3, we now see emerge another polarity. Clearly there is a great gulf. This is not just a matter of degree, nor are the two categories muddled by ideas like inherent enlightenment. One is one and the other is the other. This is religious consciousness writ large. Making a point of the complete difference between the two is an important foundation for what Dōgen is going to say in subsequent sections.

Here, also, the general idea of the power of non-self becomes prominent and the dualism of self and other is asserted with 'other' having priority. When a person affects to enlighten the myriad Dharmas, it is an act of attempted appropriation. However, the myriad Dharmas cannot, in truth, be so colonized. It is the very fact of their separation from self that makes them Dharmas. From that position, or distance, they can come forth and endlessly enlighten us.[1]

Thus the two dichotomies – enlightened and deluded, plus self and other – help to explain one another. It is in the relationship between self and other that the matter of enlightenment and delusion manifests. This is an important point. Often enlightenment is presented as though it is a characteristic of the individual and the form of much Buddhist practice seems to suggest individual effort and individual accomplishment. Śākyamuni Buddha was enlightened when alone, but he was enlightened when he saw the morning star and he called the Earth Mother to witness. Modern people who have been taught that the world is inanimate may easily miss the significance of this. It is 'all Buddhas' who are endlessly busy enlightening delusion. The picture that Dōgen is painting of the world – or, actually, taking for granted – is one in which in all directions there are Buddhas who are busy enlightening us, if we will but allow it.

Dōgen is building his argument. Awakening occurs as a function of a particular way in which the sides of the self–other dichotomy reach out to one another. There is a right way and a wrong way, an enlightening way and a deluded way. In the

1 'Coming forth', here, echoes the notion of the Buddha as Nyorai, the 'one who comes'.

deluded, common way, the self tries to dominate and the other is treated as inanimate – as an 'it'.[2] In the enlightened way it is the other that comes forth and the self that is receptive. In this mode the yang power lies with the other. To appropriate the yang position unnecessarily is to reduce oneself to one's own power solely, which is saṃsāra, whereas playing the yin part enables one to participate in the power of the whole universe. This is like playing an instrument in an orchestra: one might occasionally have to play a solo, but normally one plays one's part and what one does is enhanced by participation. We will see more on this in due course. For now we can note that there is power in the sheer otherness of the other, a power to teach and enlighten. The apparent power in self is delusory, or, at least, puny.

II.2 DISCUSSION

SELF-AGGRANDIZEMENT

On the one hand, Dōgen is pointing out how common the deluded state is. On the other hand, he is saying that the alternative is simple in concept, even if it is rare in practice. Our self-centredness is ingrained. Line 1 told us of the approach in which there are all the concepts of delusion and enlightenment, ordinary beings and Buddhas and so on. These are all wonderful teachings, but when we appropriate them, the danger of falling into spiritual materialism is high. We start to rely upon our own light, our own cleverness, our own concepts. We collect teachings so that we can use them to sustain our own self-building project, and we think that when this project is complete we shall be Buddhas, when in fact, the converse is the case. Delusion is a kind of colonization.

This is not a trivial problem. If you are reading this, you have probably attended Buddhist meetings. If you have stayed around and chatted, you have probably found yourself listening to somebody who appears to think that he knows a great deal about Buddhism and has a mission to impart this knowledge

2 We might compare the ideas in Buber, Martin 1970. *I and Thou*, W. Kaufmann (trsl.), New York: Charles Scribner's Sons.

to you. This missionary zeal may well go far beyond what you asked for. Why is this? Presumably the person in question is caught in the trap Dōgen describes in line 5. In fact, probably most of us have ourselves been caught in this trap on occasion. Rather than the teachings coming forth and enlightening us, the ego has gone forth and appropriated the teachings. Then, without realizing that it has happened, one is taking refuge in self rather than in Buddha. When one feels a clamouring need to have one's point heard, one has probably fallen prey to this tendency.

A person in this condition wants to tell everybody else. He is not learning because he sees himself as the teacher. He becomes a know-all. Real enlightenment, however, is a state in which one is continually learning (lines 2 and 5). The Dharmas that are other than self enlighten us, and the appearance of Dharmas *as* other than self *is* enlightenment. So the person who takes the teachings and makes them into an ego-*lakṣaṇa* – a prop for his own self – is, in fact, greatly deluded about the nature of enlightenment, not because his ideas are wrong, necessarily, but because he does not understand how it works.

In our Western civilization, to a degree, we are taught this kind of delusion in school. There is a premium on being clever, soliciting praise and achieving popularity. So most of us do tend to be deluded about enlightenment. We value the concept more than the practice, and we value it not so much for its intrinsic value, but more for its utility in supporting our identity. On the other hand, as always, there is also the opposite pitfall, that of pretentiously affecting to have abandoned all conceptual knowledge and falling into a kind of intellectual nihilism. Dōgen would not have approved of that either. Ideas are important, but they should be used in the correct manner.

ON BEING YIN

Many people, even immediately after having read line 5, will read line 6 as an instruction *to themselves* about what they must do as, or when, they become Buddhas, rather than as being about how the Buddhas help us. When we read, "All Buddhas are busy greatly enlightening delusion", do we identify ourselves as the enlightener, or as the deluded? As yang or as yin? If we are in the yang position, we have an ambition to be the Buddha who is going to do the enlightening. If we are in the yin position, we feel grateful for the presence of the Buddhas who come to enlighten us. In this case, the self-power position is yang and the other-power position is yin. I think that in this passage, Dōgen is advocating the yin position.

Other-power, for Dōgen, is manifest in the myriad Dharmas and, by implication, therefore, the 'Buddhas of the ten directions'. Hōnen, by way of simplification, had emphasized one Buddha – Amitābha. For some people this means that Hōnen was monotheistic and Dōgen pantheistic, but though their formulations differ they are not really in disagreement at a more fundamental level – it is all other-power manifest. To worship one Buddha is to worship all Buddhas and vice versa. Everything can teach us the non-self principle of Śākyamuni Buddha; everything, that is, except the self itself. The desire to be an all-powerful self able to enlighten everybody else is conceit. Those in the yin position can be enlightened by every rock, tree and blade of grass. Dōgen is not saying that every blade of grass is inherently enlightened, but he is saying that every blade can enlighten us.

Therefore, in all times and all places we can be enlightened by the myriad Buddhas, whether this time is *mappō* or not, but, in our deluded state, impelled by karma, we may block this light. The Dao is mysteriously functioning as the world. When people fail to understand or appreciate this grace that enfolds us, they are ordinary beings. When it appears – genjō – they are enlightened beings. However, it is more important that it appear *in* them than *to* them, as we shall see. When it appears in them, then they are already, wittingly or not, Buddhas who are busy greatly enlightening delusion.

When is this happening? When things are in a state of kōan. The state of kōan implies that one enjoys what is present when it is present, fulfils one's role when one has one, does one's duty without fuss, conforms to and plays one's natural part, which is, almost always, the yin part. All these ideas echo themes from both Daoism and Confucianism. Dōgen's Buddha, the supreme sage, not only reveals one religion, but clarifies the meaning of all religion.

So the basic paradox here is that it is by adopting the yin position that one achieves the yang position, but by clinging to the yang position one ruins everything.

HUMILITY AND MATURITY

These lines, therefore, are about humility, which is clearly a central element in Dōgen's view of enlightenment. We are to perform, but not overrate, our own part. Such humility is a form of maturity.

Entering into spiritual practice often involves a form of regression. We slip back into the infantile craving for omnipotence. Within all of us, this craving is still alive. We think that through practice we shall become something very special. We shall acquire special powers, special knowledge, special privileges in the universe. We approach spirituality as if it were a substitute parent, which is not an entirely misguided thing to do, but it does carry the real risk that we ourselves regress. If this regression is ephemeral – *reculer pour mieux sauter* – then there is no harm done, but if it becomes an enduring orientation then we do not grow up and mature in the Dharma, but remain overly dependent, trying to attract all attention to ourselves.

In the fairy story of Snow White, the wicked queen looks in the mirror and asks 'Who is the fairest of them all?' wanting the magic mirror to say, 'You, Queen, are the fairest of them all.' Instead it says that Snow White is the fairest. The queen flies into a rage and plots how to destroy Snow White. If the queen had been more enlightened, when the mirror said that she, the queen, was not the fairest of them all, she might have said, 'Oh, thank goodness for that.' Being the fairest, most intelligent, strongest or greatest of anything is not the most wonderful thing to be. It carries a lot of responsibility. It is much easier not to be so outstanding. Dōgen's contention is that the noblest thing is to accept reality. If you are the fairest, then you should take on that responsibility. If you are somewhere down the rankings, then accept that. Be in accord with reality. Realize that these things are only tinsel anyway. The important things in life are deeper.

DHARMA AS EDUCATION AND RESEARCH

The Buddha taught mindful investigation of Dharma. Mindfulness and investigation of Dharma are the first two 'factors of enlightenment'.[3] Mindfulness means to keep what one has learnt in mind. Investigation then means to go beyond it.

Buddha often referred to his teachings as the 'Dharma Vinaya'. Vinaya has come to mean the rules that monks adhere to, but the basic meaning of the word is 'education'. So this is a maturing process. Receive teachings, test them and explore further. To investigate is to let reality come forth and educate us. It requires patience, observation and restraint. Do not jump to over-hasty conclusions. Listen and watch first. That way one learns what is required of one.

Generally, we fail to see things in their real nature and so miss their message because we invest them with 'self'. Our own conceit blinds us. To 'investigate' means to be attentive and let things present themselves rather than to force them into a predetermined schema.

Thinking of Buddhism as education in this way can help us to understand it. Teachings are received. For that we have to be humble enough and curious enough to have an open mind. We delight in receiving new knowledge, then we engage in 'discovery learning' or 'research' but, here again, we are required to empty ourselves of preconceptions as much as we can. Much research is spoilt because the researcher has an investment in what he or she thinks the results ought to be.

One of my roles is to assist students in their doctoral studies. There are two extremely common pitfalls in choosing a research subject. One springs from grandiosity and is the tendency to choose a subject that is far too vast to yield a realistic research study and the other is the desire not to find out something new, but to prove an existing cherished prejudice.

---

3 For the seven 'factors of enlightenment' see: *Majjhima Nikaya* 118.36 in Ñāṇamoli and Bodhi 1995: 946–7.

When the researcher is trying to obtain a desired result, that is not real research. In order to do real research the self has to be set aside. Sometimes this is called 'bracketing'. We have to put our ego in brackets so as to get it out of the way. Then the Dharmas – the real truths – can come forth and enlighten us.

The great genius Leonardo da Vinci believed that one of the most useful things one could do was to go out alone and study the forms of nature. They would reveal to you all that you need to know. Leonardo became a great artist by copying the forms that he found in nature. Similarly, Albert Einstein said that he had arrived at astonishing conclusions not by having vastly superior intelligence, but by being willing to continue looking longer.

In Buddhist terms, we can say that the Dharma came forth and instructed these great men and was able to do so because their attention and interest was wholly upon it and not upon themselves. However, in putting self aside, sometimes we need help.

MILAREPA

One of the greatest teachers in the Kargyu Tibetan tradition of Buddhism is Milarepa (*c.*1052–*c.*1135). Milarepa's teacher was called Marpa. Milarepa went to Marpa in the first place seeking the power by which to get revenge upon those who had cheated his mother and himself out of their inheritance. Marpa agreed to take him on and gave him many Herculean tasks to perform. Little by little Milarepa was transformed. In a certain sense, Milarepa came and showed Marpa his particular manifestation of hell, which was like the tantrum of a child. Marpa took him on and gave him another hell, different in kind but just as bad, designed to make him grow up again. Slowly, Milarepa came to recognize that despite his apparent harshness, Marpa loved him deeply. Milarepa's attitude changed. Instead of taking on those tasks as a way of gaining the power to kill his enemies, he did it out of love for his teacher. When his attitude had turned around, this naturally carried over to other parts of his life. When one can love hell, it is easy to love all the other options.

Marpa then started to give him other practices – more obviously spiritual ones that he would never have been willing to take on when he first came to Marpa, or which, if he had done, he would have subverted exactly as Dōgen is warning us about. Milarepa became one of the greatest Dharma teachers in the history of Tibet. We can see that initially he regarded Marpa as a father figure. He was already in a rather regressive state and initially became more so, but gradually he changed and became mature.

HUINENG

We can see from this next example that it is not always the best policy for a teacher to give a disciple lots of books to read and many hours in the meditation hall. The sixth Patriarch of Zen in China, Huineng 惠能 (638–713), was not Chinese, but possibly Vietnamese. As far as the Chinese were concerned he was a barbarian. Yet, he had an innate affinity for the Dharma and he had had a first satori by hearing somebody reciting the Diamond Sūtra in the street. He asked the person in question what he was reciting. The man said that he was not really sure what it was all about, but that the master at the nearby Buddhist monastery had said that it was good to recite it so he was doing so. Huineng asked the way to the monastery and hurried off to go and pay his respects to the master, Hongren. The master quickly weighed up Huineng. He did not send him to the library to read about the Diamond Sūtra. He did not send him to the meditation hall. He did not give him a kōan exercise in the Rinzai sense. He sent him to the temple storeroom to pound rice, remarking that "This foreigner is too clever for his own good."

We might think that these are very special cases, remote from our own experience, but are they? Many people come into spiritual practice seeking power of some kind. They may think that by practising meditation they can become a great guru. Or they think that they are going to realize their own perfection. Popular spirituality is full of rhetoric telling us that we have God nature or Buddha nature, that our essential being is perfect, and so on. It is very common to construct a cover story that makes one out to be a marvellous person and disguises one's actual nature.

Perhaps we think that by becoming spiritual we are going to save all sentient beings. This is a very grandiose fantasy – a case of being greatly deluded about realization. If we do end up saving them it will be in a very different way from the one we expect.

THE EVIDENCE OF ONE'S LIFE

Spiritual progress, therefore, involves realizing how deluded one is. This, of course, is an almost impossible thing to do in detail. We are blind to our blindness. Yet, perhaps we get a tiny glimpse from examining the evidence of our life. In Japanese, this is *naikan* ('inward inspection').[4] We say 'inward' but it is hardly really 'inward' because what is required is that one look at evidence and most of the evidence lies all around one. One can ask oneself, what troubles have I caused? What burden has my existence placed upon others? What do I rely upon? What have I received that has enabled me to survive and grow? All of this is an enquiry into dependent origination and, therefore, into the fundamental teaching of Buddha, but in a very practical way.

We live in a world in which, in all sorts of ways, things have come forth and helped us. If they had not done so, we would not have survived. The human infant is totally dependent. If somebody does not come forth and pick her up she will hardly survive a single day. We have received much tangible help. We might have all kinds of emotions about it ranging from gratitude to resentment. Feelings, however, are not always a good guide. It is generally tangible consequences that bring us up short. That is what teaches us about our own delusion. It is the Dharmas that are not self that are most informative. They are like a mirror. We look into that mirror and it can tell us things. We can become aware of our delusion or we can magnify it. To be aware of one's own delusion is already to be more enlightened than most people are.

A great saint is not generally somebody who is conscious of his own virtue, but rather one who is conscious of his shortcomings. St Francis of Assisi is said to have wept for his

---

4 Reynolds, David 1989. *Flowing Bridges, Quiet Waters: Japanese Psychotherapies, Morita and Naikan*, New York: State University Press.

sins every day and this was one of the most virtuous men in Christendom, while there have been innumerable hypocrites who think themselves far more virtuous than is in fact the case.

BEING DEPENDENT

The idea of 'dependent origination' was the core of what Buddha understood on the night of enlightenment. Everything that depends upon conditions is necessarily impermanent since when conditions change it changes, and those conditions themselves depend upon conditions and so on. Nirvāṇa, the holy grail of Buddhism, is 'beyond conditions' and, therefore, not impermanent, but always available. As we have seen, Dōgen operationalizes this idea of 'always available' by the way in which he regards the myriad Dharmas.

The myriad Dharmas are 'other than self'. This does not mean 'interdependent with self'. Self is illusion. If they were interdependent with illusion, they would also be illusion and there would be no Dharma. For purposes of spiritual practice, the notion of 'interdependence', although it has an attractive similarity to some ideas about ecology, rather tends to overstate self-importance. It may be a lot safer simply to realize how much about one's life is dependent in a unidirectional sense.

When we think in a sober way about our life we are liable to see that we receive far more than we could ever repay. We cannot repay the sun for sunshine and we did not earn the air we breathe. We probably did not build the house we live in. The education and culture that we have received is the work of millions of people, mostly now already dead, who received little or nothing from us. If we were to draw up a karmic profit and loss account, we would find that we have received vastly more than we have given. Yet how many people go around with a chip on their shoulder, believing that the world owes them a great deal more than they have received? We take a lot for granted and this blinds us to the extent to which we are wilfully ignorant.[5]

---

5 'Wilful ignorance' is *avidyā*, the root element in the formal theory of dependent origination. The 'will' involved here is mostly unconscious.

DELUDED WITHIN DELUSION

We can analyze lines 5–9 as follows:

Delusion and enlightenment			
Ordinary beings	think themselves the teachers of myriad Dharmas	greatly deluded about enlightenment	delusion within delusion
Buddhas	myriad Dharmas come forth to train and enlighten the self	greatly enlightening delusion	enlightenment within enlightenment

Wanting to be Buddha means wanting to teach and illuminate the myriad Dharmas. Much of Buddhism, as we find it in popular literature nowadays, is structured around the desire of individuals either to be somebody special or to solve their own personal problems. Often the teaching of the great contemporary apologists for Buddhism begins with the observation that 'Everybody is in search of happiness.' This suggests that Buddhism is the way to find it. Then you can get exactly what your body and mind supposedly want. When Rujing said to Dōgen, 'Let body and mind fall away,' he was disabusing him of this notion. People begin in the position of desire, but can one get beyond it?

The very desire to obtain something for one's own body and mind – for self – is going to frustrate the desired goal. Such a desire is a sign of being greatly deluded about the nature of realization and this delusion then leads to more delusion. A Buddha has no particular ambition to be Buddha, but is Buddha because he is endlessly fed by myriad Dharmas. Thus he is 'realized' whether he realizes it or not, and within that state of realization, he is continually getting new realizations by being so fed.

ALL BUDDHAS ARE GREATLY ENLIGHTENING DELUSION

What is it that enlightens delusion? All Buddhas – *sho butsu* (see also line 2). If we become enlightened, it is not really by our own effort. We should make efforts and, if we are inspired by the Buddhas, we naturally shall do so, but not in order to get something to indulge our own body and mind. One ought to be like the good servant. The good servant does not serve for the sake of personal advancement. He serves for love of and loyalty to his master, just as Milarepa learnt to do. Of course, the good master may well advance the loyal servant in various ways as he sees fit. However, if the servant is only posing as a good servant in order to gain advancement, then this means that, fundamentally, he has no real respect for the master, but regards the master only as a means to obtain his, the servant's, own personal ends. The truly sincere servant only wants the master's ends to prosper. The true Buddhist only wants the Dharma to flourish in the world for the benefit of all sentient beings. If she, herself, as one of those beings, also benefits, this is merely incidental; too much thought about it will only get in the way.

Similarly, if we have no real respect for the Buddhas, then we are not really Buddhists. We may be posing as proper Buddhists, thinking that by doing so we shall advance ourselves in some way, but at the spiritual level this is all a sham – a patch of weeds, not a real flower garden. Many people are so deeply steeped in worldly thinking that they find it difficult really to imagine anything other than personal profit. Even people on a spiritual quest, like Dōgen on his way to China, are generally afflicted with the same disease in one way or another. Nor is Buddhism a means to advance social or economic ends, however 'politically correct'.

We might think that talk of 'masters' and 'servants' is old hat and not relevant today, but, in fact, the great majority of people nowadays work as 'servants': the 'masters' for whom they work are governments and corporations. Commonly, these vast institutions have become remote and abstract and it is probably, therefore, even more usual today for workers to have a self-seeking, instrumental attitude than it was when the 'master' was a known person. It is thus quite normal for modern people to think that 'personal profit' is a primary reason for doing anything, especially now that most things carry a monetary value. To escape from this taken-for-granted kind of selfishness is not easy.

Also, we can see from the logic of all this that *sho butsu* are '*ware ni arazaru*' – 'all Buddhas' are 'Dharmas that are not self' – because it is the not-self Dharmas that advert to enlightenment. The Buddhas are Dharmas that are not-self and those Dharmas are the Dharmas of those myriad Buddhas. The secular Westerner can easily miss the pervasive religious sense of Buddhism, but without it, all this becomes simply a self-serving intellectual exercise.

IF YOU ARE DELUDED, BE DELUDED

The implication of not-self is a kind of dualism. It is in the spirit of Dōgen's general thesis to say that when one is a deluded being, one is a deluded being and when a Buddha, a Buddha. The servant does not try to be the master and the master does not try to be the servant. To be a genuine devotee is not to try to be the Divine oneself. That would be self-worship and it would actually show a lack of faith in and respect for the Buddhas. The two domains do not intrude upon one another. When you find yourself to be a deluded being, it is no use trying to be something else. If one happens to be a Buddha, the same holds.

Here again is the basic paradox. If a person finds (genjō) herself to be in the position of being a deluded being and truly accepts her lot (kōan) then, by that very act of acceptance, she becomes one who throws much light upon delusion, and so becomes a Buddha. Yet, if a person thinks that he is Buddha and goes out and tries to illuminate myriad Dharmas, he promptly falls into delusion within delusion. This is the same as the principle in the *Yijing* that when something is carried to excess it soon turns into its opposite. This is also the meaning of the black dot in the white section of the yin-yang wheel symbol and of the white dot in the black section. A good teacher is a good learner; a good guru is a good disciple.

I think we can conclude from the above that if one were to become Buddha it might be best not to know that it had happened. Then one would go on experiencing the state of Buddha. When self-consciousness creeps in all may be lost. However, if such a person really were Buddha, then they would not mind being so or not being so, so the flow would not be impeded. In practice, in my experience of great masters, they are some of the time great masters and some of the time ordinary beings. Some of their disciples may mind, but they themselves do not.

Nonetheless, in the case of Dōgen, we should not underestimate his tendency to separate the opposites. It might be a popular modern idea that all dualities should be merged, but even if this should prove to be true in the ultimate dimension, Dōgen sees a considerable danger in jumping too quickly to that way of thinking. His statement that some people are enlightened within enlightenment and some are deluded within delusion is a strong one. He is forcefully telling us not to muddle the two. In this, he is particularly refuting Nōnin as well as all those who took the Tendai 'original enlightenment' to a non-dualistic extreme. He is saying, in essence, 'that's all very well, but some people *are* enlightened and some are *not* and the rite of practice *is* necessary'.

ENLIGHTENED WITHIN ENLIGHTENMENT, DELUDED IN THE MIDST OF DELUSION

This idea can be understood at the individual level, the collective level and the one-to-one level. At the individual level, we can see that the enlightened person is a good learner because self does not get in the way. When the enlightened person finds she has made a mistake, she is pleased and interested because now there is something to learn, whereas when the deluded person makes a mistake, they are ashamed and try to hide it or deny it altogether. Learning is, therefore, much more difficult. The self obstructs. Because the person is prioritizing his own reputation – with others or with himself – it is more difficult to learn. Everything goes through a filter. The enlightened person is simply interested in reality and thus has a naturally enquiring mind. Everything is interesting. Nothing gets in the way.

At the collective level, it is easy to see that in much social interaction we are all caught up in shared delusions and half-truths and all support one another in playing this game. Much talk is not really concerned with conveying information, but with maintaining a comfortable level of collusion between the people involved who share a 'culture'. This is why taking refuge in sangha is important in Buddhism. If one keeps good company, the effect rubs off on one. Goodness is just as contagious as madness. Sometimes people assert that in spirituality 'everything comes from within', but this is not really true. Much comes from the conditions and circumstances around us. Buddhism not only asserts the importance of keeping good company, it is also the case that Buddhist communities have generally always been interested in creating a fine environment. One can think of temple gardens in Japan. They are miniatures of heaven. Here we see how the individual and the collective level interact. If one has the image of heaven or of the Pure Land in one's heart, then one will naturally incline toward replicating such an inspiring environment in one's house, temple, garden, neighbourhood, etc., and this environment will itself be inspiring for others. Similarly, one is oneself calmed and uplifted by entering such a domain. Thus in both the physical and the communicative dimensions, living in the midst of radiance enlightens, whereas living in the midst of folly corrupts. It is, therefore, important to allow Dharmas to come to us and enlighten us. When creating such a garden it is not just a matter of imposing a blueprint on Nature, but of asking the plants how they want to be.

From this we can see how in a one-to-one situation the same principles apply with particular force. In a one-to-one relationship one is deeply affected. How two people affect one another is, therefore, supremely important. Dōgen asserts, in fact, that it is precisely in a one-to-one situation that enlightenment unfolds. In the relation between a teacher and disciple there can be a transmission of great love. This love has a rather special 'empty' quality, because it is selfless. The person who loves creates space for the other and does not get caught up in the game playing of delusion. This is how the Dharma is transmitted from generation to generation. The disciple, simply by being with the teacher, is in the midst of enlightenment. This contrasts sharply with being amidst deluded people who collude with and encourage one's faults and failings. If one has a problem in life, the common friend may take you out to get drunk on alcohol. The skilful friend, however, is there for you in a different way, a way that enables you to find the truth of your life and to find that it is the truth of all life.

III

LINES 10–11: YOU NEED NOT KNOW EVERYTHING

> 10. When All Buddhas really are All Buddhas the self does not need to know All Buddhas.
> 11. So, thus, we can say, enlightened Buddhas go on enlightening Buddhas.

III.1 COMMENTARY

This section builds on lines 6 and 8...

> 6. All Buddhas are busy greatly enlightening delusion.
> 8. So people who are enlightened are continually being enlightened within enlightenment.

The point here, however, is that lines 10–11 are a Buddhist version of the Daoist principle that it is because the sage lays no claim to anything that his ends are fulfilled, and because he never thinks of himself as virtuous that his virtue never deserts him. All Buddhas – *sho butsu* – go on enlightening beings whether those beings are consciously aware of All Buddhas or not, and whether the beings who do the enlightening realize that they are Buddhas or not. The compassionate action of All Buddhas is endlessly unfolding in the world. Yet, those who truly appreciate all the Buddhas, thereby themselves become Buddhas. Therefore, at the end of the day, it is all Buddhas together with Buddhas.[1] There is also here again an implication that enlightenment is not something that happens alone. It takes 'Buddhas together with Buddhas' to manifest.

In this and the previous section, Dōgen explains how easy everything can be. Simply adopt the yin position, appreciate the Dharma all around one and stop being self-centred. That is all. That is kōan and genjō happens. All is then Buddha with Buddha and one does not even need to know it is happening. In fact, it is self-conscious awareness that gets in the way.

III.2 DISCUSSION

DHARMA RAIN

Most interpreters of this passage take it to mean something like: Even though one may be Buddha, one does not need to know that this is so, yet, since it is so, one goes on and on becoming more enlightened. Although this way of construing the verse is not entirely wide of the mark, I think it misses the fact that in the Mahāyāna Buddhist religion, *sho butsu* – All Buddhas – is one name for the object of worship. The emphasis is not so much upon the Buddha that you yourself might be, but on the Buddhas that are all the time available to enlighten us. So, even though it may be the case that one will one day become enlightened and become part of *sho butsu* oneself, to interpret this passage as being about oneself as Buddha is not quite in the right spirit. The whole drift of the immediately preceding section was that life is 'not about oneself'.

In this religion, 'All Buddhas' is/are the source of grace. They are endlessly benefitting living beings. They cannot help it and never cease. This is not a religion based on the idea of judgement. It is, rather, rooted in the idea of a continual rain of blessings. The beneficence of Buddhas is not a function of the state of mind or effort of the practitioner except in a rather indirect way, as will become apparent. The self may be completely oblivious of All Buddhas, but All Buddhas are still pouring down blessings.

Thus, in the Lotus Sūtra, as Dōgen would have known well,

1 *Yoibutsu Yobutsu* is the title of another essay by Dogen and also a quotation from chapter 2 of the Lotus Sūtra.

there is the parable of the herbs.[2] There are many kinds of herbs ranging from tiny mosses to great oak trees and many others in between. However, the rain falls on all alike. The Dharma rain is no different. The blessings of All Buddhas fall on all beings, whether they are virtuous or not, good meditators or not, accomplished bodhisattvas or not, and whether they are conscious that they are being rained upon or not.

Among those who are in receipt of these blessing there are beings in different states, as we learnt in lines 7–9. There are those who are greatly deluded who have difficulty receiving these blessings, however freely available they may be, and there are others who are awakened, who go on being enlightened within enlightenment because they are the ones who fully receive what All Buddhas provide. So, as a result, the enlightened ones benefit most. All Buddhas go on enlightening Buddhas, whether those Buddhas know that they are Buddhas or not.

THE REAL ALL BUDDHAS

Line 10 starts, 'When All Buddhas are really All Buddhas...' This implies that it could be the case that All Buddhas might sometimes not really be All Buddhas. I think this is an allusion, on the one hand, to the fact that the idea we have of All Buddhas may be wide of the real thing and, on the other, that many things that we do not recognize as Buddhas do still function as Buddhas. There is also in this, perhaps, a hint of the Confucian principle of the 'rectification of names'. This principle is the idea that a son should be and behave like a son, a father as a father, a mother as a mother, a priest as a priest, and so on. This is very close to Dōgen's idea of playing one's proper part. One's part might not always be what one would freely choose, but if it is one's lot at a given time, then that is what needs doing. This whole, rather Confucian, philosophy, that is quite central to Dōgen, is at odds with modern ideas of choice, achieved status and freedom. Dōgen's idea of freedom is freedom from the angst and alienation involved in having to choose and achieve.

---

2 There are many translations of the Lotus Sūtra into English. See, e.g. Kato, Bunnō, Yoshirō Tamura, and Kōjirō Miyasaki 1975. *The Threefold Lotus Sutra*, Tokyo: Kosei: 126 et seq.

So Buddhas are Buddhas when they do what Buddhas do – when they play their part. This may or may not be particularly conscious or chosen. The self does not really need to know about it and is only likely to get in the way. The performance of a role is most fluid when self-consciousness drops away.

We can also analyze this from the perspective of the non-Buddha. The non-Buddha has a part to play vis-à-vis the Buddha(s). This is easier when the Buddhas are doing their bit too, just as dancing is easier when one has a good dancer as a partner. Thus, it is rather more important that the non-Buddha see the Buddha as Buddha than that the Buddha him- or herself do so. Or, to put the same thing a little differently, it is more valuable for me to see your Buddha nature than to see my own, and it is more important that you see mine then that you see your own. Buddhas are not just ordinary.

This is a bit like the Christian injunction that if you have true faith it means that you realize that God is God. When a religion has an object of worship – as all religions do, one way or another – there is always the danger that the setting up of ritual procedures, whether these are ceremonies, prayers, meditation sessions, performing thousands of prostrations, and so on, may lead the practitioner to think that by such procedures he or she can bring the Holy under personal control. The attitude is: what is in it for me? And how can I get it?

The practitioner thinks that, by doing the practice, he exercises some control over the holy beings – in this case, 'All Buddhas'. However, this is superstition. The person who thinks that way – and most do, at least subtly – has an idea of All Buddhas, perhaps, but the All Buddhas to which he is relating are not the real All Buddhas. The real All Buddhas are untouched by our efforts to manipulate them. Again, this is an instance of radical separation.

Dōgen will expand upon this characteristic of being untouched in due course by using the image of a mirror that is untouched by what it reflects. Any effort to manipulate All Buddhas is superstition or magic – it is not true religion. They pour down their compassion in their own way, irrespective of the machinations of the practitioner, and do so whether we know it is so or not, but if we play our part, we reflect and magnify the effect for the benefit of others, and this is only likely to happen when we have escaped from our addiction to self – self-worth, self-esteem, self-assertion, self-entitlement and all other forms of trying to rearrange the universe so that we ourselves are the centre around which it revolves.

This addiction to self is manifested in our desire to be in the driving seat. The Buddhas offer us a great vehicle, but we would rather have a small one under our own control. This manifests in an over-valuation of consciousness, including, and especially, self-consciousness.

ON NOT KNOWING WHO OR WHAT ONE IS

When Bodhidharma, who is generally regarded as the founder of Zen, arrived in China he had an interview with Emperor Wu Liang. The emperor asked, 'Who is this who stands before me?' Bodhidharma answered 'I do not know.' However, the phrase here translated as 'I do not know' could just as well be translated 'I am not conscious', or 'I have no consciousness (of myself)'. Immediately before this exchange, the emperor had asked what merit he had gained by all his works in support of Buddhism and Bodhidharma had replied 'None'.

This dialogue is generally presented as leaving the emperor confused and demonstrating the zany nature of Zen. However, it is possible to unpack the meaning more constructively. When Bodhidharma says 'None', he is expressing the doctrine of Daosheng that 'good deeds invoke no retribution'. The principle is that *any* 'merit' is still a form of 'retribution' since it entangles one in karma. To say 'None', therefore, was, in this context, the highest praise that Bodhidharma could give to the emperor, that his deeds were so pure that they invoked no karma. Karma is what goes on attaching us to saṃsāra. Truly good deeds, therefore, are those in which there is no karmic element at all. They are completely clean.

However, karma is also what causes us to be born into this saṃsāric world. So, it is possible that the emperor may have been a rather advanced Buddhist who grasped Bodhidharma's meaning perfectly and replied, 'So if you understand things so well, how is it that you have the karma to be standing here before me?' This is an instance of what can be called 'Dharma combat' in which enlightened masters test each other's depth of understanding. To this riposte Bodhidharma responds by saying that he is not self-conscious. In other words, here in this conversation, he is simply a mirror of the situation. He is not trying to put on airs. So when the emperor says, 'Who are you then?' he is quite genuine in saying that he is not trying to be anybody in particular. Bodhidharma thus was a clear mirror.

It may well be that the emperor was not at all puzzled, but rather enjoyed his encounter with somebody who understood the Dharma as well as he did himself.

We can take from this story a number of things. The most important is that Bodhidharma demonstrates the importance of unconsciousness, and unselfconsciousness in particular. The enlightened person is not trying to be someone or something in particular. He is just playing his allotted part (kōan). When he does so, the truth appears (genjō). In this case the truth that appears shows the meaning of emptiness as supreme goodness. It manifests as one mirror mind meeting another. Further, it does not manifest in a static way, but it goes on. Each revelation caps the previous one. Dharma is dialectical. This means that we can have faith in going forth, since we shall be shown what we need to know when the time comes.

IV

LINE 12: BE A MIRROR

> 12. Though one may deeply understand the forms of body and mind, though one may deeply understand what body and mind are saying, still this is not like a reflection in a mirror, nor like the moon in water, which is only realized on one side when the other side is dark.

IV.1 COMMENTARY

Here we come to the crux of the matter. The functioning of a mirror depends upon a certain relationship between yin and yang. One side is bright and the other side is dark. In this circumstance, reflection happens and the appearance of things changes. No amount of contrivance can produce such an effect, and however much we work on 'personal development' we shall never arrive at what is effortlessly accomplished by the appearance of the mirror mind.

If, as is likely, Dōgen did have the parable of the herbs in mind in the previous section, then we can understand that the effects of the Dharma rain can be various. It may be that it permits 'growth' and 'self-actualization' in the plants (ourselves), or it may be that we ourselves become mirrors and transmitters. The former illustrates the Buddhas' indiscriminate beneficence, but the latter is distinctly preferable. Buddhism, in Dōgen's view, is a matter of playing our part in the second way. Then we are children of the Tathāgatas or servants in the great house, not just self-satisfied consumers.[1]

"Body and mind" refers to sensory existence and also to the life of desire. We desire things in order to satisfy body and mind. By studying experience we can clarify a lot about body and mind. This is a positive result of psychotherapy, or any kind of 'personal growth work'. It is also a process of learning. It involves a gradual accumulation of knowledge and experience. By our own effort we understand something for ourselves and get to know things about ourselves. This is considered important in humanistic psychology and in religion alike, but it is not what religion is ultimately about. Here Dōgen is making a distinction between gradual accumulation of experience, which is, in principle, something that can go on forever with no natural end, and spiritual awakening, which happens suddenly, just as water that has been transparent suddenly becomes a mirror when one side becomes dark. The image in the mirror does not arrive gradually as the other side darkens. There is a tipping point. At a certain moment the image is there and when it is there it is completely there. The moon reflected in water, or a reflection in a mirror, are well-established tropes explaining the nature of Buddhist spirituality,[2] but here Dōgen is exploiting the sudden and complete aspect of the appearance of the image in contrast to the gradual accumulation of learning. A water surface that is reflecting the sky or the moon appears completely different from one that is not doing so. Whether it does so or not is a function of the balance between the light above and below.

Dōgen acknowledges that learning and experience are valuable, but asserts that the awakening of true religious consciousness is something else. It works in a different way. However much knowledge or experience you have, they will not, in themselves, ever make you enlightened. Only when you have the mirror-like mind of nirvāṇa will that be the case,

1 I have written about this issue from a psychotherapeutic point of view in Brazier, David 2009. *Love and Its Disappointment: The Meaning of Life, Therapy and Art*, Ropley: O Books, J Hunt Publishing.

2 Dogen will, for instance, have been aware of the text 'Jewel Mirror Samādhi' (寶 鏡 三 昧 歌), which elaborates the idea of the mirror mind and tells us that dark encloses brightness, but when there is brightness no light shines.

and for a mirror to exist, one side – the self side – has to be dark. Accumulating learning and studying experience is a self-asserting procedure. In such self-examination one uses the self to study the self. However, in the example of the moon and water, or that of the mirror, things work quite differently.

Reflection only occurs when one side of the glass or water is dark, and it is a sudden phenomenon. Either it does reflect, or it does not. When one side is dark, the image will be realized by the other side. To make a mirror, one can paint one side of glass black. When this is done, the other side reflects. What does this analogy tell us? That in spiritual work, as opposed to in therapy, for instance, the self side has to be black, dark. In order to reflect the Dharma of All Buddhas, the self has to be completely eclipsed, has to be black. Self-study has its uses but spiritual awakening goes beyond it, or, we could say, cuts through it, and is quite a different phenomenon.

IV.2 DISCUSSION

THE PIVOTAL IMAGE

I take this to be the pivotal image in the essay. It is by turning one side of ourselves – the self – dark (yin) that the other side becomes a mirror and thus we come to reflect the moon, which is the myriad Dharmas.

In *Eihei Koroku*, 1.19, Dōgen says,

> There is one phrase that encompasses the eight directions.
> There is one phrase that is crystal clear on all eight sides.
> If you can say it you are not a fettered person. An ancient Buddha said, 'Buddha's true Dharma body is like the empty sky. According with things, it manifests form like the moon in water.' The ancestral teachers in each generation could only express the principle of accord, but could not express the manifesting form.[3]

This is an important expression of Dōgen's metaphysics. It is also an expression of his mission in *Genjō Kōan*. He is going to tell us about the *Dharmakāya* (Buddha body) manifesting form "like

3 Leighton and Okumura 2004: 91.

the moon in water" by telling us how it is that water sometimes reflects the moon and sometimes does not reflect the moon.

This explains many things:

1. It provides a sense in which the 'original enlightenment' exists, but not as a property of self. We become the carriers and reflectors of it when our self goes out of consciousness.
2. It indirectly tells us Dōgen's position regarding the controversy about 'sudden' and 'gradual' enlightenment.
3. This message is wholly in line with the teaching of Śākyamuni Buddha in the form in which it is found in Mahāyāna Buddhism. The Tathāgata comes to us as a spiritual light, but we may or may not be in a condition to reflect that light. Sometimes the Buddha body manifests and sometimes it does not.
4. It tells us that there is something for us to do, but that this is to do with self-effacement rather than self-development. This is in accord with some of the basic teaching of Theravada Buddhism.
5. Thus, following points 3 and 4, the image has some potential to reconcile different competing interpretations of Buddhism, while challenging or provoking many popular ideas that take the Dharma as a form of self-improvement.
6. It thus yields a more religious perspective in which one's function is to reflect the light rather than try to be it oneself.

We can recast the image by thinking of the glass window of a room. The window looks out onto the world. We can think of the inside of the window as one's self and the outside as one's relation with others. When a person outside looks at our window there are two possibilities according to the balance of light. If there is a light on in our room, then the person can see into the room – they see our self. In this mode, what we present to the world is our self, made by our self, for the sake of our self. However good or bad our self is, it makes no difference to the basic fact that it is our self that is presented.

When this is the case, the vast majority of our life energy will go into a self-perfection and self-presentation project, because we are painfully aware that it is what others see. It is also what our society encourages, and a natural attraction, repulsion or competition between selves results that provides the dynamic of much social intercourse. This energy that we keep investing, however, keeps the light on in our room and perpetuates the situation. If we switch the light off, then the person outside does not see into the room. The person sees a reflection. It may be a reflection of themselves or of the moon or of the landscape, but the self has become black, hidden, unconscious. In Dōgen's day they did not have electric light in rooms, but I believe that this is the idea that he is trying to convey.

When there is no light in the room, the window functions as a mirror because there is more light outside than inside. The light outside comes from the sun or the moon. The sun and moon are well-established images for the Dharma. When we switch the light on inside our room, the effect of the sun and moon disappears because the light inside is brighter than the light outside. This is true even though the sun and the moon are actually much greater lights in themselves. In the same way when the little light of self is shining, the great light of the Dharma ceases to function. The moonlight may still be falling all over the world on all places alike, but it is not noticeable where we are because our little light occludes it locally.

Furthermore, when the light in our room is bright, we cannot see out. When we are inside a lighted room and look at the window we only see our own reflection. We become like Narcissus looking into the pool. We do not see the myriadfold Dharma that lies outside of the room of self. Sometimes one may find a group of people all talking vigorously, but with no communication actually happening because each is in his own little room talking to his own reflection. To listen to the other, one has to dim one's own light.

In the same way, relying upon self-power we give ourselves a little light, but deprive ourselves and, even more, those we encounter, of the great light of the Dharma. A little candle flame held close enough to the eye will prevent one seeing a great light further off. The other-power of the myriad Dharmas is vast and wonderful, but we, with our little selves, deprive the world of it and live in delusion.

A COMMON MISTAKE

Translators have often misconstrued this passage. The problem is partly linguistic, but it has a major impact upon the sense. It has often been taken that the dark and light characteristics apply to the sounds and forms appearing in the mirror, and not to the formation of the mirror effect itself. This results in translations of the type: Though you see one side of something the other side remains dark. If that were a correct translation then it would have little or no relevance to Dōgen's general thesis in this essay and would not easily fit into the flow of his ideas at this point.

Most translators want to see Dōgen as supporting a self-power message. Western culture has reached the point where self-study (of the self, by the self, for the self) is regarded as a good thing to such a degree that the assumption is taken for granted. Clearly, however, Dōgen is writing about the eclipse of self, not just in this passage but throughout the essay, as, indeed, was Śākyamuni Buddha in all his teaching.

Some commentators think that this passage is about ordinary persons having faulty internal maps of reality of which they need to let go in order to be Buddhas. While this idea is interesting, I do not think that it is accurate as far as the interpretation of this particular passage is concerned. I think that what Dōgen is saying implies that whatever map you have, attachment to the idea of having the right map will prevent your mirror from forming. The Buddhas will still shine upon you, but you will not reflect that light. Some say that you just have to let your map go. This is closer to the mark, but I do not think it is quite right. Dōgen is not talking about maps in this passage.

Then there are ideas to the effect that this is something to do with the division of subject and object. Again, I think this misses the point. The only subject that matters is All Buddhas and their myriadfold Dharma.

IS INTIMACY WITH BODY AND MIND A GOOD THING?

Does the text imply that self-study and being intimate with body and mind have any value at all? Dōgen is acknowledging that these things do have a relative value but, as far as the argument of *Genjō Kōan* is concerned, that value is a side issue. However, it had not been a side issue in his life; rather, it had been his obsession. If we take this passage as Dōgen talking about his own experience, then he seems to be telling us that he learnt a good deal from his various practices and studies, from receiving teachings and doing meditation, from introspection and studying, but that these were not the main thing. Dōgen's essay is about how spiritual awakening is not simply a matter of accumulating knowledge or self-understanding. Self-understanding can help if it leads to self-disenchantment, but the real tipping point is not a result of any kind of accumulation.

Dōgen and Hōnen were two of the most learned people in Japan in their time, yet both taught that it is not such learning that matters. Learning and the acquisition of skills and knowledge have intrinsic value, but do not constitute enlightenment. Nor is the purpose of enlightenment to know more and more about oneself. Such self-knowledge can aid one's navigation of social situations and bring some personal profit, or it can be used in helping others in various ways if one has such a motivation. However, enlightenment is not a result of any such accumulation. In any case, in practice, such self-knowledge tends often to be used more in the service of self-inflation than in really helping others.

Many people think that by training they are making something of themselves and it is probably for these secondary benefits that the majority of people do their daily meditation or light incense and make prostrations before the altar. However much one may be told that zazen is not for such self-development purposes, people do not take such advice seriously and make their own judgement.

This is a very relevant issue these days. Increasingly, methods and techniques are being taken from Buddhism and used for all kinds of quasi medico-psychological purposes, to cure stress, aid relaxation, build personal effectiveness, ease depression, calm anxiety and so on. In terms of what Dōgen is advocating, this is all very well, but it misses the main point of the exercise. It is spiritual materialism.

The longstanding humanism of our Western tradition goes back all the way to the Delphic injunction 'Know thyself' and even earlier. In Dōgen, as we shall see, the only sane reason for knowing oneself is to get to the point where you can forget about it, not for creating from it a foundation for one's personal successes. As we really get to know ourselves we find that we are less fascinating than we had thought. Study that yields such a realization is valuable to that extent.

THE SELF IN THE WEST

The Western obsession with self-development was especially crystallized by the philosopher René Descartes. His famous assertion *cogito ergo sum* – I think, therefore I am – placed personal being and personal knowledge at the centre of things. This approach has underpinned modern empiricism and, in due course, consumerism, since the important thing became the self's clear perception of things. Of course, we know that perceptions can be misleading, but this has not diverted the stream of modern thinking much. We value perception and, by extension, transparency. When I have explained Dōgen's mirror metaphor to people, they commonly think that it would be better that the water be transparent than that it become a mirror. Dōgen, however, thought differently.

An early critic of Descartes was the Italian philosopher Giambattista Vico, who believed that we do not really understand something unless we can make it. Thus only God understood most things, especially things like life. Vico, unlike Descartes, thus believed that there were inherent limits to what it was possible for humans to understand. In the twentieth century, with the advent of the theory of relativity and then the uncertainty principle, some leading thinkers implicitly started to come round to Vico's position. Vico was not opposed to science. Rather, he proposed a different framework for it, one that was more modest and in which one took a realistic view of human capacity. Where Descartes's philosophy led to us displacing God, in Vico's approach, as we reach a better approximation of God's perspective, we ourselves become less and less until we become nothing.

Thus, the sense that wisdom involves the occlusion of self is not entirely lacking from the Western tradition, but it has, at least since the Renaissance, tended to be a minor current. In the East, however, things have been seen differently and the need has been to explain how self-occlusion, and thus enlightenment, occurs. This is Dōgen's purpose here in *Genjō Kōan*.

ANYBODY CAN DO IT

Hōnen had pointed out that if salvation depended upon making lavish offerings to temples, only the rich could be saved; if it depended upon understanding the scriptures, only the intelligent could be saved; if it depended upon accumulating vast merit, only the saintly could be saved. He wanted to offer a practice that could be done by anybody. Dōgen will not have been unaware of this standard set by his famous predecessor. The practice that Dōgen offers is similarly one that, in principle at least, is open to anybody. *Genjō Kōan* was written for a busy layman. If salvation depends upon attaining some specific degree of being psychologically 'sorted out', then many people are going to be excluded. Dōgen is not advocating polishing the self to a point of brilliance, quite the reverse. Dōgen and Hōnen both believed that living a good moral life is intrinsically a good thing, and did not see the practices that they respectively offered as going against this, but neither of them thought that actual salvation hinged primarily on moral rectitude. Dōgen advocated keeping the precepts, but zazen was to come first, and the mirror relationship with a teacher who embodied the Dharma was to come even before zazen. In any case, for many, zazen did not mean long hours of monastic yoga, but a stillness and silence that were inner. In *Genjō Kōan*, zazen as a yoga ritual is not mentioned. The practice here is self-effacement, which is something that, in principle, anybody can do, no matter what their previous track record or present circumstance.

GRADUAL AND SUDDEN

Like Daosheng, Dōgen shows an appreciation of the value and usefulness of gradual cultivation, but both then assert that enlightenment is something else. People may be enlightened while having much learning or little, at the beginning of their career in the spiritual life or at the end of it, or not at all in spite of endless study and self-development. Dōgen himself had been devoted to developing his 'body and mind' until he heard Rujing's injunction to let it go. Learning and accumulated experience are, from the perspective of enlightenment, only secondary faculties. They can be useful in the work of helping others, but they are not and cannot be the key point, which is a sudden change. Here we can see Dōgen following Daosheng, who said, "Those who have realized the Dharma are darkly merged with the self-so-ness"[4]. The use of the term 'self-so-ness' echoes the Daoist *Dharmakāya* principle of naturalness. One becomes 'dark' by being unostentatious.

There is a story about two monks, Nangaku and Baso. Baso has been practising meditation for ten years. Nangaku comes along:

> Nangaku: What is the use of meditation?
> Baso: To make a Buddha!
> Nangaku picks up a tile. He starts to rub the tile.
> Baso: What are you doing?
> Nangaku: Making a mirror.
> Baso: You can't make a mirror by polishing a tile.
> Nangaku: You can't make a Buddha by meditating.

Baso is enlightened.

This is a very important story and it was dear to Dōgen. It tells us that gradual study (polishing, meditating) is endless. It has no natural limit, like polishing a tile. You will never get to the point where it turns into a mirror. A tile cannot become a mirror. However, in Dōgen's sense, the tile is a mirror, since it showed Baso to Baso. Therefore, the tile was a mirror already. The mirror is a mirror before it is polished and it is a mirror after it has

---

4 Kim, Hee-jin 2004. *Eihei Dōgen: Mystical Realist*, Boston, MA: Wisdom Books: 36.

been polished. The polishing is also a mirror. The polishing is a mirror when the tile turns into a mirror and also when the tile does not turn into a mirror. When the tile does not turn into a mirror, it mirrors not turning into a Buddha. Mirroring in this way it turns Baso into a Buddha. When Nangaku and Baso are both Buddhas they are the same. They are the same as mirrors, but there is nothing the same about these two mirrors. Baso becomes Baso. When Baso becomes Baso he forgets he is Baso. Forgetting he is Baso, he becomes a mirror. This mirror, however, is still just a tile. Therefore, there is no need to polish the tile. On the other hand, the mirror can become a tile when Baso is enlightened. When Baso is enlightened, not only the tile, but rivers, mountains and trees all become Buddhas and Buddhas become rivers, mountains and trees.

RITUAL PERFORMANCE

In performing a ritual one has a role. Different people may perform the same ritual and each will do it slightly differently according to differences of body and mind, but the important thing is the rite itself. In order to give a competent performance of the rite one has to let body and mind fall away. What matters are the essential elements of the rite itself, not the idiosyncrasy of one's individual performance. If one takes the whole of life to be such a rite then this consideration applies in all situations. To perform the rite one lets go of body and mind.

When one performs a rite the holy appears. Even though those who perform the rite are ordinary beings, still the sacred appears through their performance. Dōgen is saying that this is like the manner in which an image suddenly appears reflected in water. To perform in order to enhance one's self is counter-productive. However, many people do carry out their spiritual practice in this manner.

THE MIRROR METAPHOR

The mirror metaphor is a wonderful way for Dōgen to make his meaning clear. He will later, as we shall see, use the image of moon and water further in this way. This is a long-established image in Buddhist discourse, so here he alludes to it and builds upon it as something with which the reader will be already familiar. As in so many cases, Dōgen takes something familiar and extends the meaning.

The strong point of this paragraph is the analogy of the mirror that only works when one side of the glass is dark. You make a mirror by darkening one side. The same physical principle works with water too. Water reflects because the depths are dark. Dōgen is saying, self-study is not the same as religious practice because in self-study the self is what becomes illuminated and enhanced whereas in religious practice the self becomes dark. The self becomes dark when we unselfconsciously do what is required. Dōgen is contradicting the many philosophers who take 'self-consciousness' to be the supreme human achievement.

It is a particularly wonderful image because it explains genjō kōan. Genjō is sudden appearance. If there is a transparent surface and there is light on the inside, then, as we have seen, the outside observer sees into the self. As the inside gradually darkens, there suddenly comes a tipping point. Suddenly, the reflection effect comes into being. At what point does this tipping occur? At the point indicated by Dōgen's use of the term kōan. Kōan is when genjō happens. Kōan means that the person accepts and plays his allotted part in the scheme of things, just as Dōgen himself had done when he entered Tiantong monastery. At that point he had a choice. He could accept the offer of a humbling position that gave him entry to the Dharma teaching of Rujing, or he could hold onto his own idea of his status and be excluded. He chose to accept his lot and thus gained the Dharma.

> Disciple: When at the top of a hundred foot pole, what is to be done?
> Master: Climb down.
> Disciple: I thought that one was supposed to jump off.
> Master: Climbing down is jumping off.
> Disciple: What should one do when one reaches the ground?
> Master: If you listen to the wind, it will blow the ground away.

Further, the tipping point happens without what appears (genjō) being added to the content of the water or the room. If you stand on the shore of a lake you may be able to look into the water and see fish or weeds or rocks on the bottom. Then the light conditions change and you see a reflection instead. Perhaps you see the reflection of a tree on the other shore of the lake. The tree does not get added to the fish and the pondweed. They disappear and it appears. Suddenly, what is inside the water becomes irrelevant. This, therefore, is not a function of the power of the self, it is the point at which the 'other' – the myriadfold Dharma – comes to be seen. It is not seen because the self has appropriated it, but because the self is no longer seen.

Dōgen is saying that we are like that. While we are self-preoccupied, there is a light on inside. As that light dims nothing changes until we reach the point of kōan. When we become kōan, genjō occurs. This is the key point of the whole text.

DARK BUDDHA

This passage follows on directly from the passage about how "the self does not need to know All Buddhas". The mirror is a mirror and the image is reflected in it. The mirror does not need to know that it is a mirror. This means that neither self-knowledge nor any particular special knowledge of doctrine or comprehension is necessary. Such things do not affect whether the Buddhas shine upon one or not.

The mirror analogy is another way of saying the same thing. The Buddhas shine upon one, but one only reflects and thereby manifests that light if one has become dark. This state of having become dark is the state of a Buddha.

The state of being dark is yin. As in Daoism, the yin position is here recommended. The worldly person is endlessly trying to be as yang as possible, but the sage prefers the yin position. Only when we adopt the yin position ourselves can we give the yang position to *sho butsu* – All Buddhas. The attitude to adopt is that one should become yang when one has to, but, as soon as possible, return to yin. Darkness as an ideal is a very Daoist notion. The dark makes no demands and so is akin to goodness. True goodness is emptiness. As Daosheng had said, "It incurs no retribution."

So here we see several key ideas coming together: the idea of the mirror mind, the idea of sudden rather than gradual awakening, the idea of self-effort and accumulation versus letting go.

Gradual versus sudden enlightenment						
Gradual	Understanding	Being bright	Accumulating	Endless	Mind store	Self-power
Sudden	Reflecting	Being dark	Emptying	Immediate	Mind mirror	Other-power

WITH OR WITHOUT ZAZEN

It is interesting that *Genjō Kōan*, a text about how enlightenment occurs, does not mention zazen. It was written for a layman and it is possible that Yō Kōshū did not practise zazen. It would probably have been rather unusual for a layman to practise much zazen in that epoch. However, if this is so, it is then doubly interesting that Dōgen tells him all about how enlightenment occurs without mentioning it. If practice means zazen, not mentioning it would seem to support the ideas of Nōnin that practice was unnecessary.

Alternatively, perhaps Yō Kōshū is an ardent meditator and so this practice is just taken for granted, but if he were, then this would be one of his main links with Dōgen so it is still a little strange that there is no mention of it.

In the terms of *Genjō Kōan* itself there is no intrinsic reason why genjō necessarily has to depend upon meditation, or, indeed, upon any particular practice. In *Gakudōyōjinshū*, Dōgen says that nobody ever became enlightened without undergoing training, but acknowledges that there are different training methods.[5]

Sometimes, elsewhere, Dōgen talks about zazen as a very specific practice. In *Fukanzazengi* he talks about posture, breathing, and so on. Sometimes, however, he seems more to be talking about the spirit of zazen as an approach to any behaviour. Thus, in a talk in 1249, he was to say:

5 Kennett 1972: 106.

> Buddha's and ancestor's zazen is not movement or stillness, not practice and realization, not limited to body or mind, not the opposition of delusion and enlightenment, not emptying the various conditions, not bound by various realms. How could it be connected to form, sensation, perception, mental formations, or consciousness?[6]

The similarity of language here to the first verses of *Genjō Kōan* also tells us how the ideas of genjō kōan remained central to his presentation throughout his teaching career through all the vicissitudes of fortune.

It is clear that Dōgen does believe that zazen is a supreme path, but it is not entirely clear that zazen in the narrow sense is the necessary and only path. It is the spirit of zazen that Dōgen is primarily teaching, especially in *Genjō Kōan*: whether it is manifested while sitting, standing, walking or lying down, speaking or being silent, in stillness or activity, zazen is to adopt the yin position.

There is a similar ambiguity in Dōgen's writings about whether laypeople can or cannot become enlightened. At the time of writing *Genjō Kōan* he seems to think that they can. *Genjō Kōan* was written for a layperson and Dōgen himself had been treated as a layperson in China. However, later, after his move north, many of his writings seem to imply that only those who live out their lives in a monastery can be enlightened. Certainly, the lay condition is regarded as inferior. Then again, it is clear that in Dōgen's mind there is some equivalence between zazen and keeping the precepts. Laypeople might not have much time or opportunity for doing zazen, but they can keep the precepts, which then become their way of doing zazen. Later in his life, once the community was well established in Echizen, administering the precepts to laypeople became a significant activity and Sōtō Jukai ('ten precepts') ceremonies remain an important step for lay practitioners to this day. In the modern age, now that laypeople have more leisure time, there has been an upsurge in lay practice of meditation so it has now become possible for many laypeople to have a zazen practice as well, but that would have been difficult in Dōgen's own day.

---

6 Leighton and Okumura 2004: 308.

However, with *Genjō Kōan*, here he is discussing the deepest aspects of practice with a layperson. *Genjō Kōan* can, therefore, be something of a manifesto for lay Zen practice, but it remains a little uncertain whether this means zazen in the literal sense of sitting meditation.

BUDDHA NATURE

This idea of the mirror effect coming into being when the balance of light reaches its tipping point, and self gives way to Dharma, very neatly resolves many of the dilemmas that have arisen around the idea of 'Buddha nature'. The Chinese invented the term Buddha nature in part to explain to themselves how the phenomenon of karma works, in that it seemed that there had to be some kind of self for karmic retribution to mean anything, yet Buddhism taught *anātma*, non-self. Various ideas grew up, but broadly the idea that came to dominate is that there is a self that is originally pristine but has become soiled by delusion. This pristine self was Buddha nature. When delusion ceases, the inherent Buddha nature then appears. The problem with this idea is that it runs very close to the original Hindu idea that Buddha had rejected. This debate goes on to this day.

Dōgen's mirror analogy suggests a mechanism that resolves these problems. The water is water before and after the appearance of any reflection. The glass is glass before and after any use of it as a mirror. There is actually nothing inside the water or glass in the nature of a soul, nothing that is to be reunited with the godhead, yet, under certain conditions, the water displays the moon and the sky. This not only advances a solution to the Buddha nature conundrum, it also suggests a distinctive reinterpretation of the doctrine of Hōnen. Hōnen did not use the concept of Buddha nature, but, rather, emphasized the deluded, foolish nature. In Hōnen's view, it is precisely for foolish beings such as ourselves that Amitābha Buddha sheds his light. It is the foolish being who realizes his or her foolishness and turns toward Amitābha that is saved. Thus, beings are saved without changing their karmically impure nature. Dōgen shows how this can be and, indeed, how even a foolish person can be the saviour of many others. They are not so by dint of their own nature or achievement so much as by the fact that they reflect the truth inherent in the myriadfold Dharma. Dōgen's ideal is here very close to the *myōkōnin* idea of folk Buddhism – a person of simple faith, deeply modest, playing his or her part unostentatiously, yet full of devotion. The emphasis is on modesty and naturalness.

Dōgen talks about Buddha nature in various writings, but not as a personal possession or achievement. Buddha nature is not so much a quality of the individual, but more the fundamental nature of the universe. The Buddha nature of the individual is his or her absence or emptiness of nature, or, we could say, its irrelevance. It is our emptiness that gives us the capacity to be reflectors. When we are mirrors, the mirror is empty. It does not mind what is reflected in it. Here, therefore, Buddha nature comes much closer to the Neo-Daoist idea of Li than it does to the Hindu *ātma*.

WHY PRACTISE? OR HOW TO BECOME A MIRROR

Dōgen's question was: if we are already enlightened, how is it that we have to train? It was not so much that he did not want to train – he thought training essential – but he felt that the doctrine of original enlightenment deprived training of any justification. In *Genjō Kōan* Dōgen does not mention the actual activities of practice and training at all – unlike in *Fukanzazengi*, for instance. Knowing the rest of his writing, we assume that it is such training, especially zazen, that keeps us 'dark', but it does not actually say so here. Running through the whole of Dōgen's work is an ambiguity about whether what he is describing is a method to attain enlightenment or simply a state of enlightenment to which ideas of attainment are alien.

In these debates about whether practice is necessary, we can compare four innovators of the time and plot where they stood on the issue of the necessity of practice.

Faith and practice		
	Faith makes practice and keeping the precepts unnecessary	Faith is expressed in and is inseparable from vigorous practice
Pure Land tradition	Shinran	Hōnen
Tendai-Zen tradition	Nōnin	Dōgen

In the West, we have historically had many disputes and arguments about the object of faith – about what one has faith in – and so we tend to group concepts along the horizontal dimension of this grid, putting those of the same tradition together, but in Buddhism, the ultimate object is always the *Dharmakāya* and the proximate object can therefore be dressed up in different ways without leading to the same degree of conflict. A Buddhist who has faith in Guanshiyin, the bodhisattva of compassion, is not likely to quarrel on that account with another Buddhist whose practice centres on Akṣobhya, the Buddha of the dawn. Faith is faith. The common Sanskrit word for it is *śraddhā*, which also implies 'wholeheartedness'. So the question here is which is most wholehearted: to have such faith that practice be unnecessary? Or to express one's faith by vigorous practice? Dōgen and Hōnen are, generally, to be found on one side of this divide and Shinran and Nōnin on the other, even though Shinran was Hōnen's disciple and all four of them originally came out of the Tendai tradition.

In a Zen monastery that follows Dōgen's style, virtually everything is prescribed. Dōgen's later writings go into minute detail about how things are to be done. Life is almost completely ritualized. This means that there is nothing for the ego to do. In such a monastery, you do not decide when to get up, how to put away your bedding, what to do next, when to go to the washroom, what to do with your clothes when in the washroom, where to sit when you come back, when to go for breakfast, and so on. All of this is prescribed. There can be hardly any religious system anywhere in the world that is as tightly ritualized as a Sōtō Zen monastery.

Dōgen saw this complete ritualization of everyday life as being one way to keep the self dark, and it seems that as he got older he came more and more to the conclusion that it could only be done in a monastery. This may have been in part due to his failure between 1233 and 1243 to attract much of a popular following. However, in 1233, when he wrote *Genjō Kōan* and sent it to a layperson, he does seem to have believed that it was possible for the self to be 'dark' in the midst of ordinary life. We do not need to go into the debates about whether, how, why and when Dōgen changed his thinking, since our purpose here is only to examine this early text, which was written before any such change occurred, if, indeed, it did occur. In *Genjō Kōan* it seems to be implicitly suggested that this is a possibility open to anybody.

Since Dōgen continued to want *Genjō Kōan* to be the first chapter of his great book and continued to use the imagery and ideas of *Genjō Kōan* in talks throughout his career, my tentative conclusion is that it is here that he sets out the fundamental principle. He himself favours the method of sitting meditation as epitomizing the kind of dark receptivity of the yin position and 'pure zazen must be done', but 'pure' zazen does not necessarily have to mean lotus posture yoga. In fact, zazen as a specific sitting practice is only mentioned fairly rarely in his writings and many other practices do receive emphasis from time to time.

The purpose of training is to be a mirror even though one is a tile. There is one sense in which a tile can never be a mirror and there is another sense in which the tile can always function as a mirror. The difference is not in the substance of the mirror, but in where it happens to stand in relation to the other. Dōgen's Zen is positional. One's 'part' depends upon one's position. It is not a matter of there being a 'right' position, necessarily, more of doing what is necessary, no matter the cicrumstances. In China he spent two years trying to get recognition for the position he had occupied in Japan. Then he gave up and accepted what was offered. That was when things got better.

V

LINES 13–18: FORGET YOURSELF

13. To comprehend what we call the Buddha Dao means to comprehend the self.
14. To comprehend the self is to forget the self.
15. Forgetting self is confirmed by the myriad Dharmas.
16. This being confirmed by myriad Dharmas causes body-and-mind – and even the body-and-mind of others – to fall away.
17. This coming to a stop is the enlightenment-trace, the evidence of enlightenment.
18. This 'stopping', the trace of enlightenment, is what causes one to be going forth for ever and ever.

V.1 COMMENTARY

Here Dōgen expands what he has said in line 12 when he introduced the mirror image and the tipping point that occurs when things are kōan. He now says how this affects one personally. When we see the self as it actually is, it loses its fascination. When it loses its fascination we forget it. It stops. The light inside our room goes out. When it stops, our preoccupation with the supposed needs of our body and mind fall away. This stopping, or self-forgetting, is the evidence of enlightenment. It is confirmed by the appearance of the myriad Dharmas in our life that now send us forth in the service of the salvation of all sentient beings.

The Buddha Dao is to see through the self. For the deluded person, the self is fascinating, but for the enlightened one, boring. To see through the illusion is not easy, but to do so means that the self essentially loses its mesmeric effect. When we meet an impostor, but are not deceived, we say that we 'saw through him'. In the same way, Buddhism is to see through the impostor that is our self. Self is a kind of trance. When the trance is broken, self falls out of consciousness. Self is a concern with, fear about and slavery to body and mind, often manifesting as the pursuit of fame and gain. It occludes spiritual truth – the myriad Dharmas that advert to *sho butsu*. So self is also a distortion of the evidence all around one, and when the hold of self ends this distortion disappears.

It is as though all the signposts have been bent by a strong magnetic field sent out by self. When self is switched off, the field drops away and the signposts all return to their natural direction, which is that they point toward the myriad Buddhas. At that point one's over-concern with body and mind, and even with the bodies and minds of others, falls away. It comes to a stop and this is the evidence of awakening. Once this has happened and one is no longer so self-concerned, one naturally goes forth, and as there is now nothing to stop one from doing so, this going forth continues without cease.

v.2 DISCUSSION

A FAMOUS PASSAGE

This is perhaps the most famous and most quoted passage in the whole of *Genjō Kōan*, perhaps in the whole of Dōgen's writing. There is fairly general agreement among translators over lines 13–14, though with differences of nuance. As we proceed through lines 15–18 there is increasing divergence, which hinges to some extent upon vocabulary and grammar, but also upon how one interprets Dōgen's essential intention. The whole passage is, however, only working out the implications of line 12.

STUDYING THE EMPIRICAL SELF

To practise the Dao of Buddha is to comprehend the self. Several translators say that this means to 'study' the self, but I think that the intention is not so much that we accumulate knowledge about the self (see line 12) and more that we observe it in a way that enables us to become disenchanted. When one comprehends something fully it drops out of consciousness. Things that we know perfectly well, we do not have to think about all the time.

Again, many people think that studying the self means to discover one's own pristine Buddha nature. However, this text does not point in that direction. It is not even arguing for any great degree of self-knowledge or understanding. In fact, regarding one's own spiritual essence as something pristine and, therefore, important, might well get in the way of what Dōgen is advocating. Here, "comprehend[ing] the self" has much more the sense of realizing that the self is not all that it is cracked up to be. This, therefore, is very different from the idea of 'original enlightenment' taken as a characteristic of the individual. Perhaps Dōgen went to China in search of his 'true self' and discovered that he did not have one, or, rather, that his self was rather ordinary, but then that there was quite a different source of wonderment, which was the myriad Dharmas ever calling for our responsive action.

If we consider again the analogy of the room at night with the light on, if one is inside such a room, one cannot see outside, one only sees one's own reflection, but if one turns the light off, then one can see out of the window, especially if there is a moon. So for us to see the moon of the myriad Dharmas, our light has to be turned off, which occurs when we have lost interest in looking at our own reflection.

If there is any implication of self-study here, it is not so much a search for an original perfection and rather a more straightforward study of the empirical self that appears in the world, that gets out of bed in the morning, eats breakfast, goes to work, interacts with other people, and so on; the self that experiences satisfaction and disappointment, triumph and dismay, smugness and shame, that gets possessive and defensive, that smiles and weeps, that knows various ways of doing things and has habits. Such study should reveal, not how wonderful one is, but rather how vulnerable, frail, prone to error, and often foolish one is. This kind of awareness reveals the weakness of self and so may help to break the spell.

So, when we say 'comprehend' here, we can mean, 'become familiar with' as Dōgen says in line 12. Things that we are very familiar with are not at the forefront of our mind all the time. What is required is not a listing of characteristics or even the kind of self-examination that one might do in psychotherapy, which is all too often primarily concerned with building a sense of self-entitlement, the complete opposite of enlightenment. Dōgen means that one should examine one's own humanity with a certain objectivity. In practice, to comprehend the self is to realize how limited one is. It is to see one's foolish nature, to see how one is easily lifted up or cast down, how one is vulnerable, fragile, prone to error, apt to overreact and so on, to reach a familiarity with oneself as an ordinary being. When one is nothing more nor less than what one is, then one will stop being preoccupied with it.

DEFEAT MAY PROVIDE THE NECESSARY DARKNESS

Perhaps it is when we are defeated that we may have an experience of waking up. We should not forget that a large part of Dōgen's experience in China was personally humiliating. His ten years of seniority as a monk in Japan suddenly meant nothing. He had great difficulty even in gaining entrance to a monastery. His pleas to be treated better were turned down. This meant that on the occasions when he was admitted he found himself junior to the most junior trainees, much younger than himself. He had to learn to swallow his pride. When Dōgen came back to Japan, as a reminder to himself, he always wore the black robe of a junior trainee, even when he was abbot of his own monastery.

In his essay *Tenzokyōkun* – 'Instructions to the monastery cook' – Dōgen includes a story. He was at the time staying on a river-boat and an old man came on board to buy mushrooms. Dōgen began to chat with him. The man was the cook from Ayuwang Mountain Monastery, some considerable distance away, and he had come because the following day there was to be a special meal for the monastic community and they had nothing good enough in stock. Dōgen found his discussion with the old monk fascinating and invited him to stay overnight on the boat. The monk declined, saying that it was his personal duty to prepare the meal. Dōgen prevaricated – surely there must be other people at so big a monastery capable of cooking a meal. The monk was, however, not to be budged from his duty. We can see that at this point, Dōgen was thinking of preparing a meal as a practical matter, maybe even a chore, whereas for the monk it was a holy duty, an important ritual. Dōgen presses his point by saying to the monk that it would surely be better to do zazen or study kōans than to spend all one's time in the kitchen. At this point the monk burst out laughing and said, "My dear foreigner, you have not got the faintest idea about the true nature of Buddhist practice and training." Dōgen was much taken aback, but this defeat was an important step on his path, as he himself must have recognized or he would not have included the story in the midst of a text that is otherwise entirely taken up with positive instructions. It is also notable that he did include this story in which he himself is shown to be at fault.

FOOLISH MORTALS

Buddhism is not about returning people to a statistically normal state, as in medicine. From the Buddhist perspective, normal means deluded. We are deluded, but the moments in which we realize our deludedness can be very important. Those are the moments when Buddhas appear.

To be deluded means not to observe the mirror that sentient beings and inanimate things hold up before us, or to observe it with eyes that are not clear and objective. Mesmerized by self, one holds onto an image that defies evidence. This is foolishness. We do not see the Dharma reflected in others. Rather, we project images upon them and these images are all fundamentally images of oneself.

To comprehend the self is to forget the self because, when we see the self for what it is, it loses its hold on our conscious attention. We are no longer self-obsessed because solving the problem of body and mind has ceased to be fascinating. In any case, it is hopeless. Body is unreliable, mind is unreliable and sickness and death are inevitable.

The fool who knows he is a fool is wise to that extent. The person who believes in his own wisdom is generally fooling himself much more. In Shakespeare's play *A Midsummer Night's Dream*, the spirit Puck says, 'Oh what fools these mortals be.' To study oneself is to get a sense of the truth of this remark. Comedy liberates by showing us ourselves.

Initially, when we discover our failings we are inclined to cover them up. We become more self-conscious and struggle to put an attractive veneer on how we present ourselves to the world. This, however, is delusion within delusion. The person who is intent on presenting him- or herself as a more or less perfect instance of something approvable is almost certain to fall into a critical mind in regard to others. While putting on a sweet face, the poison of passive aggression seeps out remorselessly. Self-aggrandizement and self-denigration are equally rooted in pride and conceit.

However, when one has a more solidly grounded sense of one's own endless shortcomings, yet realizes that this is simply the fruit of karma without beginning and is the lot of everybody, one naturally becomes more accepting and compassionate in one's view of others. One becomes generous of heart because when one sees another go astray one realizes how easily one could be similarly rash or foolish. Compassion is then simple fellow-feeling of one fallible mortal for another.

Again, virtually everything that we think of as 'self' came from somewhere else. It is not really 'me'. It is simply what has ended up here. These ideas, these feelings, these attitudes and so on are mostly contagion. They are not the substance of my being – more the disease I happen to be suffering from at the moment. However, we are inclined to think that this congeries of imperfections is something truly marvellous.

Evidently, a great deal of our fascination with the spell of self has to do with our attempts to handle and navigate our relations with others. Here, therefore, Dōgen, in an aside, tells us also that when body and mind fall away it is not just our concern with our own body and mind that does so, but also our concern with those of others. Endless 'processing' of one's own and other people's problems becomes boring. Occasionally a true insight may arise and be interesting to share, but the habit of constant examination of self and other gives way to more practical concerns.

This does not mean that we then become careless of others, it means that we are no longer caught in the dance of mutual preening, rivalry, envy and manipulation that distorts so much interaction between people.

WEI WU WEI

In the Daoist classic *Dao De Jing*, a central principle is *wei wu wei* – to 'act without acting'. What this means is to be unpretentious – to act (behave) without acting (performing, as if on a stage). However, we should also note that at a very early stage in the transmission of Buddhism to China, the term *wu wei* came to be a standard way to render the Indian Buddhist term *asaṃskṛta*, which means 'unconditioned'. *Wei wu wei*, therefore, can also be read as 'unconditioned action'.

Now, performance, in the theatrical sense, is action that is not what it appears – actors are pretending; it is also action that is performed for an audience. These two dimensions give us quite a good practical idea of what 'conditioned action' is. If one's actions are performed for effect rather than for their inherent purpose, then one is conditioned by those upon whom the effect is to be worked. If I do the washing-up because it needs doing, that is straightforward, but if I do it in order to impress the other members of the household, that is conditioned. My hidden motive makes the action not really what it appears to be. Thus, Buddhist wisdom is called *prajñā*, a term that suggests seeing into the real meaning.

If one's life is really a continuous performance for the benefit of real or imaginary audiences, one is not liberated. One is a slave. This is especially the case where a person is under the spell of relationships that have long ceased. This can be very much the material that psychotherapy deals with, and in this respect, usefully so. We all inevitably tend to 'transfer' attitudes that were formed in relation to significant others in the past into the present. We thus perform for our boss in ways that have more to do with how we interacted with our father or school-teacher than with the real relationship with the actual person who is our boss in the present. This kind of fantasy-based activity is normal, but it can be a great liberation to be freed from it. One can free oneself in two different ways. One way is the painstaking work of deconstructing one's illusions and the other way is that of coming to the point where one's own self is simply less important. In any case, to act without acting is very close to what Dōgen is advocating. The person who is not acting (in the posing sense) simply reflects the myriad Dharmas.

RITUAL PERFORMANCE AND SELF-PERFORMANCE

We are now in a position to explore a significant distinction important to understanding Dōgen's meaning. If 'acting without acting', or, we could say, 'acting without performing' is important, does that not mean abandoning ritual? Evidently not, since Dōgen advocates correct ritual performance. To Dōgen, there is a world of difference between performing according the script of self and performing in a way that enables Buddhas to appear. It may be that herein lies the origin of the common erroneous notion that Zen has no rituals. The truth is that Zen makes all of life into a ritual.

Li, the correct performance of the right kind of rites, is an ideal in Dōgen's system and covers not only formal ritual, but everyday life as well. In Dōgen's Zen, washing the dishes is a rite, chopping wood and fetching water is a rite, entertaining a guest too. All these activities are things that have prescribed form and, therefore, are rituals. Many modern people purport to want to have nothing to do with ritual, yet if you examine their life you find that almost everything *they* do is a ritual of one kind or another too, and since life is full of ritual, it is important to do it well.

The right kind of ritual, however, is quite different from putting on airs in order to impress others or in order to avoid personal embarrassment. Whether the self shines or is embarrassed, triumphs or is defeated, is of no account in Dōgen's approach. Keeping in mind his own humbling experience in China may help us appreciate this point. There, he learnt to perform as required and to give up self-advertisement. After three years of trying to be acknowledged, he eventually gave up and followed the course offered, which was to enter the monastery at the bottom grade. This then quickly led to unexpected success. He was then no threat to anybody and no longer an irritant in the system and Rujing, recognizing his new humility, invited him in. It was like a homecoming. This is the Buddhist equivalent of 'Blessed are the meek, for they shall inherit the earth' (Matt. 5:5). To be meek is to be of mild spirit, gentle and humble. It is the opposite of self-assertion.

These two kinds of performance are actually opposites and alternatives. Each excludes the other. *Wei wu wei* refers to self-display, but this does not exclude correct performance. An actor performing as Hamlet has to let go of self in order to give a good performance. If he is in the frame of mind of 'Look at me! See how well I am performing Hamlet,' he is likely to mess it up. Right performance (Li) is impeded by self-consciousness. We shall examine this point more later.

ALONENESS

Self-performance is meant to impress a real or imaginary audience in some way. To let go of self-performance, therefore, is, in a special and important sense, to be alone. In Buddhism, this is called *ekaggatā*.

So we can ask, what am I when I am alone? Leonardo da Vinci wrote that a person is only completely himself when alone. When with even just one other person, he said, one is only half oneself. Dōgen had a similar idea. He thought that one is only completely oneself when doing zazen. This is very similar to Leonardo's idea. When one does zazen one is alone, no matter the other people sitting on the same bench beside one. My Zen teacher used to say, 'When you are sitting facing the wall, there is only you and the wall – and there is nothing wrong with the wall!'

Not only is one alone, but one is not doing anything. One is just sitting still looking at a blank wall. One is rightly performing doing nothing. This is like death. In life we play many different roles, but before death we are all the same. When sitting in zazen, Dōgen thought, we are all the same. It does not matter whether you are the abbot or the most junior trainee in the temple, when sitting in zazen you are simply yourself and social standing matters not at all. Zazen, therefore is *wei wu wei* in prototypical form.

Is this true? In Dōgen's idea there is a kind of ideal. In practice, the vast majority of people sitting in zazen are not in this ideal state that Dōgen is talking about. They are just as wrapped up in being somebody as they ever are. Zen monasteries are replete with ranks, duties, roles and standardized ways of doing things in which one can succeed or fail. So, although the ideal that Dōgen has in mind is very similar to the idea of Leonardo, I think it is rarely reached in practice. Nonetheless, the ideal is meaningful. It is a state in which concern with all the artificial things in which we get caught up in regular social life has dropped away.

If we take it that *Genjō Kōan* is also telling us how to do zazen, then the relevant image is that of still water. When a pond becomes still it becomes a mirror. When the surface is broken, the reflections are more difficult to discern. In the stillness and silence of zazen one becomes a mirror. One displays the Dharma in the world. This is not because one is trying to do so, nor is it because of any particular excellence in oneself. One is just sitting. However, just as the Buddha statue is both a supremely holy object and also merely a lump of rock, so the meditator, while still being nothing more than an ordinary human being, is, just by sitting there, exemplifying the eternal wisdom of Buddhism.

This is the meaning of ritual. Ritual is action by ordinary people that, nonetheless, makes something extraordinary appear. The ritual may be an elaborate ceremony or it may be sitting still doing nothing. It may be any of the 'rituals' of daily life. When we live together in community, life is full of rituals. Their proper performance is, therefore, also a recipe for harmonious community – for the kind of ideal society for which Dōgen, like Confucius, longed.

THE IMPORTANCE OF FAILING

In practice, this means that Zen monasteries become places where one sits 'in the state of Buddha', realizing the great extent to which one does not do so. With the ideal comes the actual.[1] By experiencing this discrepancy, people do indeed learn a great deal. With luck, they encounter their humanity to a sufficient degree that the lure of fascination with self dissipates and drops away.

One of the things that one experiences repeatedly in Zen training is getting things wrong. Even the zazen is a difficult exercise in which the correct posture is almost impossible to sustain. People perhaps enter Zen training on the promise that by their own effort they will attain satori. This promise is realized, but not at all in the way that the person expects. The satori comes at the point where self – body and mind – drops away, and it does so when one is sufficiently despairing of it. This despair comes as a result of trying to do the impossible, which is to attain satori by one's own effort. Similarly in kōan practice, taking kōan in the sense meant by Rinzai, not by Dōgen. Kōans are impossible. By taking on kōan practice one sets oneself up for failure. If one fails sufficiently to make a difference, then one is said to have 'passed' that kōan. Usually one is then given another. Dōgen failed his first kōan in the Tendai monastery, his second in the Rinzai monastery and his third on the boat selling mushrooms. Then he had his really big failure in Rujing's *zendō* and thus came satori. That satori was sufficient to darken his self enough to make a mirror of the other side. The other side reflected the myriad Dharmas, which enabled his return to Japan and all his prodigious efforts to bring the Dharma to people in his own country, doing the work that Myōzen had intended.

---

1 "With the ideal comes the actual" is a line from the text *Sandōkai* (參同契). See Kennett 1972: 225.

TO KNOW IS TO FORGET

Dōgen says that to comprehend is to forget. The better we know something, the less conscious we are of it. The more familiar we are, the more at ease. When you learn to drive, initially, at the beginner's stage, you are highly conscious of every action. Later, when you know how to drive, you do it all without thinking. The same is true of many things. When a bird learns to fly, it has to engage in a lot of trial and error, but once it has learnt, it does not have to think about it; it just flies. When you know it you lose consciousness about it, whatever the 'it' is. It becomes second nature.

Some people seem to think that the aim of spiritual practice is more and more consciousness, as though one is going to be on the alert all the time. That is a mistake. It would be exhausting. It is not the condition of an enlightened being, it is the state of a person who is a nervous wreck. We are nervous wrecks because we are trying to sustain an illusion – the ego ideal. We are self-conscious because the 'self' that we are conscious of is not real and so is highly liable to let us down. This fear of being let down by our favourite illusion manifests as conceit, manipulation of others, the half-truths of social intercourse, stress, and all the hypocrisy of ordinary life.

When we know the self for what it truly is, we do not need to keep it in our consciousness all the time. We are no longer on guard. We can trust natural unfoldment. Thus the myriad occasions of daily life are all trustworthy. The facts are friendly.[2] *Wei wu wei* is a safe place – a true refuge – whereas hyper-consciousness goes with self-performance. Enlightenment is not a self-performance. Enlightenment is a life from which such artificiality has dropped away. So the enlightened person is one who dwells at ease and to do so means not having to be self-conscious all the time.

The most fundamental Buddhist teaching is refuge. To become a Buddhist one 'takes refuge'. One takes refuge in Buddha, Dharma and Sangha. This conjures the notion of us all as refugees, in flight, seeking safety. What are we fleeing?

2 "The facts are friendly" was a favourite saying of the American psychologist Carl Ransom Rogers.

The self. Where is safety? With the Three Jewels. What happens when we feel *truly* safe? That safety becomes the ever-present, taken for granted, backdrop to life. It drops out of immediate consciousness. We can bring it back at will, but we do not have to be thinking about it because it is the hidden jewel in every element of experience. It becomes our faith.

Everybody has faith of some kind – faith that the sun will rise tomorrow, and so on. We then invest that confidence in various things, many of which – status, money, relationships, etc. – are not so reliable because they depend upon conditions. Buddhism teaches us to seek a refuge beyond conditioned things. Dōgen, here, is making that a practical proposition.

ON OVER-VALUING CONSCIOUSNESS

It is very common these days for spiritual enlightenment to be identified with 'consciousness' and, since Freud, consciousness means 'awareness' and stands in distinction to 'the unconscious'. In particular, there is a tendency to think that consciousness means self-consciousness. However, from a truly Buddhist perspective, self-consciousness is, in most situations, a handicap. We can see this by thinking about public speaking. People fear to speak in public because of the overwhelming pain of self-consciousness. Accomplished public speakers have to train themselves to keep their mind on the audience and the subject matter, so that it not stray onto themselves and induce paralysis.

In common contemporary spiritual discourse, we are likely to come across ideas such as: nirvāṇa is nothing more than being awakened to the enlightened nature of our consciousness. If we take Dōgen seriously, however, such ideas are exceedingly misleading. According to Dōgen, enlightenment comes when self-awareness leaves consciousness and becomes invisible, black, forgotten. It is precisely that blackness that creates the mirror effect and enables us to become reflectors of the myriad Dharmas, without us even necessarily knowing that we are doing it. Even saying this much is overestimating the cause–effect element, since the converse is equally true, that enlightenment leads to self-consciousness dropping away. They are two names for the same thing.

Consciousness is a big item in Western psychology, but it is not the essential feature of Buddhism that many people assume it to be. Meditation is nowadays often taught as a consciousness enhancement technique. However, in the Parinibbana Sutta – an important Buddhist text describing the last three months of the life of Śākyamuni Buddha – there is an incident described in which Śākyamuni is meditating and is so deep in samadhi that he does not even notice a lightning storm that is so fierce that it kills two farmers in the adjacent field. This story is told as a way of demonstrating the depth of Śākyamuni's meditation. So much for awareness of the here and now! The term *dhyāna*, which is the linguistic root of the word 'Zen', might well be better translated as 'rapture' than 'meditation', given the change in meaning that the term meditation has undergone due to popular fashions in spirituality.

Not only is Dōgen saying that what we now call the unconscious – forgetting – is very important, he is also saying that the resulting "going forth" is not really a personal choice, but more a natural and inevitable consequence of a process that is essentially unconscious. This is, surely, right. When somebody does something, we make some sort of assessment of how 'genuine' it is. When we sense that it is based on a conscious calculation, we rate it as less genuine than when it is spontaneous.

Spontaneous actions are unpremeditated, which means, in psychoanalytic terms, that the impulse for them is unconscious. This is what Dōgen is proposing – that we arrive at a state where our compassion and other virtues are not the result of contrivance, but have become natural, and he is saying that they become natural when our life reflects the myriad Dharmas, and that this is something that happens automatically when the self has become dark. It is not a decision. It is not something over which one has any control. In no sense does an enlightened person think, "Now I will reflect the myriad Dharmas". He has no control over it. It is not conscious. It is natural empathy.

It is difficult to stress this point sufficiently. Enlightenment does not appear in this text as an extension of consciousness. It is not a matter of being aware and alert twenty-four/seven. It is not a particular kind of attention. Buddhas sleep well. They do so because they are not on high alert all the time. They are at peace. They are at peace because they are not defending the ego. The high-alert way of living has stopped. This stopping is the external evidence, 迹, *shaku*, or 'trace' of satori.

SHAKU (迹)

Lines 17 and 18 talk about the 'enlightenment trace'.

> 17. This coming to a stop is the enlightenment-trace, the evidence of enlightenment.
> 18. This 'stopping', the trace of enlightenment, is what causes one to be going forth for ever and ever.

The word *shaku* means 'trace'. A trace may be a track left behind, an indicator that something has happened. Interestingly, the word '*mārga*' that occurs in the fourth of the four truths that are commonly taken as the foundational statement of Buddhism, and which is generally translated as 'path' or 'way', more strictly means 'track'. While path, way and track are near synonyms, the subtle implication of path and way is that the emphasis is upon where they lead, whereas track suggests more something left behind, like car tracks or animal tracks. The fourth truth is the eightfold track. It is not so much a 'path to enlightenment', more an 'enlightenment trace'. Śākyamuni did not attain enlightenment by following it; he discovered it by becoming enlightened, and, being enlightened, this was the trace he left behind as he proceeded.

The word 'trace', therefore, also refers to the enduring effect after the first experience of change has worn off. When we think of satori, we perhaps like to think of the moment of realization. Actually it may be more than a moment – perhaps a state of a certain kind of ecstasy that may last for some days or even, as in the case of Śākyamuni Buddha, a few weeks. This all sounds rather marvellous and attractive. However, it fades. The immediate experience wears off, but a trace remains. Trace is an insufficient term. We are talking about the evidence in the life of the person. When body and mind have fallen away and self has receded into the unconscious, the person becomes a bright mirror of the myriadfold Dharma and, with his own light dowsed, he can see the moonlight outside and, even more importantly, we receive the moonlight reflected from him.

We can understand that this is a marked change of orientation. This is what happens in spiritual awakening – in genjō at the point of kōan. The person's energy and attention is no longer all bottled up in their own room, but is drawn outward into the world where everything appears by grace of the Dharma moon.

This change of orientation carries one forth into the world full of gratitude, generosity, patience, love, energy and compassion, bestowing peace and wisdom, not because one has oneself suddenly become superlatively wise and strong, but because the tipping point has been passed. Now, unselfconsciously, one follows the old track.

When a disciple comes to a master and describes wonderful spiritual experiences – or even horrible ones – the teacher listens carefully, but is unmoved until they see the trace – the evidence of change in the person's life. If that is not there, then there is no evidence of satori. However, it is possible for a satori to have happened with no spiritual fireworks at all, but simply some experience has occurred that has had a deeply sobering effect upon the person. They might not even be consciously aware that it has taken place, but the trace is visible. It is evident to everybody else that something has happened. The person in question is suddenly on a different track, noticing the needs of others, less boastful or self-denigrating, less self-obsessed altogether, more engaged with things around him or her, more open to spirit. There is a lightness about the persion in both senses of the English word – less heavy and more radiant. The person him- or herself may not think anything of it, but satori has occurred.

GOING FORTH

Line 18 says: "This 'stopping', the trace of enlightenment, is what causes one to be going forth for ever and ever." So this is quite a dynamic 'stopping'. What stops, we might say, is the obstacle. What is the obstacle? Self-concern. The ordinary person lives defensively, but the psychological castle that they build in order to defend themselves becomes their prison. Locked up within its walls, they feel that they have no choice.

What are you doing with your life? Some people have a clear sense of purpose or mission, but they seem to be the minority. Sometimes I ask people this question. Sometimes, they say such things as, "I don't know, I expect something will come along," or "I don't think about that. I don't have much choice."

My impression is that some people think that they have freedom and often they feel rather frightened of it, and most people think that they do not have freedom, complain about that, but actually have far more freedom than they are willing to think about and really would rather not.

Freedom and choice are lauded as 'goods', and lack of freedom is said to be bad, but most people do not exercise the freedom that they do have. It seems to be easier to believe that 'there is no alternative'. Many secretly prefer not to have a choice because then they do not feel responsibility. Life can go by and when one reaches judgement day one perhaps hopes to be able to say, "It was not my fault." I am sure that many people who think that they have stopped believing in God and 'judgement day' still go on living as though they still do. Is that not strange?

I am now 69 years old. The time I have left could go in a trice. What am I going to do with it? As best I can I shall study, teach, and practise the Dharma. That will be my contribution to world peace and the wellbeing of the world after I have gone and it is what I will be able to feel happy about and grateful for. That will probably mean writing a few more books and maybe undertaking a few projects. It might mean travelling. It will involve helping those who want to study and practise, and supporting their faith. It will probably mean living at my retreat in France for the immediately foreseeable future, but perhaps going back to England, my home country, at some point as I become less capable of managing to live out here. However, these practical details will, no doubt, arrange themselves in their own way. Five years ago I did not expect to be living where I am now, so who knows? One can have a sense of direction, but it can all be swept away in a moment. Perhaps, next month, my whole scheme will be turned on its head.

Details depend upon conditions, but one's basic refuge should, I think, provide an answer to that awkward question: what are you doing with your life?

THE EXAMPLE OF ŚĀKYAMUNI BUDDHA

Going back to the example of Siddhārtha Gautama is, I find, always helpful. That does not mean that one should live exactly as he did, necessarily, but his courage and spirit are inspiring. Siddhārtha Gautama's first 'going forth' occurred after he saw the 'four sights'. Going out of his palace, he saw a sick person, a person decrepit with age, a corpse, and then a holy man full of poise and peace. These four sights disturbed his self-seeking and self-indulgent attitude and caused him to leave home. How could one be so poised and at peace in a world of aging, sickness, and death?

However, this first leaving home was still self-centred in a fundamental sense. He was still seeking the solution to *his own* problem – his own suffering, his own confusion, his own mortality. What he was concerned about was his own body and mind. This first going forth was exactly what Dōgen did in going to China. Both Siddhārtha and Dōgen set out on difficult personal searches, trying to find the answer to their own spiritual unease.

Siddhārtha then went to see a variety of teachers. Each time he learnt something, but nothing was ever really good enough for him. Just as he had abandoned his family, he now abandoned one teacher after another. Just as he abandoned teachers, so, later, he abandoned even his friends upon the spiritual path. Eventually he was alone, more or less down and out, and defeated. At this point Sujata the innocent milkmaid had pity on him and fed him. In a way this must have been humbling. He had to face the fact that he was human and dependent. His arrogance fell away. During the following night his self-concern, which had been his guiding light up to that point, went out, and in that great blackness appeared the reflection of all the Buddhas. Siddhārtha was enlightened.

He remained in this ecstatic state for a few weeks, but then he felt divine inspiration to go forth again. This time his going forth had a completely new quality. It was not driven by his own inner conflict, but inspired by a divine voice that said that there was a job to do. No longer was he seeking something for himself. From then on he was rarely alone. Always he was in the midst of people, helping to liberate them, spreading goodness in the world, fed by his communion with all the Buddhas of past, future and present, sustained by that great lineage and protected by the gods.

We can see the parallel with Dōgen. He goes to China, experiences repeated defeat and setback, searches here, there and everywhere, gathers information about Buddhism in many temples and other situations, but is still driven by a nagging discontent, and nothing actually solves his problem of body and mind until he meets Rujing. Rujing shows him kindness, takes him in and then shows him that it is his concern with body and mind that is itself the problem. Letting it go, he is filled with new energy. He laps up everything that Rujing has to tell him and feels vibrant and keen to return to his native land in order to assist beings there.

This is the great turning around that Buddhists talk of. For Śākyamuni and Dōgen it came about in a similar way. Both were sobered by repeated defeat, yet along the way learnt a great deal about spiritual methodologies of various kinds, and then when all seemed lost, were shown kindness just at the moment of their greatest despair.

There has been debate among scholars about whether Dōgen did, in fact, ever experience satori in China. He gives no dramatic account of a spiritual experience in his writings, so we do not know whether his satori was accompanied by descending hosts of angels or just happened quietly in his sleep. However, we do see the 'trace', the *shaku*, and that is all the evidence we need.

LOOK AND THEN STOP

This section of *Genjō Kōan* has an interesting relationship to the two primary forms of meditation in Buddhism, which are generally called *samatha* and *vipassanā*. *Vipassanā* is 'insight meditation' and *samatha* is 'tranquil abiding'. These terms, however, are the result of a long process of refinement and the formulating of these two into techniques and methods that can be taught as formal spiritual procedures. There is, in our modern world, a tendency toward packaging, technicalization and commodification. If things can be packaged, they can be sold. This leads to the setting up of schools for the distribution of spiritual 'commodities'. Basically the terms simply mean 'stop' and 'look'.

Now, it is commonly taught that *samatha* is a preparation for *vipassanā*. The idea is that what really matters is insight, and tranquil abiding might be needed to prepare the ground for this more important form of meditation. However, it is clear from this passage that Dōgen thought otherwise. Here, insight – comprehending the self – is, if it is necessary at all, merely a step in the direction of that 'stopping' in which the self becomes dark and forgotten. When this darkening of self occurs, there is a 'stop' and this stop is the real indication of enlightenment. It causes the true going forth, that then continues ceaselessly. In Dōgen, therefore, it is stopping rather than insight that is the more important of the two.

LEARN LIFE BY LIVING

It is the dark side of the mirror that makes the reflection of Dharma possible. The real manifestation of Buddhism goes on out of sight, even to the person him- or herself. When realization has become complete, one does not remember it, or only does so occasionally. This is because it is completely internalized. This is just like any challenging activity. A person who fights many battles might become brave, but he did not fight battles *in order to* become brave, and he probably does not often think "I am brave and I became so in such and such a way." If he is interviewed by a newspaper that wants to do a feature on bravery, he might be able to come up with something, but it may not be very clear or comprehensive. In the same way, a person becomes genuinely enlightened by encountering life. If somebody later says, "How did you get that way?" the master may say something like, "By chopping wood and fetching water." All the assembled disciples then think that this is very profound and mysterious, but what he means is that he became fully alive by living.

NO NEEDS

Having 'body and mind drop away' has a special meaning for Dōgen since, according to Keizan, Dōgen had his big awakening experience when Rujing used these words. Some scholars dispute this story, saying that Keizan must have made it up. Who is right? We do not know, but I am willing to accept the traditional story. We have already seen that Dōgen went to China with a preoccupying question about what, if all beings are inherently enlightened, the real justification for training or studying Buddhism can be. The inherent enlightenment teaching made Buddhism seem like a long, arduous journey to return to one's starting point. It also implicitly said that enlightenment is something to do with achieving the right state of mind.

When Rujing used the phrase, "Let body and mind fall away", Dōgen realized that up to that point he had been in pursuit of enlightenment conceived as something to be gained, something that could become a possession of the body or of the mind. Many people think that way. They believe that enlightenment is going to be something they can *get*. When they have got it, it will be established either in their body or in their mind.

'Dropping away of body and mind' sounds rather esoteric. Nowadays we would probably talk about 'needs'. Dōgen is saying that there are no 'needs' in the absolute sense. A need is always relative to a purpose. In order to make tea I need hot water. Hot water is a need in relation to tea. However, we tend to think that we have 'needs' in a more unconditional sense. In fact, this is not true. I need air in order to breathe. I need to breathe in order to stay alive. I need to stay alive in order to... what? People do not always choose to stay alive. Sacrificing one's life is sometimes noble. Reflecting upon the question 'what is a real need, and what for, and when?' can be productive and challenging.

For Dōgen, spiritual awakening means being without neediness. This is another way of defining his idea of kōan. The *bhikṣu* does not start from his own needs; he starts from what comes freely. Concern with the 'needs' of the body or the mind drops away. The whole matter of the nature of spiritual practice turns around. One sees it from the other side. One asks, "What am I supposed to be doing now? What is the right thing to do next?"

Airs and poses are based on our desires. We have many layers of desire and a corresponding repertoire of poses. It is as if we wear many layers of disguise. Shedding even one layer makes us feel lighter. This is no different from the standard teachings of Buddhism. However, I think we can say more. On the one hand, there is what we may call incremental Buddhism, which involves taking disguises off one by one. On the other hand, there is 'sudden awakening', which is what happens when all the disguises fall off at once. The dropping away of body and mind seems much closer to the latter than the former.

I think that Dōgen did have a major and sudden awakening experience. Rujing saw through his disguise. That he did not write about spiritual fireworks proves nothing. He came back with a driving impulse to bring what he had received to the people of Japan, so there we see the *shaku*. For him, dropping off body and mind was a lot more than a clever idea. After encountering Rujing it penetrated the marrow of his bones.

SUMMARY SO FAR

1. The image in line 12 is pivotal to the whole message of the essay. The mirror works because one side is dark. What must become dark? The self. Thus the self becomes no self. In this way, principles of Daoism and Buddhism are united.
2. On the bright side of the mirror are All Dharmas (line 1) but on the dark side our self-effort has ceased (line 2).

3. The self becoming black, the falling away of neediness of body and mind and the 'stopping' in lines 17 and 18 all refer to the same thing.
4. Dōgen is writing about a process that is often largely unconscious, as in line 10. Our task is to conform to this hidden Buddha Dao (line 3). To conform to it is to perform life as its rite or dance. With the idea of right performance (Li) of the rite of life, Buddhist and Confucian principles are united.
5. Performance is hindered by self-consciousness. Right performance (Li) is all-important. Therefore self-consciousness must drop away. It does so when we 'comprehend' self. Li originally meant 'sacrifice'. When the self is sacrificed, everything else is made sacred.
6. This is all about how to relate to the sacred object of worship – the 'Buddha Dao' in line 3, 'myriad Dharmas' in line 5, 'All Buddhas' in line 6, 'enlightened Buddhas' in line 1, and, metaphorically, 'the Moon' that is reflected in our dark water.
7. The passage in lines 13–18 is rightly famous, but only correctly and fully understood in light of line 12.

In the remainder of the text we shall continue to encounter the notions of the Dao and its Li and a further series of images, all of which, I believe, confirm this interpretation and give to the text a coherence that is otherwise difficult to grasp.

VI

LINES 19–20: PUT YOURSELF OUT

19. If, when a beginner seeks the Dharma, he positions himself as far away and nowhere near to the Dharma's edge,
20. then, when the Dharma is correctly transmitted to him, he is soon playing his part like a natural.

VI.1 COMMENTARY

Dōgen describes two stages. Firstly, there is the establishment of religious consciousness. There are delusion, satori, practice, birth, death, Buddhas and sentient beings, just as in line 1. Secondly, there is 'being a natural'. The first stage sets up the second. The person is separated from Buddha. Unless one realizes that one is not Buddha, one does not get anywhere. Prematurely playing with ideas of non-duality, Buddha Nature, original enlightenment and so on, and thinking oneself wise ahead of one's actual knowledge only leads to disaster and insulates the practitioner from any possibility of progress. To learn, one has to know that one does not know. If one starts from a humble position, then there is a sound basis.

Transmission implies separation. For something to be transmitted, it has to go from A to B. However, when there is transmission, the sender and the receiver are playing their proper parts. In fact, 'transmission' *is* two people playing their proper parts. When the light is reflected in a mirror, the light and the mirror are both playing the parts for which they were designed. The light has already been playing its part for eternity, waiting for the mirror to show up. However, the mirror-to-be – the practitioner, ourselves – had not become a mirror yet because the self side was illuminated by karma and had not fallen dark.

To position oneself as a beginner far from the Dharma's edge is the correct course. It is humility, without which one will get nowhere. Later, in fact, we shall see that the humbler one has been at this stage, the deeper enlightenment is.

VI.2 DISCUSSION

TRANSLATION PROBLEMS

Some translators interpret line 19 as a description of the unfortunate state of the beginner. They take the implication to be that it would be better not to be so far away. However, my impression is that Dōgen is actually telling us the correct attitude, which is one of extreme deference. The further away we place ourselves, the better. If we have first established this humility, then when later the Dharma is given to us we shall receive it as a precious gift and feel grateful. If we start off from a position of arrogance, whatever progress we do make is likely only to fill us with more pride and smugness.

AWAY FROM THE BOUNDARY OF THE DHARMA

When we begin our study of Dharma, it is only natural to think of it as something that is far away. We know we have much to learn. Buddhism then seems like an educational programme and enlightenment is a kind of credential that will be awarded to us when we pass the exam. Or we think of it as a spiritual journey to a distant destination. In the Lotus Sūtra there is the parable of the 'illusionary city'. In the parable we are told that Buddha has compassion for those who are flagging on the journey and conjures up the mirage of a city not too far away in order to keep them going in the right direction. In this sense, the ordinary idea of enlightenment is a 'carrot'. We read in a Buddhist book about the wonderful experiences that people have had at the time of satori and we desire to have such an experience ourselves, and so we become willing to practise. Our practice is motivated by this desire and we are then willing to put up with sore knees, or temple circumstances that at any other time we would regard as gross privation, because we want what those enlightened people have.

In thinking this way, however, we are still prey to a 'gaining idea'. Our initial humility is tarnished by greed. We may have to try and try and try again before we realize that this is not the right procedure. Better just to be humble and grateful for what we already have.

The Dharma may be far away, like the moon in the sky, but its light comes to us already. While we try to grasp it, it eludes us. When we stand in awe before it, it bathes us in silver light.

ON BEING A NATURAL

The term used here is 本分人.

人, *nin*, means person. It is a picture of two legs – humans walk on two legs. So it is also like the suffix '-er' or '-or' in English, in words like 'actor' or 'seeker'.

分, *bun*, means a part, share or lot. The word for a Buddhist monk in Sanskrit is *bhikṣu*, which means a person who has his share. This is generally taken as indicating a share of the alms food, but Dōgen here gives it a different twist. The traditional monk was a mendicant who begged for alms. This was a crucial element in the way that the Buddha trained his people. You never knew what, if anything, was going to be put in your bowl. This meant living a life of complete acceptance. If there is nothing, you go hungry. If there is nothing for a long time, you die. If there is plenty, you share it. These simple acts, complete acceptance and complete dependence, encapsulate the whole attitude of the *bhikṣu*. There is no declaration of rights here. The *bhikṣu* relies upon the goodwill of others. Dōgen builds on this principle of relying upon providence.

Dōgen's modification of the term kōan changes it to mean one who keeps to and fulfils their share or lot, so 分人 means a person in the condition of kōan, in Dōgen's sense, and that means a person who is at the point of genjō, the point at which a radical change in perception and presentation occurs.

本, *hon*, means 'original' or 'root'. It refers to the natural or 'root' state of something. It is a very important word in Chinese philosophy and in Buddhism. The symbol 木 means a 'tree'. It is a picture of a tree. The addition of the horizontal stroke at the bottom turns it into 'root'. In these East Asian philosophies there is a great concern to get to the root of things. In the term 'original enlightenment', 'original' is 本. So 本 can mean 'fundamental' in a logical sense, or 'original' in the temporal sense. In Eastern cultures the past is generally the better or best time. The world is conceived as gradually degenerating from a former golden age. In the golden age of the past people were naturally virtuous. Therefore, if people were to go back to their 'original' state, all would be well. This is one reason why the idea of original enlightenment caught on and seemed to capture so much of the Japanese native sense of spirituality at a stroke. 'Original' did not just imply something that you were born with, it implied something from ages past, something incalculably better than what one normally encounters. '*Hon*', thus, does not just refer to the authentic state of the individual, as we in the West with our individualistic society might be inclined to take it. It refers to a person in that time of old when all is believed to have been so much better than today. As soon as the term '*hon*' is included, there is some sense of reference to ancient wisdom and an ideal world. This general association is true for Dōgen too. Thus, 本分 means 'dutiful', 'staying within one's bounds' as well as 'original part'. The kind of modern person who gets involved in Zen perhaps does not readily equate enlightenment with being dutiful, but for Dōgen this is a natural association. Here, the best kind of person is dutiful and therefore is 本分人. Enlightenment is therefore a condition in which one becomes dutiful not through a heavy sense of obligation, but through a change in perception (genjō) that makes being so quite natural because the self-centred resistance has fallen away.

THE THEATRE ANALOGY

To play one's proper part correctly is to be a good actor. We have already touched on this in our discussion of *wei wu wei*. Consider again the situation in which an actor – let us call him John Smith – is playing the part of Hamlet. What does the audience see and experience?

If John Smith is a poor actor, he will be self-conscious. He will either be showing off or he will be embarrassed. If he is in either of these states, what the audience will experience is John Smith and his emotional struggle. They will have difficulty getting into the play. Afterwards, they will talk to their friends about John Smith and his performance.

If, on the other hand, John Smith is a good actor, he will be so much in role that he will not be self-conscious. The audience will not experience John Smith; they will experience Hamlet. They will receive the message of Shakespeare. They will be caught up in the problems of the state of Denmark, the dilemmas of unrequited love, the question "To be or not to be?" and so on. Afterwards, they will still be moved by these themes and the tragic dilemma that was represented on stage.

In other words, there are two completely different alternatives. What the audience see is one or the other. Whether they see one the other depends upon whether the actor is self-conscious or not. When the actor plays his part like a natural, John Smith disappears and Hamlet appears. That John Smith should disappear is what Dōgen means in lines 17 and 18 by "coming to a stop". On stage, this is the mark of a good actor. In the case of religion, it is the mark of a good practitioner.

This switch from one mode to the other is exactly the same as the switch that occurs when the water's surface ceases to be transparent and becomes a mirror instead. In one state we see into the water, just as in one case we see into John Smith. In the other state we see the sky, just as in the better performance we see only Hamlet.

In the classical sense of literature and art, the artist disappears and that is the mark of his accomplishment. This is also Dōgen's ideal. In modern times we have evolved other, more self-indulgent, self-serving ideas, and have become a culture in which we are as much or more concerned with 'celebrities' than with the art. Dōgen's ideal is the complete opposite. To seek to be a celebrity is the diametrical opposite of what Dōgen advocates.

Genjō kōan equates with the Buddha Dao and its Li. Li is correct performance, which is doing what is needed like a natural. When there is correct performance, the Buddha Dao appears, just as Hamlet appears, or just as the sky appears in the lake. Kōan is the playing and genjō is the appearing.

It is worth noting here that the 'appearing' to the audience is more significant than what appears to the actor. Line 10 said: 'When All Buddhas really are All Buddhas the self does not need to know All Buddhas.'

John Smith plays his part. If his part is that of Hamlet, then he probably does know the whole play, but if his part were that of Marcellus, the soldier who appears in the first scene and knows about ghosts, then it would not be necessary for him to know the whole play. He would need only to play his own part well. Then he would have done what he needs to do in the presentation of the whole play.

In the theatre of life, we each have a part to play. We do not need to know the whole plot nor the deep message in order to play our own part. That is what is required and that is all that is required.

TRANSMISSION

These two verses tell us that the Dharma can be 'correctly transmitted' (正傳). The term *den* (傳), translated as 'transmitted', implies propagation. This is like cultivating plants. New Dharma is propagated from existing healthy Dharma. It comes from outside the self. It cannot be otherwise because self is delusion. How can delusion enlighten itself? Delusion can only be deluded. Receiving the Dharma through encounter with what is not self, if one is humble, one learns one's part. At the same time, '*den*' carries some implication of being a special kind of person. The element 專, *zhuan*, means 'exclusive' or 'special'. Here again we see the paradox. The least self-conscious person is a special person. They learn more quickly. They are easier to be with.

The Dharma is transmitted to us by others. We pick it up. The way that they transmit it to us is by being other. It is the very fact that they are not a function of myself – that they do not play my games – that makes them effective as agents who may awaken me. They puncture the balloon of my egotism.

All Dharma is not self. In myself there is impermanence and affliction. Most of the time, people seek the Dharma in the first place thinking that when they find it they are going to arrive at a self that is free from impermanence and affliction. They do not seek liberation from self, they seek the perfection of the self. This is like heading north to go south.

In transmission one is receiving from another. While one is in the self-power mode one thinks of transmission as getting something. This is like Ānanda in the second chapter of Keizan's wonderful text, the *Denkōroku*. Keizan was Dōgen's eventual successor. He wrote an inspiring work that gives the histories of the ancestors in the Zen transmission line. The first ancestor after Śākyamuni was Kāśyapa. Kāśyapa understood the Dharma in a famous incident when the Buddha held up a flower and smiled. When Buddha Śākyamuni died, Ānanda was still not enlightened, despite having spent many years at the Buddha's side. Ānanda was then enlightened in an encounter with Kāśyapa.

Ānanda asks Kāśyapa what he received from Śākyamuni. This is like asking, "What did you get that I didn't get?" Most people are initially caught in the kōan of the apparent contradiction between, on the one hand, "Unless I get something out of it there is no point in practising", and, on the other hand, "If I'm just trying to get something for myself then I am not really practising". Desiring to give up desire is self-defeating.

Kāśyapa replies to Ānanda by saying, "Cut down your flagpole." A flagpole is where we hoist our ensign, the symbol of our identity. As long as one is attached to one's identity one will always be seeking personal advantage. Life, then, is always a matter of contention. What Kāśyapa got was freedom from attachment to self. So in saying, "Cut down your flagpole," he is both challenging Ānanda and telling him what he did receive. Ānanda was enlightened.

In India they had a tradition of debate. Debating competitions were a big thing and drew large crowds. This led to the development of sophisticated principles of logic by which to determine which arguments were stronger. When there was a debate, the two contestants would each set up a flagpole with their standard on it. The one who lost had to take down his flag and the one who won celebrated.

In this instance, there was transmission between Kāśyapa and Ānanda. Ānanda became special when he stopped trying to be special. In Keizan's text, transmission occurs in an encounter. We can see that receiving the transmission is also a defeat. When the ego is defeated and goes dark, the mirror mind comes into existence.

A great deal has been made of transmission as a personal empowerment, which is an obvious hook for power-hungry people. However, Dōgen would have said that power-hungry people are far, far from even a glimpse of the Dharma. Transmission occurs when the myriad Dharmas live in us. Yet it is easy to misunderstand this idea because for them really to live, we need to have a religious consciousness – mindful of the sacred presence – and then be defeated. Now, one cannot plan to be defeated any more than one can plan an accident. This means that there is no technique or method that can guarantee satori. Nor is there any method of training disciples that invariably works. People came to see Śākyamuni Buddha and he did his best for their sake. However, not everybody who came to see him was enlightened. Many were, but some were not. If even Śākyamuni could not enlighten everyone who came to see him, then it is unrealistic to expect anybody else to have an infallible formula.

THE EDGE OF THE DHARMA

Seeking is a self-project, therefore. The person seeking the Dharma is, for that very reason, outside the Dharma, but this is precisely what is needed, if one is honest about it. The text does not just say that we move away from the Dharma; it says that we move away from the edge of the Dharma. What is the edge or boundary of the Dharma? The Daoist classic says that "with desires one sees the boundary; without desires one sees into the wonders."[1] Because of our desires we only see the Dharma from outside (cf. line 1). However, the Buddhas are ceaselessly working to try to rescue us. Dōgen is telling us that, although we are full of desire, still we can be rescued if we begin from a humble position. He had gone to China full of desire to get the Dharma, but had only been rescued by Rujing when he climbed down from his initial position of arrogance.

The use of the term 'edge' again lays stress on separation. Not only separation, but great distance, and, in the long run, the greater the distance the better. So here again we see the strong sense of 'religious consciousness'. This is certainly not about merger or identity. In order to receive the transmission, it is important to place oneself far away, or, one could say, in as lowly a position as possible.

THE PARADOX OF DESIRE

There is an important sense in which desire is a necessary stage. Desire is love in primitive form. The best known of all the wonderful parables in the Lotus Sūtra offers the image of the burning house. Inside the house the children are playing. They do not realize their danger. The father lures them out of the house by offering toys, each according to his or her desire. Having got them to safety, the father, who here stands for the Buddha, does not actually give the children the toys that they desired, but gives each of them the best one. The analogy to the spiritual path is further intensified by the fact that, in the sūtra, the toys are also vehicles – carts and chariots. The Dharma is thought of as a vehicle or *yāna*, hence the term *Mahā-yāna*, literally, 'great vehicle'.

Thus desire is our part in what gets us out of the burning house. The spiritual path is that of a gradual maturation in love, from initial desire to ultimate altruism. However, although we can think of this as a gradual progression, in the parable

1 *Dao De Jing*, chapter 1: "故 常 無, 欲 以 觀 其 妙, 常 有, 欲 以 觀 其 徼".

of the burning house, there is still a point of abrupt change – a tipping point – when the children actually get clear of the fire. Only then is the father-Buddha in a position to offer them the ultimate 'great ox' vehicle. Only at and after the tipping point does the great way appear. So this is a parable about the ultimate common ground of different schools or religions as well as being one about individual salvation and its variety of courses, which depend upon different natures. It also illustrates a process parallel to that described by Dōgen, with his notion that reflection starts abruptly at a certain point. In all cases, however, the intention of the Buddha (father) remains simply the expression of love. Salvation in this case does not depend upon the children themselves achieving a particular sublimation of desire through their own effort (or practice) but is rather something that builds upon their initial relationship with the father and his skill in exploiting their natural desire in a good way. This, therefore, is essentially an other-power story. All the children have to do is have faith in the father. Later in the sūtra there is the parable of the 'prodigal son', which answers the question of what the Buddha must do in the case of somebody who does not have – or rather loses – faith. In that parable too, the son follows his desires, but the Buddha, again represented by the father in the story, gradually coaxes the son back into a position from which he can receive his rightful inheritance.[2]

In the story of the burning house the children have faith in the father. In the story of the prodigal son, the son fails to recognize the father, but by accepting to work for him unwittingly allows the father to influence him. Under this influence, he gradually gains faith until his real relationship can be revealed. In each case, the practitioner is in the position of the child who either already has or will gradually find faith in the father and, when he finds it, the necessary transition occurs. Dōgen will have been very familiar with these stories and their meaning.

---

2 The sūtra deserves to be read. It is one of the most readable of the major Mahāyāna Sūtras and there are plenty of translations: Hurvitz, Leon 1976. *Scripture of the Lotus Blossom of the Fine Dharma (The Lotus Sutra)*, New York: Columbia University Press; Kato et al. 1975. *Saddharma-Pundarika or The Lotus of the True Law*, New York: Dover; Kubo, Tsugunari and Akira Yuyama 1993. *The Lotus Sutra*, Berkeley, CA: Numata; Murano, Senchū 1974. *The Lotus Sutra*, Tokyo: Nichiren Shu.

VII

LINES 21–5: THINGS ARE NOT AS THEY SEEM

21. When a person goes riding in a boat, if he turns his eye toward the shore, he erroneously thinks that the shore is moving.
22. If he observes the boat closely, he will see that it is the boat that is going forward.
23. If we try to discern the myriad Dharmas from the perspective of our confused idea about body and mind, we make the error of thinking that it is our mind and our own nature that are permanent.
24. However, if we go back to studying the acts of our own daily life (*an ri*) intimately we shall see that the myriad Dharmas themselves are not therein.
25. Then the Dao 道 and its proper performance (Li 理) will become clear.

VII.1 COMMENTARY

We have already seen that Dōgen's style in this essay is to establish polarities. He makes it clear that there are different states with no overlap. Now he talks about the relationship between them and, in particular, how we can sometimes mistake one for the other. Especially, we can blame others for things for which we ourselves are responsible. We can assume that we are steady, constant and reliable and that the vicissitudes that we experience are caused by others, when, in fact, it is we who are creating the trouble.

What needs to happen is that we need to become less entranced by the self. This happens when one becomes realistic about it. When one knows it just as it is, it recedes, just as anything that is familiar does. When one keeps to one's lot and simply fulfils one's part one is acting not only like a good Buddhist, but also like a good Confucian or good Daoist. In any case, Dōgen is saying that at that point one's way of construing things undergoes an abrupt reversal, just as when one realizes that it is one's own boat that is moving. The shore is what is stable. Here, the shore represents the Dharma all around us. That is what is unmoving and reliable. That is the Buddha Dao. These lines, therefore, further expand those that immediately precede them.

We are all familiar with the illusion that it is the shore that is moving. This illusion arises because we implicitly take it that we ourselves (and our boat) are the point of reference. So this is a different metaphor, but the point is the same. Thinking one's own boat is static is the same as having the light on inside. Our self-aggrandizing tendency occludes the Dharma apparent before us in myriad manifestations. Self is a dependent variable that cannot be relied upon.

One can see exactly the same illusion when sitting in a train stopped at a station and the next train seems to start moving backwards when what is actually happening is that the train that one is in is moving forward. Dōgen uses this phenomenon as an analogy for the mistake we make in relation to the myriad Dharmas. We think that we are the point of reference and everything revolves around us, but this is not the case. We can come to see things as they actually are – genjō – or not.

In the boat or the train, after a while we are forced to realize that it is we who are moving. In the same way, by examining the stuff of daily life we can arrive at a more realistic picture and see that the fault is on our side. It is not that the myriadfold Dharma have failed to arrive for us, it is that we have not done what is necessary in order to receive their eternal light that has been shining all along. Thus, there are two parts and it is important that we play our part and not blame the other for our failure. However, when we play our part, by realizing that the source of the light is not in ourselves, we shall understand how the whole thing works and why.

The path begins with separation (line 19). The already present Dharma is waiting for us, but we can only see it when we drop our affected ways and return to being naturally dutiful (line 20). This is virtually the same as what Laozi is supposed to have said to Confucius in the famous story of their one and only encounter which we can summarize as "Give up affectation!"[1] The reconciliation of duty and naturalness, conformity and creativity, has been a perennial preoccupation of Chinese philosophy. This awakening means climbing down from our conceit in which we fail to take responsibility for our part in things, a blindness that also blinds us to the Dharmas that are waiting all around for an opportunity to enlighten us if we would but see.

The way to make this change is to examine the evidence of our life in a careful and honest way. When we are able to face ourselves as we truly are, we stop thinking that we are 'God'. When we have climbed down in this way we are in a much better position to receive and dance with the Dharma. Then we move with the Dao and its purpose becomes our meaning.

VII.2 DISCUSSION

YIN AND YANG POSITIONS

When in a boat, you move forward, but you do so taking into consideration the constraints imposed by the shore. In the relation between boat and shore, the shore is yang and the boat is yin. The boat watches the shore and conforms to its requirements. The shore is indifferent to the boat, as if blind, but the boat must pay attention to the shore or it will be wrecked.

Dōgen is saying that the deluded person goes through life with this relationship the wrong way around. Such a person is blind

---

1 This well-known legend can be found in many sources, e.g. Suzuki, Daisetz Teitaro and Paul Carus 1964/1974. *Lao Tze: The Canon of Reason and Virtue*, La Salle, IL: Open Court: 69–71.

and indifferent to others, and especially to the myriad Dharmas, and so never receives what they offer. We can understand this by once again using the analogy of a dance.

The Dharma is already waiting to play its part, like a dancer waiting for a partner. We can say that the music is the Dao (道), the dance is Li (理). Yin and yang are the steps of the dance – left, left, right... left, left, right... or some other variation – but we can also say that they are the two dancers who also must oppose one another, yet cooperate.

In this dance we ourselves are the yin partner, receptive and dark, while the myriad Dharmas are the yang partner, bright and in control, whisking us into the flow of the music. The devotee has it in him to join the dance, but it requires that one adopt the yin position. It is no good insisting upon leading the dance oneself. For one thing, one does not yet know the steps. The Dharmas come forth and teach us the dance.

Of course, in a dance, there is a certain unity between the dancing partners, just as there is a certain unity between a mirror and the object that it reflects, but the idea of unity can be overemphasized. In the unity – the Dao – there are two parts – yin and yang. If we concentrate too much on the unity we will miss our own responsibility. Either we seek mastery, trying to be the leader of the dance, or we fall into passivity, avoiding the need to respond to life's invitation. Life is a tango in which one is in the female (yin) role most of the time.

A METAPHOR THAT DOES NOT WORK

An interesting point that can be quite confusing in reading Dōgen is that he presents what seem to be metaphors, yet when one examines them carefully they often do not work. In this passage, Dōgen talks about the boat and the shore. He rightly says that it can happen that one thinks that the shore is moving. He then says that the way to dispel this illusion is to examine one's own boat carefully. Then, he says, one will realize that it is one's own boat that is moving. In fact, in the case of real boats – or real trains, for that matter – this is not correct. The way to dispel the illusion is not to examine one's own boat or train, but to look out of a different window and set one's eye upon something that one does trust not to be moving. If one is in a train and the train on the next track to the right seems to be moving, one can be quite unsure what is the case. However, if one looks out of the left-hand window and sees the platform one immediately knows which train is stationary and which is not.

Why does Dōgen make this 'mistake'? I think that the reason must be that he is not very concerned about the metaphor itself. Once he has established the notion of boat and shore as representing self and Dharma he is no longer talking about boat and shore. In the case of self, he wants to tell us that we shall make progress by examining ourselves and seeing how lacking we are. We think that the Dharma is in us and that we are the truth and the measure of things, but when "we go back to studying the acts of our own daily life (*an ri*) intimately" we do not find the Dharma therein. This should bring us up short.

SELF AND OTHER

Others have their own lives and their own reasons. They are not here in the world simply to make life easier or more difficult for me. They are other, independent, just as the shore is independent of the boat. Recognizing the other as other is an important stage in becoming mature. Recognizing that one's parent is a human being and not just one's parent is an important stage in growing up. This is about respect. In order to become mature people it is necessary to respect others and allow them to be other. They are not obliged to take note of us any more than the shore has to take note of the boat, but the boat does have to take note of the shore. This might seem 'unfair' but that is how it is. Otherwise one alternates between conflict and co-dependency. So separation is an important step.

There is an unfortunate tendency in psychology to blame the parents for almost everything that seems to go wrong in a person's life and, for the small amount of trouble that cannot be laid at the door of mother and father, to blame other people in the client's life. This is delusion within delusion and serves only to keep a person in an infantile state. It is no use blaming the shore for the failure of one's own navigational skills.

There is a similarly pernicious tendency in the spiritual world to overdo the notion of interdependence to the point of asserting that everybody is a part of everybody else and that all separation is a fantasy. This idea is often related to various misinterpretations of the Buddhist doctrine of dependent origination. Buddhism is certainly concerned with how people relate to one another and it is true that currents pass through people from one to another, but to take the idea of inter-existence to an extreme is a mistake. Such ideas merely confuse people and lead to an avoidance of the important spiritual work of taking responsibility for one's own life and arriving at respect for the independent existence and dignity of the other.

If we think that the boat is static, then we assume that the sense of change, movement and effect that we experience is created and caused by the actions of others. We blame them. In reality, others are mostly too busy getting on with their own lives. We attribute a much greater degree of stability and consistency to ourselves than is warranted by the facts. When something goes wrong, or does not happen as we expect it to, we are inclined to find somebody else to blame. All of this is a distortion based on our attachment to ourselves, which is to say, to our body and mind. Regarding oneself as the only source of stability and wisdom, one attributes all fault to others. This is the insanity of the ordinary person.

Attachment to body and mind thus leads us to avoid responsibility. Seeking to establish in our body and mind something that will make us always right, always justified, always wise, always the winner, we move further and further away from being a natural human being. We do not really observe, listen, nor learn. Śākyamuni originally blamed his problems on his family and left them. Then he blamed them on his teachers and left them. Then he blamed them on his companions and left them. It was always somebody else's fault. In the end he was alone. Who was there left to blame? Eventually he snapped out of it.

STOPPING ONE'S BOAT IS NOT AN OPTION

One might think that the thing to do is to stop one's boat. If I become still, then I will no longer live in a world where I subvert others to my selfish purposes. Many people do approach spirituality in this way, seeking to make themselves so pure that they cannot be implicated in the bad things that happen in the world. This, however, never works. It fosters one's sense of one's own specialness. It is another instance of trying to be the one right thing in the universe.

So we can see that there are two extremes. One extreme is to avoid responsibility by failing to respect separation. The other extreme is to try to separate oneself to an unrealistic degree in order to make oneself into an island of purity, untouched by anything. However, one's own little boat will always keep sailing along.

The answer is not to stop the boat, but to recognize that it is the boat that is moving. We cannot avoid being implicated in the things that happen in the world as long as we are alive. There is, in this, a great grief. However kind I may try to be, I will still be implicated in killing and cruelty. However honest I try to be I will always still be implicated in theft and exploitation. It is not possible for one's hands to be completely clean. Even if I decide to be a vegan, thereby, perhaps, trying to escape from the responsibility for killing animals, the loaf of bread that I buy from the shop is still made from wheat that was cut by a harvesting machine that killed a large number of insects and small animals as it ploughed its relentless course across the field. Even if I try to have the most politically correct attitudes and become a total pacifist, I probably still switch on the electric light using power generated from oil won by my country by means of terrible wars in far-away countries. Just by being alive one puts a burden upon others, because life is a dependent condition. This does not mean that there is no value in trying to minimize harm, but it is important to be realistic about our existential situation. Furthermore, it is important to recognize that one is not always that strict or correct anyway. We may have ideals and good resolutions, but often we do not live up to them and this is not all bad either. A certain amount of give and take is called for. Buddhism is a middle way. Recognizing this is one of the things that helps us to become disenchanted with the ego. The personal purity project is a big ego builder. It is a matter of setting up one's own light rather than receiving the Dharma light.

CONTRITION

In lines 23–5 Dōgen tells us how the Dao and Li become clear to us.

> 23. If we try to discern the myriad Dharmas from the perspective of our confused idea about body and mind, we make the error of thinking that it is our mind and our own nature that are permanent.
> 24. However, if we go back to studying the acts of our own daily life (*an ri*) intimately we shall see that the myriad Dharmas themselves are not therein.
> 25. Then the Dao 道 and its proper performance (Li 理) will become clear.

This passage describes us climbing down from our inflated sense of ourselves and doing so by studying our daily life and its effects. We could say, by studying the evidence. If we really study the evidence of the effect of how we generally carry on, we will arrive at a change of heart. When that happens we shall see what we need to do.

In Western renderings of Buddhism, contrition is often ignored or minimized. Westerners do not like it. I have seen famous teachers avoid the subject even when questioned directly about it. Yet in Asian Buddhism it plays a crucial role. Contrition, *sange* in Japanese, is the indispensable gateway to the Dharma. I remember a Japanese Buddhist teacher coming to our temple and seeing the contrition verses in our service book and being startled. "Oh, that is very Japanese!" he said, remarking that he had not found it elsewhere in his visits to other Western Buddhist centres. I hope that this is now changing.

The problem here has its roots in Western history and ideas of eternal damnation. In Buddhism, karmic consequence does not have quite such a dreadful implication, but we are still wary of ideas about confession and contrition. Although modern people often no longer believe in hell, the attitudes of self-justification and judgementalism persist.

In these lines about the boat and the shore, Dōgen is, firstly, talking about us taking responsibility and realizing that our nature is all too human. Here are Dōgen's words recorded in the text *Shūshōgi*:

> Contrition before the Buddhas brings purification and salvation, true conviction and earnest endeavour... Here is the way in which to make an act of perfect contrition. "May all the Buddhas and Patriarchs, who have become enlightened, have compassion upon us, free us from the obstacle of suffering which we have inherited from our past existence and lead us in such a way that we may share the merit that fills the universe... All the evil committed by me is caused by beginningless greed, hate and delusion. All the evil is committed by my body, speech and mind. I now confess everything wholeheartedly."[2]

He goes on to say that through contrition we open the way for the Buddhas "to help us naturally." Contrition thus functions to make us open to receiving help. Contrition itself does have a purifying function, but the aim is not to transform us into a 'justified' state since, in Buddhism, there is no final judgement, no punishment or forgiveness, only karmic consequence, which is inexorable.

How, then, does contrition work in Buddhism? Let us consider an example. Perhaps, in the course of the day, I lose my temper and say some things that later I regret saying. I see the unfortunate consequences of my loss of control. I feel contrite. We need to distinguish between two levels in this experience of contrition. The first level is regret. This may involve a criticism of myself and a resolution to try to do better in future. Clearly it will be better for everybody if I keep my anger under control. I shall do better next time, I hope. This is the superficial aspect of contrition. There is, however, a deeper level. Studying the acts of my daily life, I see that I am made this way. Perhaps I

2 Kennett 1972: 130.

shall indeed curb my temper, but there will be other things. No matter how hard I try, I will still be human. Furthermore, even my attempt to improve is ego-driven. The reason that I decide to curb my anger is to have an easier life myself and appear in the world as a better person. Even my attempts to do good are shot through with self-serving motivations. Thus, the deeper level is to see that there is no escape.

Buddhism is not a matter of exhausting all of our near infinite stock of karma. That would be completely impossible. It is about a change of perception, or genjō, that happens when we truly realize that we are not the most radiant star in the universe and start to play our proper part in the scheme of things.

In Christianity, the main concern in relation to contrition is forgiveness. Catholics believe that divine forgiveness follows confession before a priest. Protestants, mostly, believe that the priest is not necessary – that God will forgive the faithful directly. However, in Buddhism there is no forgiveness. In Buddhism, therefore, recognition of our nature can lead to a kind of despair. Karma is inexorable and one is never going to be 'forgiven'. There is no sūtra on forgiveness: forgiveness is not really a Buddhist concept. Plenty of modern people want to insert it, but Buddhism solves these problems in a different way. Although we cannot avert karma, contrition does open the way for the Buddhas to help us because it extinguishes, at least for a little time, the blinding light of ego. Contrition is the gateway to enlightenment.

In Christianity, the person who is forgiven returns to an innocent, 'justified' state. In Buddhism, this does not happen. There is an important Buddhist story often used by Dōgen about a monk who spent many lives as a fox because he failed to understand that even the enlightened still have their karma. Enlightenment does not wipe out karma, nor is it the result of karma being exhausted. Karma is never destroyed. However, the Buddhas have vowed to help the karmically oppressed.

The word 'contrition' in European languages comes from a Latin word meaning 'crushed'. We say this in common speech sometimes: "When I realized what I had done I felt completely crushed." In Buddhism, the state of 'feeling crushed' is precious.

These are moments when the ego loses its grip and the gateway to liberation stands open wide.

It seems that, in practical terms, the Christian and Buddhist approaches are quite similar. What is different is the metaphysics. The framework of ideas used to explain the situation and provide a sustaining image is different, but the liberating intent is much the same. Many Western Buddhists want to believe that Buddhism promotes an idea of 'original goodness' in contrast to the Christian idea of 'original sin' and this idea sustains them in their adherence to Buddhism, but if one looks deeper there is really less difference in practice.

Ideas such as 'Buddha nature' have been recruited into the cause of asserting 'original goodness', but in this development of Dharma theory there lies a serious danger of grandiosity that is alien to the Buddhist approach, which has more to do with the value of those times when the ego is crushed or abandoned.

In any case, in this passage about the boat and the shore, Dōgen is emphasizing that the Buddha body in relation to us is as the clear blue sky in relation to a dewdrop or, here, as the continent in relation to a small boat. One is only slightly more than nothing. It is no use the sailor cursing the land because it 'keeps moving'. One has to accept and play one's proper part in the scheme of things, and this is a humble one. This, therefore, involves a complete self-abandonment. When the Christian writer Thomas à Kempis wrote, "I would far rather feel contrition than be able to define it",[3] he was expressing a sentiment that would have been completely acceptable to a medieval Buddhist also. Dōgen would probably also have approved his, "If you desire to know or learn anything to your advantage, then take delight in being unknown and unregarded."[4]

THE DAO (道) AND ITS LI (理)

The thing that is said to be most like the Dao is water, because it always seeks the lowest place, always finds the way down toward the great ocean, is infinitely patient, yet, in the end

3 À Kempis, Thomas 1952. *The Imitation of Christ*, L. Sherley-Price (trsl.), Harmondsworth, Middlesex: Penguin Books: 27.

4 À Kempis 1952: 29.

turns out to be the strongest force, wearing away mountains and moving past all obstacles.

Dao is the music of the universe. It manifests in the myriad Dharmas. Each Dharma has its Li, its particular rite. Thus, the manner in which one raises a cup of tea to the lips, the way that one washes a pot or holds a fan, the way that one speaks or remains silent, can each be a perfect instance of conforming to the Dao. Another way we can think of it is by saying that when one considers the teachings and actions of Buddha one can readily discern that they include a great variety, but it is as if in all this variety we always find the same taste, the same tone, the same atmosphere. This common taste is, in much of the Chinese interpretation of Buddhism, designated by the term Li.

Dōgen often talks about practice as 'vigorous'. When we read about duty and being in the yin position, we may start to think of something in which passivity implies dullness or a lack of energy, but in Dōgen this is certainly not the intended meaning. Even sitting still should be imbued with strong energy: "Time flies like an arrow from a bow and this fact should make us train with all our might, using the same energy we would employ if our hair were to catch fire".[5] If Li is a dance, then it is, perhaps, a form of tango, a vigorous dance in which our whole being is engaged.

The terms Dao and Li also reflect the Chinese way of dealing with immanence and transcendence. There is, as Laozi says, something mysterious and wonderful (*miao*) going on and it manifests in the ways of ordinary things. Thus the holy is both completely transcendent and totally immanent at the same time. More than immanent, it *is* the actual working of things themselves in their allotted place (kōan) in the scheme of things. Conforming to one's allotted place one becomes a mirror for and *an instance of* the Buddha Dao unfolding.

ON NOT KNOWING THE PLOT

Of course, if I consider myself and others, there are a lot more of them than there are of me. Insofar as we are related, it is true that I am much more an element in their stories than they are

5 Dōgen in *Gakudōyōjinshū* (Kennett 1972: 103 et seq.).

in mine. This is another example of the boat and the shore. It is the opposite way round from how the ego likes to think. Since I am more part of their stories than they of mine, it follows that I do not know the plot. Whereas formerly I thought that I was the only one who knew the real plot and became distressed whenever others were not playing their parts properly, as I supposed, now it seems quite natural that unexpected things happen and instead of finding them annoying I find that they give me hints about the part I am supposed to be playing. In fact, I find them delightfully interesting because they give clues to my destiny. Each is an instance of Buddha, complete and radiant right here.

Taking up again the analogy of the boat and the shore, I may try to sail my boat in a straight line. However, I do not know what the coast is going to be like beyond the next headland. Rounding the point, I get new information. I have to adapt my plans, trim my sails and find the right course. If I omit to do so, then either I will wind up on the rocks or I will be lost out of sight of land.

As we play our part in the stories of many beings, we learn a great deal, but when we consider that each of them has a whole world-view, of which we only ever see a tiny and tangential part, we know that our knowledge is tiny. Dōgen will have more to say about this later when he talks about the ocean not being merely square or round, but first he wants to take us in another direction.

VIII

LINES 26–36: THERE IS NO GOING BACK

26. Firewood becomes ash.
27. It cannot become firewood again.
28. However, we should not see it as ash after and firewood before.
29. We should understand the Dharma position of firewood: it has a before and an after, the before and after exist, but it is cut off from them.
30. As for the Dharma position of ash, it has a before and an after.
31. The firewood has become ash completely and cannot become like firewood again.
32. After the person dies away, he does not come alive again.
33. So, the definitive Buddhist teaching is not to say that life becomes death, but rather to say 'no appearance' or 'no birth' (*fu shō*).
34. Death cannot become life.
35. The definitive transmission of the Dharma Wheel is to say this is 'no disappearance' (*fu metsu*).
36. Life is one position in time and death is also one position in time, just like, for example, winter and spring. Do not think that winter becomes spring. Do not say that spring becomes summer.

VIII.1 COMMENTARY

A person is vulnerable to greed, hate and delusion just as wood is vulnerable to fire. However, when the fire is burnt out, the ash cannot go back to being wood. No more does a Buddha go back to being an unenlightened being. The person who is like firewood is like that because he is in a trajectory that has a karmic past and future, but he does not see it. The person who is in the position of ash sees it, but it no longer seems important to him. Being now completely ash, he will not become wood again. What has died away does not come back. The old person has gone forever. However, the person who is ash is now in the realm of the Unborn. What he has discovered did not come into being because he became ash. There is no regression from this spiritual death. What he now is and has will never pass away, will never disappear. These are different states occurring at different points in time, like winter and spring. Winter is winter. Spring is spring. They are not the same. No appearance (*fu shō*) means not regressing. No disappearance (*fu metsu*) means that illumination does not cease.

VIII.2 DISCUSSION

TRANSLATION PROBLEMS

I have studied a number of existing translations of this passage and generally they take it as being about a theory of past, present and future and how they do or do not relate to each other. Many commentators try to interpret this as to do with the theory of time in the way that Western philosophy would make such a theory, but Dōgen, like Śākyamuni, was interested in salvation, not ontology.

Generally, people think that Dōgen is talking about being in the present moment, this being a popular view of Buddhism these days. I am not convinced that this is the real meaning. Most translators take the examples of wood and ash rather literally, but I am sure that Dōgen did not mean to refer to these substances in this way. If you take them literally the text does not make sense. These are code names for spiritual states.

Dōgen has no interest in real firewood. He is interested in the flames of passion and the going out of that fire.

Again, modern interpreters have difficulty in seeing that in these figures the favoured states are ash and death, not firewood and life. We see here again, and very clearly, the clash between religion and humanistic psychology. The favoured metaphors of the modern age do not apply here. Dōgen is consistent throughout the essay. The little light of self locally occludes the great light of Dharma. When that little light dies – is switched off – the mirror comes into being. When the dangerous firebrand person becomes ash he or she becomes fertile. These are just so many figures for the same thing and the whole essay is thus consistent.

METAPHOR OR CODE?

In our examination of the figure of the boat and the shore we saw that it did not really work as a metaphor, at least, not in the way that a modern writer would use metaphor. We should, therefore, be prepared for the fact that this figure does not always work as metaphor either. In fact, Dōgen is not really telling us anything about firewood or about ash. These are code terms rather than metaphor. It is not what happens in a bonfire that matters. Here firewood means the person who is capable of being inflamed with passion, and ash means the person who is not. The former is the ordinary being and the latter is the Buddha. Dōgen emphasizes the complete difference between them. The ordinary person is on a karmic trajectory, but is blind to what is happening. The Buddha has a past and a future, which is that of all Buddhas. Once Dōgen has made his code clear, he is no longer talking about real wood or real ash.

DUḤKHA SAMUDAYA

I think, therefore, that this passage is about the four truths, the teaching given in the Buddha's initial turning of the Dharma wheel. The four truths are *duḥkha*, *duḥkha-samudaya*, *duḥkha-samudaya-nirodha*, and *mārga*. In this respect, *duḥkha-samudaya* is firewood. It is the inflammatory element in us. *Nirodha* is ash. It is what we have when the fire of *duḥkha-samudaya* has been completely consumed, which is a common understanding of the meaning of '*nirodha*', the third truth. In my understanding of the four truths, *duḥkha* gives rise to *samudaya*, which is to say, the things that happen in the world stir us. In the ordinary person, *samudaya* generally only leads to more *duḥkha*. The first two truths are truths for everybody. However, for 'noble ones', i.e. the enlightened, there are two more truths. The first of these is *nirodha*. *Nirodha* implies mastery of the fire. In Buddhist usage, ash is a symbol for *nirodha*. *Nirodha* leads to *mārga*, the eightfold path, the 'trace' of enlightenment, the life of the enlightened person.

Now, my understanding of the four truths[1] is not the common one. The interpretation generally given is that *samudaya* causes *duḥkha* and that *mārga* is the way to overcome *samudaya*. However, there is no need for us to go into these differences here, nor my reasons for differing from the commonly presented interpretation, which are all presented elsewhere. I think that it is reasonable to state, however we interpret the four truths, that firewood is a good analogy for the unenlightened person who is liable to burn with passion and that ash is a good one for the person whose fire has died down due to enlightenment.

The image of fire is apt. When we are disturbed by something our temperature rises. Buddha talks about this sometimes as fire, and sometimes as fever. There is nothing original in Dōgen's use of this trope. The whole of *Genjō Kōan* is full of instances of well-known Buddhist analogies about which Dōgen gives his view. This is simply another.

Life involves fire and fever. Buddha is suggesting that such fire be reduced to ash. Fire is destructive. Ash is fertile. So ash is useful and fire is dangerous. Also, ash is left when the wood is completely consumed – in other words when the fuel is all used up, when we completely 'comprehend' the self (line 13). If we keep feeding our fires, then they will burn endlessly, but if we let them take their course, they die down naturally. There is also, here, a parallel with lines 13–14 in which when self is fully comprehended it falls away.

---

1 This is set out in more detail in my books *The Feeling Buddha* (1997; London: Robinson) and *Not Everything is Impermanent* (2013; Malvern: Woodsmoke Press).

Dōgen is not talking about real fire, nor about the nature of time. He is talking about the practicality of realization. He is saying that while it may be the case that at one point a person is deluded and later he is enlightened, it is not the case that enlightenment is a later stage of delusion. Delusion is one thing and enlightenment is another.

THE PAST AND FUTURE OF FIREWOOD AND ASH

Firewood means the person who is liable to catch the fire of greed, hate and delusion, the person about whom Śākyamuni Buddha talks in the 'Fire Sermon', recorded in the Ādittapariyāya Sutta. In the sūtra the Buddha says that "All is aflame... with the fire of passion, the fire of aversion, the fire of delusion". He goes on: "Seeing thus, the well-instructed disciple of the noble ones grows disenchanted", and: "Disenchanted, he becomes dispassionate", and: "Through dispassion, he is fully released".[2]

People are liable to be inflamed because they are on a karmic trajectory. However, generally speaking, they have little or no insight into this fact. A person flares up on the spur of the moment. They may rationalize afterwards, but really they do not have much idea of why they are as they are. They just notice that they 'become upset'. Our particular propensity to blaze up is related to a past in which our intentional actions laid down karmic seeds. This aspect of ourselves also has a future, which is not ash. Actions based on passion in the present lay down further karmic seeds for the future. Fire breeds fire.

When a person has become ash, this ash also has a past and a future. However, its past and its future are not really its own. The person who has become ash proceeds in faith. His life reflects the Dharma. His faith and practice are not aimed at achieving anything for his body and mind, but are a celebration of gratitude for the grace that naturally falls into his life. Faith and practice of this kind, once established, do not again become worldly fever. That person simply plays his part. Sailing his boat, he does not blame the shore. He is part of the life of all the Buddhas. His life is no longer his own.

---

2 Saṃyutta Nikāya 35.28.

DYING TO SAṂSĀRA

Nirodha – ash – is, in Buddhism, regarded as a kind of death. To become enlightened is to die. Contrition is to be crushed. When the text says that firewood that has become ash completely cannot become like firewood again and after the person dies away, he does not come alive again, we should not think that Dōgen is, gratuitously, and apropos of nothing in particular, throwing in an opinion about the doctrine of rebirth. When Dōgen speaks of boats and the shore he is not talking about real boats; when he talks about mirrors he is not talking about real mirrors; when he talks about firewood he is not talking about real firewood, so there is no reason to suppose that when he talks about death he is talking about literal dying.

The two halves of the sentence are saying the same thing. Ash not becoming wood and death not coming back to life, both mean that an enlightened person does not once again become an unenlightened person. We should also, I think, see a parallel between becoming ash, dying, and becoming the dark side of the mirror.

The person who has experienced the death that is *nirodha* does not return to being an ordinary human being again. The person dies and a Buddha is born. The Buddha does not go back to being a deluded person. However, it is not really that the deluded person has turned into a Buddha. The deluded person has become dark, been forgotten, dropped away. This does not mean that the person has completely ceased to exist, but he or she has ceased to be the centre of the person's attention. Śākyamuni Buddha was still Siddhārtha Gautama, and he still had the karma of Siddhārtha, but he did not make the concerns of Siddhārtha his priority any more.

THE ROOT OF COMPASSION

As was discussed in the commentary on lines 1–4, the four truths are often called the 'four noble truths', but can better be rendered 'four truths for noble ones'. The enlightened are still human and they have karma. *Duḥkha* happens. When it happens, an enlightened person is not immune to pain, suffering or passion. His or her stock of firewood has its past and its future. However, the enlightened person has four truths, not just two. She or he has the capacity to be fertile ash. So, an enlightened person incorporates a being of passion, yet is not just a being of passion, is not the being that used to be just a heap of firewood waiting to explode into flames.

When *duḥkha* comes along, the person who experiences ash still also experiences firewood catching light. However, this fire is contained and used to good purpose, not least to understand deeply others who are also heaps of firewood. If this were not the case, then an enlightened person might be wise, but could not be compassionate.

NO DEATH

'*Fu shō, fu metsu*' (不生不滅), literally 'no birth, no death', or 'no becoming, no ceasing', is a phrase in the Heart Sūtra, but the terms also appear in the Lotus Sūtra, where they are part of the assertion of the "eternal life of the Tathāgata".[3] *Tathāgata* means Buddha, but highlights a particular aspect of Buddha. The word can be construed as *tathā-gata* or as *tathā-āgata*. In the normal Japanese rendering, *Nyorai*, it is understood as *tathā-āgata*. *Āgata* means 'come'. *Tathā* has no equivalent word in English and is sometimes rendered as 'suchness'. The implication is of Buddha come to us as saviour. and come as or from 'suchness'. Dōgen considers suchness equivalent to *wu wei*. So, 'no birth' means that Buddha is not born out of the deluded being – Buddha nature already exists and has always existed – it is unborn, it is suchness. If this were not so then Buddha nature would be a function of conditions and therefore transitory.

Fu metsu implies that the Tathāgata will never pass away. Dōgen often quotes from the Lotus Sūtra so it is probable that he had this in mind. When he says, "death cannot become life", he means that the Tathāgata (death) does not pass away, i.e. does not turn into a deluded being. Life is the product of karma and the Tathāgata produces no karma. To produce no karma is true goodness as was made clear by Daosheng, but if one is outside

3 Lotus Sūtra chapter 16. See, e.g. Kato et al. 1975: 249–56.

of karma one is outside of birth and death and, hence, eternal.

Modern readers are easily misled in this passage because of our cultural assumption that death is negative. Here 'death' signifies the state of a Buddha, *nirodha*, and it does not pass away. It is the dark side of the mirror.

Many modern readers may also be disturbed by the notion of 'eternal life' because of its associations in our Western religious history. However, we will never understand Buddhism or Dōgen if we skirt round and try to ignore all associations that raise our hackles. The Lotus Sūtra is pivotal to Mahāyāna and especially Far Eastern Buddhism and, if one wants to understand, one has to take it on its own terms.

NO BIRTH

Similarly, line 33, "So, the definitive Buddhist teaching is not to say that life becomes death, but rather to say 'no appearance' or 'no birth' (*fu shō*)", refers to the fact that the Buddha (death) may seem to appear at a particular point in time, as when Śākyamuni had his awakening experience under the bodhi tree, but, in reality, the Tathāgata has been in existence from eternity.

"The Buddha's true Dharma body is like the empty sky."[4] The appearance at a point in time is how enlightenment seems to the worldly mind, but Śākyamuni did not manufacture enlightenment – he found it. What he found had always been waiting to be found. So it is an established custom in Buddhadharma not to say that it was the deluded Siddhārtha who became the enlightened Śākyamuni Buddha. In *Yui Butsu Yo Butsu* (Just Buddha Together With Buddha),[5] Dōgen says that if realization were to arise through the force of thoughts prior to realization it would be an unreal or unreliable realization. Something happening in delusion cannot be the cause of non-delusion. The state of being deluded and the state of being awake cannot be in a relationship of causality. In passages like this we see clearly that this is a religious text, not simply a humanistic reduction of Buddhist teaching.

4 Leighton and Okumura 2004: 91.
5 *Yui Butsu Yo Butsu*, in Nishijima and Cross 1994, vol. 4: 213–20.

With his analogy to the seasons, Dōgen is saying that delusion and enlightenment are like winter and spring. Winter does not cause spring. Spring happens and it comes after winter, but it is not in causal continuity with winter. Winter has reasons for being winter and spring has reasons for being spring.

Siddhārtha Gautama 'died' when the way of ash was discovered. Yet that way of ash had a past – an extremely long one – and a future – also similarly great. Becoming enlightened may be like winter giving way to spring or spring giving way to summer, but the summer of the Dharma is an eternal summer.

In this passage Dōgen brings together the most fundamental teaching of Hīnayāna Buddhism – the four truths for noble ones – with the most sophisticated teaching of Mahāyāna – the eternal life of the Tathāgata. He unifies the Nikāyas and the Lotus Sūtra. This is typical of Dōgen and is exactly what he would want to do in the first chapter of his great work. This is what the whole work was going to be about: the complete integrity of the Buddhadharma and the wholeness of its encompassing spiritual vision.

THE KŌAN REALIZED

This passage is not a theory of time, nor one about mortality, nor is it a jumble of juxtaposed interesting comments lacking coherence. It is a tightly worded unification of the Buddhist principles of the necessity of practice and the eternal nature of that in which practice involves one. It is, therefore, another reflection upon Dōgen's solution to his own kōan. The universal religious problem is the link between the transitory and the eternal, the absolute and the personal. In Buddhism, the personal is exemplified in the teaching of the four truths for noble ones and the absolute in the eternal life of the Tathāgata. The word 'religion' can be construed as meaning to link together. Religion is, therefore, about the bridge between these two, and this is no less true in Buddhism than in any other religion. The confusion in most Western interpretations of *Genjō Kōan* and of Dōgen generally often arises from the desire of modern interpreters to present Buddhism devoid of its religious core. If one approaches religion from the personal side, then it appears as an exercise in building the bridge. If one thinks about it from the absolute side, then the bridge is already there, always has been, and always will be. The resolution of this apparent contradiction is that religion is about discovery not construction. That discovery is genjō and it occurs when there is kōan.

IX

LINES 37–41: TRUST THE DHARMA TO APPEAR

37. A person's satori is like the moon lodging in water: the moon does not get wet and the water is not broken, but it is like a vast light lodging in the smallest bit of water – the whole moon and firmament, even in so much as a dewdrop on a blade of grass.
38. Just as the moon does not pierce the water, so satori does not break the person.
39. Just as the sky and moon in the dewdrop is no hindrance, so a person's satori is no impediment.
40. As for the depth (of illumination), it shall measure as the height (of the Dharma/moon).
41. Whether for an hour or a moment, look closely and you will see, in great waters or in small, the full scale of the sky and the moon.

IX.1 COMMENTARY

Śākyamuni Buddha was still Siddhārtha Gautama, but his personal self was eclipsed by the light of the Dharma. The moon of the Dharma lodges in the person like an image in water, completely filling it without ever breaking it. The person is mortal, the Dharma is not. Conditioned and unconditioned do not hinder one another, so great Dharma is not a hindrance to the karmic nature of the person.

Satori is as vast as the Dharma itself. It is not a compromise with self, in the manner of a partial awakening. Yet the components of the old self remain at hand to be used by the newly awakened person. It a question, necessarily, of being a great man or woman. The full reflection of the whole Dharma can be seen in great lives, but especially in modest ones.

The Dharma is not contaminated by our imperfection any more than the moonlight by the water. The Dharma remains completely the Dharma just as the image is the image of the whole moon, whether the water is small or large. Even in a dewdrop it is the same. The moon does not damage the water. Satori does not hinder – it enhances. Satori should be as deep as the Dharma is great, just like the moon and its reflection. It does not matter what sort of person you are. Look and see. Even a short glimpse will show you.

IX.2 DISCUSSION

TRANSLATION PROBLEMS

Line 40 in Japanese only says: "As for the depth, it shall measure as the height." In order to render this comprehensible in English one has to answer the questions: 'depth of what?' and 'height of what?' I think it is clear that what is referred to is the way that the depth of the reflection is the same as the distance from the object to the reflecting surface. Some translators take it that 'depth' refers to the depth of the dewdrop, but I think this is a mistake springing from our wish to think of the illumination as being in some sense a function of our own capacity or effort. The implication of Dōgen's text is that it is not. Our part is minimal and consists of being humble and steady. By this I mean that, if we think about the dewdrop, we can see the image in it when the drop is perfectly still. When the dewdrop is doing its zazen, we can see the moon – the Dharma – in it. Similarly, when we are not activating our ego, others can see the Dharma in us. This is not because we have become Dharma-sized. It is because we have become a better reflector. Thus, the depth of the illumination is a function, not of our depth, but of the Dharma's height. This refers us back to line 19, which talks about the importance of establishing a great distance between oneself and the Dharma. Now we see why. Putting oneself far from the edge of the Dharma is an act of humility and on that basis, when the Dharma is reflected, it is so much deeper.

DARK SIDE OF THE MIRROR

Here again we have the same analogy as in line 12. Dōgen relies upon its familiarity to the reader. He does not need to say that the moon represents the radiance of the Dharma. He assumes that we know that.

As we saw earlier, the expression "Buddha's true Dharma body is like the empty sky. According with things, it manifests form like the moon in water," was important to Dōgen. He is showing how satori never becomes a possession or property of the person, just as the image does not belong to the mirror. The mirror has no control over what the image does, even though the mirror is filled with it. In the same way, the person of faith has no control over what the Dharma is going to do with him, nor can he talk about the Dharma appearing in him as his own Buddha nature. There is no ownership here.

This is deeply parallel with the Christian "Thy will, not mine", and the biblical idea of kenosis (in Greek, κένωσις), which means 'emptying'. In Philippians 2:7 it says that Jesus emptied himself – became nothing – in order to be filled with the will of God. In Dōgen one enters emptiness, *śūnyatā*, by becoming 'dark', so that one then reflects the Dharma.

At the same time, the former characteristics of the person due to his or her personal karma are not destroyed. The old person still exists, but now her or his characteristics are used in the service of the Dharma, and no longer as part of a script of self-pity and blame of others. The whole thing has turned around. It is as though, when body and mind have fallen away, they are still available to be used, but not in the old way. A skilful practitioner of the Dharma uses whatever is to hand in the work of great compassion.

TONGLEN

The Tibetans have a practice called *tonglen*, which is a meditation in which one imagines while breathing in that one takes in all the harm, grief, sorrow and delusion of others and that when one breathes out one breathes out compassion and love. Many Western people dislike this practice because they hold to the idea that one should only take in what is good for oneself. I know of one famous Buddhist teacher in the West who has spoken strongly against it, and of people who have become disciples of that teacher, leaving Tibetan Buddhism in order to do so, because of this point. However, *tonglen* is substantially consistent with what Dōgen is saying in this text. Actually, Dōgen goes further. In the Tibetan practice, there is a sense that it is we who are breathing out compassion, whereas Dōgen is saying that the compassion was never our own. The love and compassion is simply the myriad Dharmas functioning. One's own part is to be the mirror that re-shines that love and compassion into the world. The Buddha Dao is thus this whole scheme including the Dharma light and the darkened self. The great Light is wonderful, marvellous and eternal and, in a sense, lacks for nothing, yet it does need something.[1] It needs us to put our little lights out so that it can fill us and turn us into mirrors.

GREAT AND SMALL AWAKENINGS

We all experience small awakenings from time to time. These are moments when we realise that we have made a mistake. These are times when we climb down from some position of arrogance to which we have clung. Many times while working on this book I have had to acknowledge that I had completely misunderstood some passage. These are also times of real learning, real progress.

There can also be a negative form of arrogance; a pose of self-pity calculated to draw sympathy or lenient treatment, say. A person might say, "I know I'm the sort of person who takes it all upon myself." What impact is this supposed to have upon the

1 "The Wheel of the Dharma rolls constantly and lacks for nothing yet needs something" (Keizan, *Kyōjukaimon*). See Kennett 1972: 213.

hearer? Something like, "I make trouble for myself and so you should look after me." This is really a manipulation. Letting such things go, we experience a degree of liberation. It is sobering. It may be embarrassing. Nonetheless, it is freeing. Defending a false position takes such a lot of energy and makes one into such a bore.

We talk of great realization or small realization and from a self-power point of view we think that this must be a function of the strength or excellence of the practice or effort made by the practitioner. To think so, however, is conceit. Our own delusion is incapable of making the wisdom and compassion of the Tathāgata greater or less. We may or may not realize how the light of Buddha is reflected in us, but that does not make any difference to it doing so. When we realize it, we may rejoice and bathe in the beauty, but we shall not think that this was our own doing.

The core of practice is not effort and achievement, but to gaze, wonder and worship. Be grateful. Sometimes I am a small water and sometimes I am a large water. Sometimes you are a small water and sometimes large. The sky and the moon continue to be reflected in either case. Spiritual practice means to keep this in mind (first factor of enlightenment), to investigate in detail (second factor of enlightenment), and to see for yourself.

GREAT AND SMALL LIVES

We should not think that the enlightened person is thereby necessarily going to become a great figure in the conventional sense. That depends on circumstances, and is not a pivotal issue. One could be fully enlightened and be the only inhabitant of a desert island. One could have had a great satori and spend one's days as cook at Ayuwang Mountain Monastery. Enlightened people do what is needed in the circumstances in which they find themselves. They no longer regard themselves as the admiral of their life. The Buddhas will find work for them. The Dharma will be radiant in them no matter whether they are kings or hermits.

If they live in communities with other people who also love the Dharma, then when such people come together there is evidently a great sense of love. The scale of this love is in inverse proportion to the extent to which members of the community are still trying to shine their own lights, by demonstrating their own cleverness for the sake of self-satisfaction or aggrandizement, or by other self-centred strategies. Enlightened people are productive because they are neither self-pitying nor self-praising. This may lead to them becoming great figures, but the way of the world is such that the path to greatness is strewn with requirements that an enlightened person would not fulfil. This is why many of the hero sages of China, for instance, were hermits who declined high office or prestigious positions. A person living a humble life, to whom few people pay much attention, may be more enlightened than a famous teacher.

ETERNAL MOON

When the moon is reflected in water this does not bring the moon into being. In the same way, a person becoming awakened reflects the light of the Buddha who has always been there waiting. The Buddha is not created from nothing, nor is the Buddha created from the person. The Buddha is *fu shō fu metsu*.

The moon is just being the moon. The Buddha is just Buddha. The light of Buddha falls into every hamlet in the land, says Hōnen, but only those who look up carry that light in their heart. Most people cannot understand this because they think that realization is a personal achievement and that Buddha nature is a personal possession. Dōgen thought so until he met Rujing. *Genjō Kōan* is the result of his new perspective.

There is another chapter of the *Shōbōgenzō* called *Tsuki*. *Tsuki* means 'moon'. However, in the title of that essay, Dōgen does not use the normal character 月 for moon. He uses separate characters for *tsu* (都) and *ki* (機) which, taken together, can mean 'the whole mechanism'. The moon appearing in water is automatic, not contrived. Dōgen starts the text of *Tsuki* by saying that it is not "three before and three after". In other words, it is not a situation where you get out what you put in. This is also explained in the chapter entitled Flowers in the Sky. Because of the way that the Dharma nature works, you get a lot more out than you put in. In fact, in rather Daoist style, he is saying that the way to get most out is to put nothing in. It is our putting something in that gets in the way. The dewdrop that does absolutely nothing gives the best image. The one that wobbles still reflects the moon and sky, but the image is less clear. Things happen in their own way so it is not necessary for us to manipulate them. In fact, if one wants a two-word definition of what living according to the Dharma is, "Don't manipulate" would be a good candidate.

Thus awakening is not like a worldly achievement. The moon does reflect in the dewdrop and the Buddha Nature reflecting in the person is no different. It simply happens. Furthermore, when the moon reflects in the dewdrop, just as the moon encompasses the dewdrop, so the dewdrop encompasses the moon. This is the same as line 11: "enlightened Buddhas go on enlightening Buddhas". Enlightened Buddhas enlighten Buddhas and those Buddhas are also enlightening the first Buddhas, as in a hall of mirrors, ceaselessly and limitlessly.

The moon has phases. Sometimes it is not yet full. Sometimes it is past full moon. We might think that these represent our own progress, but that would be like thinking that it is the shore that is moving. Dōgen also uses the boat–shore analogy in his essay *Tsuki*, but then adds a similar, but slightly different, cloud–moon analogy. When the clouds are moving, it looks as though it is the moon that is speeding. However, the moon does what it does. It is not we who make the moon bigger or smaller, faster or slower. However, as soon as we accept this then we too are clouds and moon and we can no longer say which moves which.

Sometimes there may be many moons. Sometimes it is the sun. Sometimes sun and moon together. Sometimes neither. In Chinese thought and Dōgen in *Tsuki* and elsewhere, sun is yang and moon is yin. However, this is not always the case. There are infinite possibilities. 'Infinite possibilities' is also a possible meaning of *tsu ki*. Dōgen will have more to say about infinite possibilities in a subsequent section of *Genjō Kōan*.

In *Tsuki*, Dōgen also says that we should not take these figures of boat and shore or moon and clouds as mere metaphors. They are instances. The clouds and moon move relatively and, strictly speaking, we should not say that it is really one or really the other that moves. In the present text, similarly, it is not just that the moonlight represents the Dharma Nature and the dewdrop represents the practitioner. Dewdrop and moon are all Dharma Nature. This is similar to the idea of self-power and other-power. To get the idea, we talk of self and other, but strictly speaking there is only other-power, nothing else.

ON NOT BEING BROKEN

The other-power is like moonlight in water. The reflection does not depend upon an effort on the part of the water or on the part of the moon. The practitioner may think that he has to break himself in the way that a horse is broken in or as Śākyamuni broke himself by ascetic practice, but actually the other-power is already and eternally present and is able to be so *because* it is effortless. The Buddha's compassion is in no way compromised (does not get wet) by being naturally bestowed upon evil or deluded beings. Just as Śākyamuni followed ascetic practices, so Dōgen risked his life and went to China. Similarly, as we discussed earlier, the moment of awakening for you or me might be a moment of contrition, but, in principle, it need not be any of these things. The Dharma light is always shining.

Nor is it as though the Tathāgata shares out his compassion so that each person gets his share. All the stars are reflected in a single drop of water, but this does not prevent them also being reflected in another drop of water, or in thousands of other drops. Every drop reflects the whole moon, stars and sky. Thus Buddha offers to save all sentient beings.

X

LINES 42–3: YOU WILL NOT FEEL FULL

> 42. When Dharma is not yet in body and mind, when practice is not fully rigorous, one thinks that he is sufficiently in the Dharma already.
> 43. However, when the Dharma is in body and mind completely and sufficiently, a person feels a sense of lack.

X.1 COMMENTARY

This passage expresses Dōgen's rejection of the ideas of those who say that practice is unnecessary because it is sufficient just to know that the Dharma is already perfect. He is saying that if you think you have enough already then the Dharma has not really filled you. If it had, then you would not be so complacent. The true spirit of Buddhism is not quietism. Such self-satisfaction is evidence that a person is not practising fully and has not been penetrated by the Dharma. When we have experienced the Dharma we are far from being satisfied with ourselves. This section follows on from line 38 and also from line 24. The unenlightened person is not destroyed by satori and replaced by a new improved model. Rather, the person's attitude to him- or herself and to everything else changes. Rather than arrival, satori is another going forth, one that precipitates one into endlessly going forth again and again.

These lines are also prefatory to a section about infinite

possibilities, so this is a way of saying that the advent of the Dharma opens one up to infinite worlds. When we just reflect ourselves, it is a small world, but when we reflect the Dharma the whole cosmos not enough.

x.2 DISCUSSION

GREAT SAINTS ARE AWARE OF FALLING SHORT

Great saints are not content with themselves. They do not bathe is a sense of self-satisfaction. They are ever vigilant. This is true of great souls of all religions.

People may think that enlightenment is a kind of omniscience. Short of enlightenment we tend to over-estimate what we know, wanting to be clever, and so we assume that being enlightened must make us even more clever. We enjoy being knowledgeable. We like to be right. Perhaps we think that if we become enlightened then we shall be right all the time. This, however, is really all only relevant for self-advertisement. However, Dōgen tells us that what we know by being enlightened is not the right answer to every question; it is, rather, the wonderful quality of Buddha reflected in each circumstance. It is not so much that the Buddha is compassionate toward others just because he sees how full of faults they are – it is more that he sees them as wonderful and radiant, faults and all. The Buddha sees reflections of Buddhas in all beings. All 'faults' are stepping-stones.

Buddhism has more to do with emptiness than fullness. The mirror 'fills' because it is empty. It can be the host to whoever and whatever shows up. Its acceptance is limitless because of its emptiness. Dōgen suggests that the enlightened person is empty in this way, open to receiving whatever arrives, accepting whatever lot falls to him or her, never complete.

LONGING

When people of deep faith from completely different metaphysical systems meet, they can find a great deal of common ground if they can avoid having the differences of concept get in the way.

Such people share a sense of longing for something that is indefinable. Each group has a vocabulary for talking about this phenomenon. Spending much time analyzing the concepts in such a vocabulary can be valuable for study within such a community. We are doing something of the kind here in this book. Nonetheless, the concrete reality of it, as Dōgen might say, presents itself in very real terms in the life experience of anybody who completely gives him- or herself to practice.

There is a subtle and intimate experience of the wondrousness of existence. Although it fills us with light, it also fills us with yearning. One feels deficient, lost, small. This may be a great disappointment to the person who thinks this is all about happiness. True spirituality is an intensification of the struggle. We need the Dharma as a flower needs water and we crave it, yet we can never possess it. Even though we lack possession, still it reflects in and upon us. Is this not to stir intense passions?

The things that enlighten people seem to be a mixture of, on the one hand, inspiration and, on the other, setback, shock or affliction. Yet even within enlightenment, Dōgen says, enlightenment goes on. Thus inspiration and affliction continue. With the anaesthetic of delusion washed away, feelings may be more intense than before. The ordinary person, therefore, lives in some degree of spiritual numbness, but the awakened are exposed to the full force of naked encounter.

The Buddha sees beings rising and falling according to their deeds. Given that those deeds are often inspired by impenetrable ignorance, is this not a sad prospect? The great Buddhist sage Vimalakīrti suffered a terrible illness. When the disciples of Buddha went to find out what it was, they discovered that he suffered from his compassion for the innumerable beings in the world who are all busy generating tormenting karma for themselves. One has only to read a newspaper.

Buddha taught that the spiritual path begins with a sense of lack (*duḥkha*). It is from our encounter with impermanence that the path unfolds. If we can have the nerve to entrust ourselves to life and not to escapism, then we may be illuminated, but this does not mean that we shall then enjoy a state of self-satisfaction or complacency.

In Buddhism as commonly taught, there is a sense that enlightenment is a kind of final destination at which one arrives and in traditional Indian Buddhism there is a widespread idea that the aim of the exercise is some kind of extinction. 'Liberation' is understood to be liberation from this saṃsāric world and the best thing that can happen is that one will not be reborn again. Although few contemporary Western Buddhists see it that way, there is a modern parallel in the attitude that the goal is something final and terminal within this life and is a form of uninterrupted 'happiness'. This can lead to a smugness, complacency or reductionism that Dōgen saw as a serious danger.

The ideal of Mahāyāna Buddhism is boundless compassion, and compassion involves feeling the pain of others. In the classic Buddhist view, if one puts others before self, then until all of them are safely delivered to nirvāṇa one cannot help but suffer with them.

FINAL KNOWLEDGE OR OPEN MIND

There is a well-known story about a seeker going to see a master, in which the master serves tea, but when he has filled the cup he keeps pouring and the tea over-runs the cup. The visitor says, "Stop, stop! No more will go in." The master says, "It is the same when a person is already full of ideas and opinions. They are so full that no more will go in." This was a rebuke to the visitor who had come overfull with opinions. This is a common problem. I have lived in a number of Buddhist communities. During those times I have often wondered at the fact that visitors, only a day or two after their arrival, are issuing lists of instructions about how the place could be improved, things could be done better – or, at least, differently – and seeming to exhibit a knowledge of everything concerning the community considerably in excess of that of the people who have been living there for some years. Such people invariably seem to believe that they are being helpful. They are like the person referred to in line 5, who poses as the trainer and enlightener of myriad Dharmas, or the one in line 42, who thinks himself sufficient.

What Dōgen is saying in these two lines, 42 and 43, is that the matter of the overflowing tea-cups is not just relevant to the student. Those who are enlightened are also still learning. In fact, they learn better because they "feel a sense of lack". The ten-year-old child who has a book about physics or astronomy feels as if he knows a lot, whereas Einstein felt that he knew very little. This is because the scope of Einstein's mind was vast. Although, objectively speaking, he knew much more than the ten-year-old, he also knew how this still amounted practically to nothing in the vast scheme of things.

XI

LINES 44–51: INNUMERABLE POSSIBILITIES

44. For instance, if you are in a boat out of sight of land and look in all four directions, you just see a circle, but the fact is that you are not seeing what is really there: this great sea is not a circle, nor a square, the virtues of the ocean are inexpressible.
45. According to the scope of one's eye it is like a palace, like a necklace of jewels, or anything at all.
46. Just for now, one only sees a circle.
47. The myriad Dharmas are like that too.
48. Conditioned by the mundane world, or by ideals, we make assumptions, but we only apprehend what falls within the capacity of our eye.
49. In order to understand the myriad Dharmas on their own terms, we have to do more than just see squares and circles.
50. The merits of the ocean and the merits of the mountains are inexhaustible, not to mention those of the incomparable domains of the four directions.
51. One should know it is like this right here, even in a single drop.

XI.1 COMMENTARY

Beings of different types, of different conditioning, different karma, passing through different realms and bardos, see things differently. To a god, the ocean is a string of jewels. To the Nāga king, the ocean is his palace. One can, therefore, appreciate that everything else is like this too. Mundane or sublime, there are always a million ways of seeing everything. This is not just true of certain special things, but of everything. Our idea of ourselves and of others is insufficient. Everywhere, including right here or even in the tiniest dewdrop, innumerable qualities are inherent.

When one looks at the sea one is impressed by the horizon, yet the horizon is something that does not exist as a real edge to the water. It is not there. However, one cannot see the sea without seeing the horizon. It is thus with everything. Not only do we have an inadequate view, we also see what is not there. This is unavoidable. There is no way to train yourself not to see both more and less than is actually there. This is not just a matter of only being able to see as far as your present accomplishment permits; it is an inherent feature of being-in-the-world. To awaken is not to arrive at flawless perception, but to appreciate that this is the situation.

It is not that we need to stop seeing horizons, nor that we must see all the myriad qualities, but we should be aware that many unseen qualities exist. The unseen world is much greater than the one we see. We tend only to see idealized forms, such as squares or circles, when reality itself never conforms to such ideals. For instance, we never know the full truth of another person, even if we live together for many years, still we see patterns that are only a fraction of what is there, and the pattern we see is more a function of our viewpoint than of the actuality. The circular horizon that we see on the ocean does not exist except in the eye of somebody standing in the place where we are. Being aware of the limited nature of our view should at least keep us from becoming too opinionated. When we are awakened to this reality we always know that, as in line 43, something is missing.

We are each in the domain that we are in for the time being.[1] Regarding it this way is liberating.

---

1 'Time being' is the translation of '*Uji*', which is the title of another famous essay by Dōgen. There are many translations, e.g. Shimano, Eido and Charles Vacher 1997. *Dōgen Shōbōgenzō Uji*, Fougères: Encre Marine.

XI.2 DISCUSSION

THE OCEAN LOOKS ROUND

Squares and circles are ideal forms. In nature there are no exact circles, nor exact squares. Standing on the beach and watching the waves, one might have an idea of the perfect wave, yet every single one is unique. There is never an exact repetition. Life is like this. While it is a fact that we do think that we see such idealized forms, it is also important to be aware that we are only seeing a tiny part of what is actually there.

Dōgen's sea crossing to China is bound to have made a great impression upon him. In our modern world it is, perhaps, difficult to realize quite what a big thing it must have been: a venture from which many never returned. Then, coming back again on another little boat while full of the experience he had had in China, he will have had plenty of time to reflect. We can imagine him standing on the deck of the boat gazing out at the endless water, and the circular horizon, wondering how it was that his life turned out this way.

We should not, however, pass over the fact that in the writing of Daosheng, Li is also characterized as 'round,' suggesting both perfection and immeasurability. So, here, it is quite possible that by 'ocean' Dōgen is again making an oblique reference to Li. Our performance makes the 'perfection' appear, even though we are not 'perfect' ourselves, just as our being in a certain place makes a certain horizon appear even though no such phenomenon exists 'on the ground'.

In 1241 Dōgen wrote an essay called *Kokyō*,[2] which means 'The eternal mirror'. The eternal mirror is round, with the same implication of perfection. Although it might at first seem that moving from the moon being reflected to the way we see the ocean is a move from one metaphor to another, this is not really the case. In Dōgen's mind this is simply an extension of the same idea. Whether ocean or dewdrop – great and small waters – both reflect the sky and moon.

Like the ocean, the mind of enlightenment is full of innumerable possibilities. One does not have them all in

---

2 Nishijima and Cross 1994, vol. 1: 239–59.

conscious awareness at once any more than the mirror has all its possible images at once. That would be impossible, but the mind becomes big, open and spacious, able to accommodate and willing to be accommodated by whatever comes along.

The mind of enlightenment sees the Buddha Dao at work in all forms, not just those that one associates with perfection. One lives one's life playing one's part in the forms that appear, since they are the Buddha Dao functioning, just as the traditional *bhikṣu* accepted whatever food was put into his bowl and slept in whatever shelter was made available. Sometimes Buddha slept on hay in a barn, sometimes in an open field, sometimes in a palace.

FAMILIAR IMAGES

As we have seen, *Genjō Kōan* would have been much easier to understand for a person of Dōgen's time than it is for modern people, since the images he uses were already familiar. He is working variations on well-known themes.

Two generations before Dōgen, there had lived the poet Saigyō who was already regarded as a saintly figure by Dōgen's time. He wrote many remarkable poems in the waka style. Waka is the form of which haiku is an abbreviation. Waka have five lines and a syllabic form 5-7-5-7-7. Generally, Saigyō prefaced his poems with a prose introduction setting the scene. Here is one of his famous poems.

> I was in the province of Sanuki and in the mountains where Kōbō Daishi had once lived. While there I stayed in a hut I had woven together out of grasses. The moon was especially bright and, looking in the direction of the [Inland] Sea, my vision was unclouded.
>
> *kumori naki*
> *yama nite umi no*
> *tsuki mireba*
> *shima zo kōri no*
> *taema narikeru*

Cloudfree mountains
encircle the sea, which holds
the reflected moon:
this transforms islands into
emptiness holes in a sea of ice.[3]

This poem has an astonishing economy of words. The few syllables that there are hint at many possibilities. On first reading, it is a description of a natural phenomenon. The reflected moonlight makes the sea seem like a sheet of ice and this, in turn, makes the islands seem like holes in the ice, concave rather than convex. However, we see here many of the same images that Dōgen uses in *Genjō Kōan*: mountains and sea, the moon and its reflection, and, in addition, clouds and cloudlessness, water and ice. Clouds refer to obscurations of mind. Saigyō uses this metaphor also in his introduction – "my vision was unclouded". Unclouded mountains are the myriad Dharmas revealed. The moon is the light of Buddha. When it is held by the sea, the sea seems turned to ice. Ice is the absence of passion, just like Dōgen's 'ash'. The islands, which might normally appear to be defects in the smoothness of the sea, are now turned into points of emptiness – especial spiritual value – a version of the theme of form becoming emptiness and emptiness form.

We can thus see that an educated Japanese of Dōgen's time would have had no difficulty in deciphering the images that Dōgen uses. In fact, they were so well established that they had almost ceased to be metaphors. When an image has become sufficiently familiar, it simply becomes another name for what it represents. When in English we say that somebody is tilting at windmills, we do not necessarily have to bring Don Quixote to mind to know what is being said. Moons, mountains, seas, reflections, cloud and ice are code words in the genre of that time.

TRAVEL

Travel broadens the mind, they say, and this is true. Being taken out of one's habitual surroundings disturbs one's sense

3 LaFleur 2003: 36.

of business as usual and opens up new possibilities. For the fragile person, deeply engrossed in ego, this can be disturbing, disastrous even, triggering, in the worst case, psychotic breakdown. The ego is, in substantial measure, an effort to keep some stability in the midst of the fluidity of reality where all ordinary things are impermanent. The truly spiritual person, however, can rely upon a different kind of refuge and so is open to the experience. Dōgen had a great insight when with Rujing, but that insight no doubt progressed further as he travelled home.

Travel confronts one with multiple possibilities and leaves one wondering at 'being here' rather than 'being there'. It is a very important spiritual reflection to ponder: "What is it to be *this* – to be what I happen to be at this moment?" And such a reflection is intensified and provoked by travel because one's identity is continually changing. Was Dōgen a monk or a layman? A native or a foreigner? A monastic or a traveller? A scholar or a servant? When other people's expectations of us coincide with our self-image and nothing changes for a while we get a false sense of stability and it is easy in such circumstances to regulate life energy to a lower level.

Śākyamuni Buddha established a sangha in which those who most seriously sought liberation gave up the static life and travelled. They were continually on the move. This is clear from all the basic Buddhist scriptures. One might think that what matters is 'in the mind', but Buddha placed great emphasis upon the practical matter of 'going forth' and leaving the householder life. This was not just something done in one's head. Dōgen, too, took his people away to the mountains. Disrupting the 'normal' was an essential part of Buddha's prescription. Not only travel, but travel with very little in the way of a safety net. The *bhikṣhu* did not even know where his next meal was coming from.

There are many people who have highly developed fantasies about being spiritual while living completely comfortable conventional lives. Śākyamuni would have scorned them. Dōgen did too. One of the major underlying – and sometimes quite overt – themes in Dōgen's message is that it is all very well to talk about non-duality or Buddha Nature or oneness or anything else, but one still has to do something about oneself and that involves practice – practical action – shifting oneself.

In my Dharma life I have travelled a great deal. People invite me and I go. You never know what you are going to encounter. Generally speaking, people are very kind. However, they are kind in their way. It is wonderful that people share their food with you. However, it is not always your kind of food. They accommodate you, but it is not your bed and the things that surround you are not your things. On one occasion, I was staying in India and a family gave up their bed so that I, the honoured guest, could sleep inside. They themselves slept on the porch. I was very honoured. My bed was a thin cloth spread on concrete. They were a poor family and were giving me their best. A month later I was visiting another country and staying in another house. I came down early in the morning and encountered my host and he said that as there was still some time before breakfast, he would take me up in his private aeroplane so that I could see around the area for half an hour or so. When you travel in the spirit of the Dharma, you accept what comes. You sleep in the bed that is offered. You do your best to fit in and to play your part.

"What are we doing today?"

"We are going to Chandrapur, sir, and, on the way, we are going to a ground-breaking ceremony."

"A ground breaking ceremony?"

"Yes, sir, for the new college that is being built. They want to lay the foundation stone."

"Interesting. Who is leading the ceremony?"

"You are, sir."

Sometimes one has to invent rituals as one goes along. This is how it goes. One learns to adapt. One tries to play one's part. When they said to Dōgen that he could enter the monastery, but as a layperson, he said, in effect, "OK, I'll do it."

Life is full of many possibilities. People generally try to minimize them by hanging onto one identity. This involves having a list of things in mind that have to be done 'their way'. We hold to a sense that 'I am the kind of person who...' but this is largely fiction and self-restriction. Paradoxically, the person who is willing to fit in and play his or her part is, thereby, much freer than those who can only function when things are done 'their way'.

DIFFERENT BEINGS HAVE DIFFERENT EXPERIENCE

The ocean is a palace to nāgas and to gods it is a jewel necklace. This is because nāgas and gods have their own Li, which, nonetheless, along with our own Li, is a local expression of the great Dao Li. We are neither nāgas nor gods at the moment – though who knows what comes next? – so the ocean is going to look different to us. Nonetheless, "it looks round" means that we sense its ultimate perfection, even though its details and transformations largely escape us. We are not ordinarily going to see what gods or nāgas see.

This last point is also a reference to another traditional illustration used in Buddhism: different creatures see the world in completely different ways. It is used to make the point that what one sees is a function of one's individual karma. Fish and nāgas may see a palace, gods an ornament, and hungry ghosts see it as pus and blood. Some schools of Buddhism say that this means that the reality of the water from its own side, as it were, is inaccessible to us. Other schools say that there is nothing on the water's own side, that all is apparition and projection of mind, and so on. It is an ancient subject of debate. Here Dōgen emphasizes that there is a lot that one does not see. The implication seems to be that *all* these innumerable perspectives and qualities are properties of the object. This is because, in the model that Dōgen is presenting, the qualities that we see are really all Dharma teaching. They are not so much qualities inherent in the object as inherent in the Dharma that the object presents. The Buddhas will give us what is good for us at the time corresponding to whatever realm of saṃsāra we happen to be wandering in.

Being aware that nāgas and gods and so on see something completely different in the same thing introduces relativism into our own appreciation of the object. It jolts us out of our taken-for-granted assumptions. If we can deeply accept and internalize this, it leads to a deeply grounded humility, equanimity and willingness.

THE DHARMA EYE

We can nonetheless still ask what it would mean to be able to see totally. How might an omniscient being perceive things? A Buddha would not be particularly interested in grasping every quality of the ocean simply for the sake of getting the best experience. He is not invested in getting himself a nāga palace, for instance. The Buddha would love and appreciate all the different kinds of beings – fish, humans, gods, hungry ghosts and all. Appreciating them, he would appreciate the way that they see things. So, the Buddha's consummate vision is not a function of his acquiring some accomplishment for himself – it is not that he is feeding his body or his mind – but of his love and compassion. This is what arises when body and mind drop away. The Buddha thus does, as it happens, get an appreciation of all the qualities of the ocean, but this is incidental. He is not on a quest for experience to feed his own body and mind. To travel in the Dharma is quite different from travelling as a tourist.

This is a bit like the experience of a good therapist. A good therapist empathizes deeply with the client. As a result she does incidentally get a vicarious experience of many worlds that she has not actually experienced herself. Perhaps she has one client who is a refugee, another who has been a violent person, another who lives in the world of heroin junkies, another who lost a limb in a war, and so on. Each of these people has a story to tell and presents a world. That world may be very different from the normal world of the therapist. To be a good therapist one has to be able to enter into all these different worlds – to enter the ocean of life from the perspective of all these different participants. Dōgen's idea is the same, only more so.

WONDERFUL QUALITIES

Coming immediately after the section on the moon reflected in the dewdrop, we can take it that the expression "innumerable wonderful qualities" refers to the same thing as is meant by the reflection of the moon, stars, and sky in the dewdrop. Even when they are there we do not necessarily see them. There is more going on than meets the eye. There are a vast number of drops in an ocean and every one may reflect many things. One might never suspect that in the dewdrop there is a whole universe reflected – or, indeed, many universes. In the same way one does not necessarily see the many worlds that converge in one's neighbour. However, when one has empathy for the nāga or the god, one sees through their eyes and, for a short time, one sees another skein of wonders. One does not do so in order to get what they have got, one does so out of love and compassion, but, incidentally, one experiences other worlds and gains the conviction of infinite others unseen.

Furthermore, we too are dewdrops. The light of all the Buddhas is reflected in every being, ourselves included. From a different angle, a different world comes into view. We do not need to notice this particularly. It is enough to trust. When the impulse to feed the neediness of one's own body and mind is no longer clamouring, then one can have faith that the light of all the Buddhas is doing its work quite naturally, one can enjoy the experiences that befall one and trust in those passed by. The Nāga King will see us one way, the hungry ghost another, but each is getting what he needs, even if he does not realize it himself, and this will be so whether we notice or not.

TWO SIDES TO THE MIRROR

We can ask why it is that Dōgen uses two examples only – palace and necklace, suggesting gods and nāgas. The example of hungry ghosts makes the point more strongly and is common in Buddhist discourse, but Dōgen does not use it. Why not? The answer must be that the image of the mirror dominates in this essay and the sea is a kind of mirror. Furthermore, the Nāga King and the gods are conceived as being on opposite sides. The nāgas are under the sea and the gods are in the sky. If the Nāga King had a sufficiently bright light on in his palace, when we looked at the surface of the sea, as Dōgen did during his voyage, we would see the nāga palace down below. However, because the world below the surface is darker than the world above, we see the reflection of the sky and the world below the waves is out of sight. The sea surface becomes a mirror because of the balance of light. This is, therefore, another instance of the image set up in line 12.

In *Kokyō*, Dōgen talks about how the mirror reflects exactly what is there, nothing else. It does not manipulate the image. He means that this is how one should be. One is fully in the present situation, no more, no less: every moment of life lived to the full without excess or pretention beyond what is actually the case. This does not mean that the past and future are ignored. We have already seen, in the section on firewood and ash, that it is the deluded person who is cut off from past and future. The enlightened person is able to occupy the present fully because future, present and past are seamlessly integrated as part of the Dao that has no boundary. Being cut off from past and future is a kind of reduction that keeps one's life imprisoned within a tight boundary. Dōgen's period as a layperson in a Chinese monastery was meaningful because he was a monk in Japan and had a mission to take the Dharma back to his country. This longer time perspective enabled him to play his part in China.

When two people with mirror minds meet, they reflect each other and, therefore, in the sense that matters, their minds are exactly the same. This does not mean that they think the same thing, have the same doctrine, have similar temperaments, or anything of the kind. They are the same in their mirror-ness.

In the same essay Dōgen uses the story of the Yellow Emperor having twelve mirrors and also receiving three mirrors from the Daoist sage Kōsei. The Yellow Emperor is one of the all-benign mythical originators of Chinese civilization. The twelve mirrors are the twelve years, months and hours that make up the cycles of time. The three mirrors are heaven, earth and human beings. Here we again see Daoism, Confucianism and Buddhism indistinguishably merged. The point, however, is that reality – time and space; heaven, earth and ocean; sacred and profane occurrences – is not just a symbol for the mirror, it is the mirror; just as the mind of the sage is. When everything is a mirror in this sense, then there is "great order". Great order because the pure mirror is the measure of things, not in the sense of calibration, but of validation. Dōgen quotes Master Nangaku (677–744) as saying "it cannot delude others one bit". For the emperor, the people are the mirror. For the people, the emperor is a mirror. At the most mundane level, we see ourselves in our politicians, and at the most sublime level, we experience genjō kōan by being true beings.

In Dōgen, the Buddha Dao is dialectical manner. In Western philosophy we are used to rather static concepts. Perfection is, to us, completeness, but in Dōgen, as in Daoism, perfection is a ceaseless unfolding. Thus, again in *Kokyō*, Dōgen reports a dialogue between two monks, Seppō and Sanshō. The topic is the mirror mind of monkeys. However, the point that I want to make is that Dōgen uses this conversation to tell us that the eternal mirror is flawless, so when a flaw appears in it, that really is a flaw, yet that flaw itself is the eternal mirror. A flawless mirror shows us our flaws flawlessly. In this kind of flowing perfection, every step is made wrong by the next one and so is made right by it. This is like a flight of steps. Each step is needed in order to reach the next one, but the purpose of each step is to be left behind. This is why it is impossible to have enlightenment as a possession or permanent knowledge (line 10).

RIGHT HERE AND IN EVERY DEWDROP

Dōgen always wants to stress that what is true universally is true in every concrete instance. The Dao enters into the immediate and is encountered there. It is in concrete situations that the holy life is lived.

"Buddha's true Dharma body is like the empty sky. According with things, it manifests form."[4] The empty sky is like the circle of the ocean. To know that perfection is all well and good, but it is more important in practice to know how it manifests form. To know about 'original enlightenment' is all very well, but it is in the circumstances of daily life that the holy life is lived.

4 Leighton and Okumura 2004: 91.

A person who pontificates about original enlightenment, or any other concept of perfection, yet is still attached to his own bed, his own food and his own favoured circumstances has not understood the Dharma.

We can have all the clever ideas in the world, but we still have to deal with the situation that comes about right in front of us. It is exactly that situation that has the power to enlighten us and change our life from being mundane to being holy, but the important thing is not whether we become enlightened or not, but how we regard that situation: whether we do so from the perspective of what we can get (enlightenment, etc.) or from the perspective of eradicating neediness. In order to have no neediness, one's mind has to be focussed on the situation that presents itself rather than on oneself. When we sit in the hall and chant, our task is to harmonize with the others, not to shine as the best singer. When one harmonizes one disappears. When one disappears the Dharma is reflected in one. The sign of its presence is the sound of our imperfect singing rolling on.

So Dōgen is saying, be here in the present moment, but do not be trapped by the present moment. The enlightening thing about the present moment is that it is passing away, never to be repeated. Cling to it and all is lost. Avoid it and you will never arrive. There are no snapshots of enlightenment.

XII

LINES 52–63: LIKE FISH AND FOWL

52. Fish swim in the water, but however far they go there is no end to the water.
53. Birds fly in the sky, but however far they go there is no end to the sky.
54. However, fish and birds, now, as of old, never free themselves from the water or sky; they just make great or small use of it according to their need, so, there is no such thing as using up every morsel or exploring every single crevice.
55. If a bird leaves the sky it dies straight away.
56. If a fish leaves the water it dies straight away.
57. If you are a fish, investigate the water.
If you are a bird investigate the sky.
58. When you are a bird, you have to be a bird.
When you are a fish you have to be a fish.
59. Birds live the life of the sky (emptiness – *kū*). Fish live the life of the water.
60. But then to go further beyond is enlightenment practice and is the way of the old living sage.
61. So, thoroughly investigate the water and, later, you will be investigating the sky.
62. If the fish or the bird tries to go through to the other domain it cannot do so.
63. The place is attained when the doing of daily activity (*an ri*) is genjō kōan.
When daily activity is genjō kōan, the Way is attained.

XII.1 COMMENTARY

Fish and birds represent the life on opposite sides of the mirror surface of the sea. They each keep to their own place and cannot live on the other side. Here, they represent the enlightened (birds) and deluded (fish). Being enlightened is as different from being deluded as birds are from fish. The two live in different worlds and there is no path from one to the other. There is no technique by which one can transform oneself from one state into the other – they really are as different as fish and fowl. So, whichever you are, that is your domain, and your practice is to inhabit and investigate it thoroughly. If you are a 'fish' and you investigate the 'water' thoroughly, you may find that, without even noticing it, you have become a 'bird'. Yet, if you are a 'fish' and you try to become a 'bird', you cannot do so. In other words, it is not by trying to become enlightened that one becomes enlightened; it is by fully inhabiting and investigating the actual life that one has. The servant who does his duty well and conscientiously may well be promoted, but the one who is always seeking promotion is more likely to be dismissed. When one simply is what one is and acts accordingly, then daily life is kōan and genjō occurs. At this point one is naturally penetrated and pervaded by the Dharma because one's unpretentious way of being has made one into a mirror. It is when we expect nothing that treasure is bestowed. As long as we remain greedy we get nothing.

Regarding line 60, the Japanese actually says 'person' rather than 'sage' but I have translated it this way as I take this to be the intended meaning. The reference to an 'old living person' is an echo of 'living Buddhas' in line 3. 'Old' and 'wise' are virtually synonyms in oriental thought. Here Dōgen is again asserting that there are living Buddhas, that enlightenment is a reality even in this time of *mappō*, that training is not futile, and that the most noble and worthwhile thing we can do is to follow in the footsteps of the spiritual ancestors.

XII.2 DISCUSSION

THE IMAGE

When you are at sea, on the boat, looking out across the expanse of waves, the sea's surface is a boundary. There are two worlds, one above that boundary, inhabited by birds, and one below that boundary, inhabited by fish. The birds do not live under water and the fish do not live in the sky. This image forms a yin-yang diagram. Once again, as in the other images, Dōgen is at pains to emphasize a complete separation, a sharp duality.

The image of the fish and the birds may also come from Dōgen's sea voyage, although here I agree with Okamura that Dōgen must also have had in mind the poem of Hongzhi Zhengjue (1091–1157) that Dōgen quotes in full in his essay *Zazenshin*.[1] This poem ends with the lines:

> The water is clean, right to the bottom,
> Fishes are swimming, slowly, slowly.
> The sky is wide beyond limit,
> And birds are flying, far, far away.[2]

In Dōgen, everything is determined in multiple ways and every phrase is the nexus of a number of cross-currents, just like life itself.

The sky and the sea each have their own forms of life. The sky is empty and bright (yang). The sea is dark (yin) and what light it has comes from the other realm. They form a duality that exists perennially, each in relation to the other, complementing one another, and each has its own life. It is no use trying to cross to the other side, but if you do what you should do as what you are, then you may, surprisingly, find that you have appeared on the other side in a completely unexpected way. Dōgen is pointing out a mysterious working of Buddha Dharma that, *inter alia*, skilfully unites the Daoist principle of mysterious processes of transformation with the Confucian one of rectification of roles.

However, even if the 'fish' is transformed into a 'bird', what is now required is not essentially different: do what is needful

---

1 Okumura, Shohaku 2010. *Realizing Genjokoan: The Key to Dogen's Shobogenzo*, Somerville, MA: Wisdom Books: 157 et seq.

2 Nishijima and Cross 1994: vol. 2: 101.

in the realm you are in at the time. Therefore, you might not even notice the change. That a humble person has become a saint might be evident to others, but may well not be evident to the person in question, whereas to the same observer the folly of the 'fish' that is endlessly trying to become, or pretend that it has become, a 'bird' is usually obvious enough.

If you are a fish, be a fish. Do whatever you do wholeheartedly. If you do, you may well find that it leads somewhere you did not expect. My Zen teacher sometimes said, "If you are going to sin, sin vigorously – that way you'll learn." Many people live their lives in a half-hearted manner.

WATER: *SUI*

The term *sui* (水) means water and the term *unsui* (雲水), literally 'cloud and water', means a Zen practitioner. 'Cloud' is another established 'code word' as we can see from the poem by Saigyō in Sanuki. It has a distinctly Daoist flavour. The true Zen practitioner lives like cloud and water. Each flows according to conditions. Water especially is a favourite Daoist image, symbolizing the way of practising that accords most perfectly with Dao (道). Thus, a Buddhist practitioner, an *unsui*, is a 'cloud-water', which is to say, a sky-ocean, or bird-fish. These compounds represent the ever-churning Buddha Dao (佛 道).

This also means that the Zen trainee is willing to be bird or fish as the case may be. It also means that when he is a fish he is already a bird and when she is a bird she is still a fish. Birds and clouds are the life of the sky. Fish and water are the life below. For the time being, one. For the time being, the other. This is the true spirit of Buddhism. In this kind of non-dualism, duality is completely and concretely manifest.

THE SKY IS EMPTY

A key to the interpretation of these lines lies, as so often in Dōgen, in a linguistic point. The word for sky, *kū* (空), also means emptiness or space, and also 'for nothing'. Birds, therefore, from line 57 onwards, are those who live in emptiness, which, in

Buddhism, means enlightened people. They are empty of self and they dwell in a domain that is empty. Here, therefore, 'birds' is not a metaphor; it is code word for enlightened people.

Such people do things 'for nothing', which is to say, without seeking personal reward. In other words, they do their duty in a light yet conscientious way. In polite conversation, a person who acts in this way and is then complimented for it, says, "It was nothing." Dōgen is talking about a way of being in which this is not just a polite expression; it is really sincere. Love is such. Love is 'for nothing'. If it is 'for something' then it is not love. If 'she loves him for his money' then it is not really love. If he loves God for having made him one of the chosen people, this is not really love. Love is gratuitous. Love is to play one's part unilaterally, in a level way, and this is what Dōgen calls kōan. Genjō is the transformation that appears when one does so and that transformation is a natural occurrence, as amazing as the sudden appearance of a reflection upon the surface of a lake.

The same year as Dōgen wrote *Genjō Kōan*, he also wrote a commentary upon the Heart Sūtra.[3] *Kū* (空), here in *Genjō Kōan*, is the same word as appears in the Heart Sūtra in the passage "*shiki fu i kū, kū fu i shiki*". '*Fu i*' means 'not different from' or 'not apart from'. *Shiki* means 'form' or 'colour'. Hence: 'Form is not different from emptiness, emptiness is not different from form.' Thus, within the emptiness there is all manner of form; non-duality includes duality, duality expresses non-duality, they are not separable, they cannot be mutually exclusive. In his commentary on the Heart Sūtra, Dōgen quotes the poem by his master, Rujing:

> Whole body, like a mouth hanging in space
> Not asking if the wind is east, west, south or north,
> For all others equally it chatters *prajñā*
> Bing-bong-bang, Ting-a-ling, Ting-a-ling.

Because the wind-bell is empty, 空, and hanging in space, 空, it responds naturally to all the different winds that blow. It emits its sound indiscriminately, pleasing anyone who cares

3 "*Maka Hannya Haramitsu*", in Nishijima and Cross 1994, vol. 1: 25–30.

to hear. It does its job, unselfconsciously, unhesitatingly, and without prejudice. It does its duty, yet with a happy and healthy indifference. It is like the mirror that does not discriminate between the images that form.

The teacher is a bit like this. In the teacher's boundless compassion, there is a kind of ruthlessness. This is not a cruelty in the service of self-interest, but a realism that cuts through the fond illusions of the disciple. This is similar to the passage in the Daoist classic that says:

> 天地不仁，以萬物為芻狗；
> 聖人不仁，以百姓為芻狗.

> Heaven and Earth are not 'benevolent'.
> They treat the myriad things as acting as straw dogs
> The sage is not 'benevolent'.
> He treats the people as acting as straw dogs.[4]

This passage may startle, since we think that the Buddha, heaven or God should be benevolent and, therefore, the sage should be so too. However, in Daoism and Buddhism we are required to become spiritually mature, not regress to being spiritual children. The sage's love is shown in ways that help to bring the person to maturity, that facilitate their realism. This is not achieved by bending the rules of the universe in order to indulge a favourite. This is a love that transcends favouritism.

In the Daoist passage just mentioned, there is the image of straw dogs. Model dogs made from straw play a part – act – in Chinese ritual. Playing one's part is kōan and doing so correctly is Li. The straw dogs play their part perfectly and never put on airs. The teacher helps us to play our part. The purpose of this is to show us how to be empty of favouritism and manipulation. The same is true in our relation to ourselves. The true practitioner is not his own favourite.

When people act in this way they are *prajñā pāramitā* and this is the sacred object most worthy of veneration. As it says in Kennett Rōshi's translation of the poem, The Most Excellent Mirror Samādhi, "Such actions and most unpretentious work all foolish seem and dull. But those who practise thus this law

4 My translation.

continually shall be called Lord of Lords unto eternity."[5]

The image of birds and sky also makes clear that although we might conventionally talk about 'emptiness' as an 'inner' quality – emptiness of self, and so on – the experiential reality is that the person lives *in the midst of* emptiness, just as the bird lives *in* the sky. What does this mean? It means that the person takes everything that happens in a straightforward way, as not 'loaded'.

In modern psychology we talk about projection. The person who is mired in self-concern sees self everywhere. Instead of seeing the Dharma in its myriad manifestations, such a person would see reflections of himself. This is what we call 'taking things personally'. The extreme of this is what is called 'ideas of reference' in psychosis. The psychotic person may think that people on the television are communicating messages to him specifically or that his own thoughts control when the traffic lights change. This is an extreme case of self-*lakṣaṇa* (see discussion of 'Myriad Dharma' in chapter I), but milder instances are normal in the life of ordinary people who easily feel slighted and take to heart comments and occurrences that may have had nothing to do with them at all.

This is all due to seeing the world as a reflection of self rather than letting self be a reflection of the Dharma, as the wind-bell is of the wind. When it is such a reflection, that is because of emptiness, but also because of the experience of everything else being empty. People in such a condition encounter Dharma everywhere without particularly being consciously aware of the fact. Nonetheless, they experience it and this gives rise to joy, inner peace, and all the other factors of enlightenment.[6] In order to see the real thing one has to see beyond one's own reflection.

This means that an enlightened person may be oblivious to the self-projections of others. A person goes to see a Dharma master and, through habit, tries out their 'games' upon him. The master does not respond in the expected manner. He does not 'play the game'. However, this is generally not because he has cleverly 'spotted' the game and decided not to play; it is

5 Kennett 1972: 228.

6 For the seven 'factors of enlightenment', see Ñāṇamoli and Bodhi 1995: 946–7.

generally because he does spot it, but is not caught by it. It is like a joke that falls flat. The master is not tricking the disciple nor manipulating him. It is precisely because he has no need to manipulate that the other person's attempt to manipulate fails. Manipulation depends upon reciprocation. In order to manipulate another person one has to play upon something that they desire or fear. Manipulation is a trade. It is as though one were saying, 'I'll play your game if you play mine.' If the master is not genuine, this becomes, 'I will make you feel like a great master if you will collude with me in my illusion about myself.' However, if the master is genuine, he does not need this. He is 'empty', and whatever comes his way appears empty to him. He can love all the winds that come – east, west, south or north – and respond accordingly. That is love. This may well manifest as seeing the best in people, but in an uncontrived way.

It is also the way in which the myriad Dharma are constantly enlightening one, so that those in the midst of enlightenment are continually becoming more enlightened (line 8) and enlightened Buddhas go on enlightening Buddhas (line 11).

BIRDS MUST BE BIRDS, FISH MUST BE FISH

Normally we think we must give up delusion and find enlightenment, that this is a task to be performed by our own effort and that we are in some way a failure if we do not achieve it. We think that there is too much delusion and not enough enlightenment, and that there is a moral duty to do something about it. However, it is from this very delusion that the Buddha Dao leaps forth (line 3). The delusion does not create the Buddha Dao, nor does the Buddha Dao destroy the delusion. The image is rather as a lion leaps forth from the forest. No forest, no lion, but the forest does not create the lion and the lion does not destroy the forest.

Dōgen says: if you are deluded, be deluded! Investigate delusion. To investigate, one must take an objective view. This is a matter of closely observing the boat (line 22). If we study the acts of our own daily life intimately, we shall see that the myriad Dharmas themselves are not therein (line 24), but the very activity of studying intimately puts us into a different mode. Study takes one out of oneself. Attention is now centred on something objective. When we are out of self, a transformation occurs. By being objective in that way, one naturally arrives at the point where daily activity is genjō kōan (line 63). Then the myriad Dharma *are* in daily activity after all.

This is why being in a 'safe space' is often so therapeutic. When nobody is condemning us for our delusions we initially pursue them, but as we do not have to defend them, we gradually become curious about them. Either they reward this curiosity or they do not. If they do not, we become bored with them. If they do, we investigate further. Either way, we soon find ourselves in a different place in relation to them.

Thus, it is more enlightened to recognize one's unenlightened state, and to investigate it thoroughly, than either (a) to think oneself endowed with original enlightenment, or (b) to be constantly hankering to be something different from what one is. Dōgen agrees with Hōnen here, that the idea of 'original enlightenment' might be true in an absolute sense, but that it can easily become a first-class way of fooling oneself and avoiding the necessity of practice.

So Dōgen is saying: do not do the practice as a way of *trying* to become enlightened; just do the practice and let things take care of themselves. You may never know whether you are enlightened or not, but being preoccupied with the issue will only get in the way, because it is inherently a concern with self. In his essay *Immo*,[7] written in 1242, Dōgen quotes Yunyan Tansheng (780–841), who is called Ungan Donjō in Japanese, as saying "If you want to attain it, you have to be it, and since it is what you are, why are you worrying about it?" Dōgen goes on to say that even the worrying is 'it'.

THE ACTIVE LIFE OF THE DOMAIN IN WHICH YOU ARE

When a Buddha is living his life he makes full use of practice and realization. He is on the job. He is at ease, just as a fish is not particularly conscious of the water. He is so at home in the

7 Nishijima and Cross 1994, vol. 2: 119 et seq.

water that he naturally swims in a way that is appropriate to a water animal. The truly awakened person is like that. Yet it is still the case that even the unenlightened person is living in the same medium as the enlightened one. It is not that they live in different worlds; it is that they relate to that world in different ways, one making appropriate usage and the other trying to pamper his body and mind.

The monk says, "Every day we have to get up, put on robes, eat food... How can we be free from all this?" The master says, "Just get up, put on robes, eat breakfast..." Freedom is not a matter of leaving the world of conditions, the element within which we have our being. Liberation happens within this world of conditions. The Unconditioned penetrates and pervades, but does not, in doing so, break the conditions.

The Buddha's teachings apply to this and any possible world because in all possible worlds there will be such conditions. The fish might be reborn as a bird or the bird as a fish, but the situation will not have changed in its essentials. Yet Dōgen sees it as important to stress that a fish is not a bird and a bird is not a fish.

If we are the birds and fish, then the birds and fish around us, the air and the water, are all life, but the question is: are we ourselves alive? Has life become us? And if it has, are we still going on? The life of Buddha is always expanding. Are we trying to be Buddha, or are we trying to advance the work of Buddha? The latter is much closer to the Mahāyāna ideal. This is so even though the original usage of the word 'bodhisattva' was to designate a person who is on the way to becoming a Buddha. There is a kind of paradox here. In order to become a Buddha one must forget about becoming a Buddha and get on with doing the Buddha's work where one happens to be.

Disciple: Where will you go in your next life?
Master: Hell.
Disciple: But you are supposed to be the accomplished one. We are all practising to avoid going to hell. If even you are going to hell, what is the point of practising?
Master: I shall go to hell because there will be plenty for me to do there.

The disciple is practising in order to get something to please or satiate his body or his mind. The master is practising genjō kōan. Actually the master does not know if he will go to hell or to some other place, but wherever he goes he will use the scope of that domain to save beings, thereby doing the Buddha's bidding. In a sense, wherever he goes will be hell if there are beings there to be saved and it will also be heaven because he is saving them.

WHEN DAILY ACTIVITY IS GENJŌ KŌAN

In line 63, 'daily deeds' – *an ri* (行李) – has a number of nuances. The compound term 行李 also means luggage – the baggage that we carry around with us. We might think that becoming enlightened means putting all our baggage down, but here Dōgen says that the baggage itself becomes genjō kōan. If you take the characters separately they suggest 'the right fruit'. We might reflect that the baggage we are carrying today is the right fruit of our past karma. As such it is exactly what we need right now. When we view it that way, then we will accept it in a natural way and it will become genjō kōan.

Also, in this line, we see the sense in Kennett Rōshi's rendering of the title of *Genjō Kōan* as 'The Problem of Everyday Life'.[8] However, there is a strong sense in which what genjō kōan is advocating is, precisely, to not problematize daily life. This is not to disagree with her – I imagine that she would wholeheartedly concur. Stripped of the delusional colouring (*shiki* – see above) imparted by taking everything personally, one falls into sanity. The kōan stories are all stories about moments when this has happened for people. Dōgen's argument with Hōnen is over the issue of whether this is still possible in the present age. Dōgen emphatically asserts that it is. In fact, this apparent disagreement is not so sharp as it may at first appear. Both Dōgen and Hōnen see the way forward as being to give up *trying* not to be a 'fish'. Both assert that the way to do that is to be what you are and have a modest attitude. The fish that tries to be a bird fails, cannot find a way, and dies as soon as it leaves its water. This

8 Kennett 1972: 142 et seq.

tells us everything we need to know about practice, and Hōnen and Dōgen agree that practice is essential. Here, practice is not anything pretentious. It is daily life carried out with an innocent mind. The innocent mind is curious, open, attentive and ever-expanding. It has no hidden manipulative agenda.

DUALITIES IN THE TEXT

This contrast of fish and birds is the last of the major images in *Genjō Kōan* and it follows on naturally from the others. I think that there is a parallelism running through all of these pairs, from the one that appears in the first two lines, and all the way through. The state in which all Dharmas are Buddhadharma and the state in which the myriad Dharmas are not self are two domains, like firewood and ash, or sea and sky. One does not displace the other. Self and the myriad Dharmas are two domains. One does not displace the other. This is the core of Dōgen's argument: that the manifestation of the Buddha Way – the Dao – occurs when this is the case; in other words, when the different domains – yin and yang – do not encroach upon one another, yet form a whole. They naturally give way to and give rise to one another and one can rely upon that without needing to overreach oneself by trying to exert personal control upon the process. It is not that we make enlightenment happen by our effort – any such enlightenment would not be worth having – but by applying our effort in the right way, as unpretentious practice. We can be in tune with this bigger dance, the Buddha Dao, and it will carry us to where we need to be. At any given time we each have our place and our lot. That place may ask us sometimes to be active and sometimes not – sometimes making great use, sometimes little, but to do so within its own domain.

Parallel images								
Light	Not-self Dharma	Sky (*Kū*)	Bird	Jewel	Gods	Moon	Yang	The Buddha Dao
Dark	Self	Sea	Fish	Palace	Nāga	Reflection	Yin	

XIII

LINES 64–8: TRUE ENLIGHTENMENT IS THE HEART'S SECRET

64. This Way, this place, is not a matter of greatness nor smallness, not about self (*ji*) and other (*ta*). It precedes the 'is not' in the 'is'.
65. Therefore, it is not in the now-manifest, yet, nonetheless, it *is*.
66. Here, in this way of penetrating and pervading, one cannot know some knowable edge, cannot get the ultimate knack of Buddhadharma
67. except by living the same life and practising the same practice, simply just as they are.
68. One should not expect to have intellectual knowledge of one's attainment. Although evidence of enlightenment is immediately apparent to the eye, the secrets of the heart are not necessarily known to the mind.

XIII.1 COMMENTARY

The Way is not reducible to the normal worldly categories of great and small or even the religious ones of self-power and other-power. It is not a matter of affirming one and negating the other. It is not part of things as they generally appear to us and, as we 'progress', the 'goal' may become less and less apparent. Nonetheless, it happens. We might want to get some sense of control by knowing where the boundary between deluded and enlightened lies, but this would be with a view to trying to cross it by our own effort. It does not work like that. What happens is that the Dharma comes, penetrates and pervades us when we give up our grasping agendas and live life and do our practice in a totally unpretentious manner. Although when satori has occurred one can see the evidence of it in the changed manner, demeanour and attitude of a person toward others, as we saw above, this is not necessarily something of which the person him- or herself is necessarily conscious. A change of heart might or might not register in the mind. What is really true in a life remains secret in the heart, sometimes secret even to the person concerned.

XIII.2 DISCUSSION

BEFORE THE IS NOT IN THE IS

In line 64, Dōgen disposes of three ideas about spirituality that he thinks tend to get in the way. Each of these ideas has some merit, but Dōgen's point is different in several important ways.

Big and small:

Firstly, there are ideas of grandeur and self-depreciation. This is the ordinary worldly view, in which enlightenment is viewed as something great and delusion as not great, and the motive for achieving enlightenment becomes a grasping one.

Or, we might think that spirituality is about humbling oneself. There is some truth in this, but it still contains a strong element of self. In the idea of genjō kōan, it is not a matter of getting the self 'right' in any way at all. It is a matter of self dropping away. Thinking that one is, in seeking enlightenment, going to become a big person or a little person is by the by. It is irrelevant. One might find oneself in one position or in another, but concern about it is only going to get in the way.

Self and other:

Since, here, Dōgen uses the characters for *ji* and *ta*, rather than ordinary cursive writing, I think there is an intended reference to self-power (*jiriki*) and other-power (*tariki*). Dōgen is avoiding taking sides in this debate. He is saying: it is not a matter of whether you can become enlightened by your own power or by the power of the Buddha; it is a matter of stopping these attempts to get somewhere, and instead living a life that is not self-concerned. This put him at odds with many of Hōnen's followers, perhaps, but hardly with Hōnen himself. Dōgen's view is that it is not by ourselves that Buddha is created (think of the conversation between Baso and Nangaku); it is by the Dharma entering into and pervading us (as the moon in the dewdrop), but we still have a part to play in this because the water only becomes a mirror when it is dark, so our part is self-effacement and sincere practice. I cannot see how Hōnen himself would have disagreed with this. The emphasis is, perhaps, different, but the doctrine is essentially the same.

Is and is-not:

Debates about 'great' and 'small' or self-power and other-power are often about advocating one and then discouraging the other, and upholding exclusive positions. Dōgen's position is more inclusive. If you are small, be small. Things will take care of themselves. Arrogant self-assertion will bring no real gain, more likely disaster.

Consciousness is the capacity to choose. When I am conscious of something, that gives me options, it enables me to adopt a different option, to refuse the present reality. This is a marvellously useful capacity that is also the root of nearly all neurosis. It produces creativity and also indecision. It endows us with a treacherous relationship to life. The process that Dōgen is talking about substantially happens unconsciously. We have seen him asserting this point over and over. You might not notice that it has happened. Perhaps, nobody else will notice either. Contemporary spirituality tends to over-emphasize awareness and consciousness, but real enlightenment is not contrived on a basis of knowledge and choice. It is more in one's bones than in one's head, more in the heart than in the brain.

Dōgen does not say that enlightenment is a matter of going beyond 'is' and 'is not'; he says that it precedes them. This means going back to innocence, somewhat like the biblical "Verily I say unto you, except ye be converted, and become as little children, ye shall not enter into the kingdom of heaven" (Matt. 18:3), except that, as discussed earlier, Buddhism is wary of inviting people to regress. What is called for is an adult straightforwardness, not a childlike dependency.

FOR THE TIME BEING

Another of Dōgen's most famous essays is called *Uji*,[1] which means 'time-being' or 'being time'. The text was written in a town called Uji. In other words, Uji was where he was for the time being. Furthermore, Uji had been the site of a major battle in the civil war when fortunes had changed in a day, so there was in that town a sense of never being able to count on the morrow. This, of course, all brings home the Buddhist teaching on impermanence.

The moral of *uji* is to live fully, whatever the circumstances, and trust that what needs to happen will eventuate naturally or mysteriously, at any rate in a manner that is not directly of one's own making. The essential attitude is to be willing to take things as they come. Genjō does not come about by any sequence of achievements that one could plan. The path is not linear. It is not any kind of accumulation, neither of knowledge nor of skill. The paradox is that this is not a pathway to awakening because if one lives this way then genjō will have already happened. The lake does not know that it is darkening and does not know that the reflection has already appeared in it.

Knowledge and skills may be useful, but they are secondary. My knowledge and skill will help me to get things done, but enlightenment is not about getting particular things done; it is about having one's heart in the right place. Then one sees what needs doing, one perceives one's 'duty' or 'lot', and one does so in a clean way, empty of desire or resentment. Too much desire only leads to depression. To deal with the situation in hand and leave the rest 'in the lap of the gods' is the correct religious attitude. The Buddhas alone can see into our hearts. Even we cannot always do so.

In *Uji*, Dōgen says that it is the passage of time – change – that wakes us up and makes us practise, but that our practice then "wakes up time", or, in other words, makes whatever is happening become vibrant.

---

1 See Shimano and Vacher 1997.

Even zazen, therefore, is not really a 'method'. To sit still with nothing happening is an instance of kōan, and so has a taste of awakening. Nothing more. Nothing less. When sitting, just sit, but *really* sit. Although zazen is an instance of kōan, it is still possible to corrupt it with pretention: 'Look how my lotus posture is so much better than any body else's in the room!' or, 'If I sit here looking sweet long enough, that handsome monk is surely bound to take notice of me eventually.'

THE WAY OF PENETRATION AND PERVASION

The moon penetrates the water and pervades it. Without one even knowing, the Dharma may be filling one. So awakening can be occurring anywhere, anytime. When the fish is not trying to be anything but a fish, it may actually be a bird. When we are completely yin, yang happens. This is a basic principle of the *Yijing*, *The Book of Change*, which is a classic of both Confucianism and Daoism.

There is always something happening, and there is no place that one cannot be in the midst of the myriad Dharmas, just as there is no place where one cannot be in the midst of delusions. They do not interfere with one another. It is not a matter of too much or too little. We commonly think that a change of circumstance will bring us satisfaction or liberate us in some way or another, but the attitude that Dōgen is advocating transcends all such thinking.

THE PROBLEM WITH EXPECTATION AND TRYING

This passage reveals what seems like a deep paradox to the beginner approaching Buddhism. The simplest Buddhist book will tell you that nirvāṇa comes by giving up desire. One then thinks: does that mean that I must give up my desire for nirvāṇa? Will the very motivation that one has for following the spiritual life impede or even completely prevent one from fulfilling it? This is an important point and it is the conundrum that gets cut through in many kōan stories.

This is a bit like climbing a mountain. When you are far away from the mountain you can see the summit. You can regard it from a distance and the whole business of climbing the mountain is still academic. If you actually decide to climb the mountain you go closer, and as you go closer, the summit disappears from view. It is no longer in the "now-manifest". As you get into the foothills you can actually see less and less of the mountain. However, this is the only way to climb. You climb the mountain by putting one foot in front of the other, step after step, yin-yang, yin-yang. Along the way, every step is complete in itself. You may more or less forget about the summit. You are just a fish being a fish. Then, after being engrossed in walking uphill for a long time, you may suddenly come out upon a ridge or plateau and there is the summit right before you. You suddenly discover that you have become a bird.

The spiritual path is like this. When one starts, one is far away from the boundary of the mountain (line 19). When one gets involved in practice, it is just practice: one unpretentious thing after another. Eventually one really does arrive at true unpretentiousness and suddenly, as though the surface of water had fallen calm and a vivid reflection had appeared, one has arrived. And what does one do after that? Continue in the same way! Why not? If the fish really has become a bird, well, there is now a vast new world of sky to explore.

Another analogy is the painting of a room. When painting a room, you take your brush and pot of paint and climb a ladder and start painting, doing the best you can. You paint the whole of the area you can reach. When you have painted all you can reach from one position, you move the ladder and then paint all you can reach from this new position. Eventually, a completely painted room emerges, almost as a surprise. However, it may be that you are standing on your ladder and you think, perhaps it would have been better to start on the other side. You get down and move the ladder. In the new place you then think, should I start at the top or at the bottom? You do a bit at the bottom but, not being sure, you stop. You look around the room. Perhaps it would be best to start at the top in the corner. You move the ladder. The ladder does not fit very well in the corner. You start thinking about going to buy a different ladder. The job takes much longer and perhaps never gets done at all. The second person has had a wider view, but it has not served him. Painting has remained largely an academic idea for him and nothing has got done. He never really became a painter and the room never got painted. This is a result of, on the one hand, trying to be too clever and, on the other hand, not applying oneself to what is right before one.

So there is a critical difference between (a) making effort in an unpretentious way, 'for nothing', and simply getting on as an act of love, and (b) 'trying' for the sake of an expectation that endlessly demands that one find the perfect method. There is no 'method' except just to do it. If you are a fish, be a fish. Do not try to get out of your life.

When we examine ourselves carefully we may be able to tease out the 'bargaining' that we are doing with fate or God, etc.: "If I am good in such and such a way, then I deserve to get *x*." Much contemporary popular psychology encourages us to think "You deserve it!" and so on. This, however, is all fantasy and a long way from true enlightenment.

GENJŌ OCCURRING

The occurrence of genjō is immediate enlightenment. Genjō is the mirror effect that occurs at the tipping point, when the light on the self side is receding and not trying to outshine everything else. To be 'enlightened' is to be in the state in which the light comes from the Dharma, not from the self. The fish lives in a realm where there is enough light to see a certain distance, but the fish does not know where the light comes from. Perhaps the fish even thinks that the light comes from himself. However, if one is a fish, it is enough simply to be a fish, and if one is a bird, be a bird. Like Alice, we can explore whichever side of the looking-glass we are on, but, unlike Alice, we do so without causing any great commotion and disturbance. The enlightened person relies upon the whole Buddha Dao, with all its yin and yang, without needing to be in the driving seat. We could say that the whole message of *Genjō Kōan* is "Don't play God. Have faith."

THE SAME LIFE, THE SAME PRACTICE

Sometimes a fish, sometimes a bird; sometimes a Nāga King, sometimes a god; sometimes a layman, sometimes a monk; sometimes a scholar, sometimes a tourist; sometimes a 'success', sometimes a 'failure'.[2] The Buddha Dao encompasses all and knows its own way.

Each domain, for the time being, has its possibilities, its range, and that is "sufficient unto the day" (Matt. 6:34). It is, as line 36 says, just a position in time. Fish do not become birds and birds do not become fish, but if you are sufficiently a fish you may be a bird. According to whichever one is at the time, that is one's life, that is one's practice. However, it is possible to know that there are also many other possibilities (line 50) and this knowledge enables one to have some perspective and thus to have a bigger mind.

All phenomena – everything that we might find ourselves being or encountering – are temporary, so that real states are crystallizations of time. They are concrete yet ephemeral. On the one hand, this is it – there is nothing more real than what one is at the moment. On the other hand, there are innumerable other things one might have been and might still be in the future. Value the present, but do not over-value it. Whatever you happen to be right now, soon you will be something else, so fulfil what you are to the full, yet do not get too attached to being what you happen to be. Sometimes one is up, sometimes down, sometimes a devil, sometimes an angel, sometimes the teacher, sometimes the student, sometimes in the holy of holies, sometimes in the most mundane place, sometimes somebody special, sometimes Mr Ordinary. Sometimes one is the whole universe.

Living the Buddhist life can be like this. One minute one is conducting a holy ceremony, standing in for Buddha, wearing a

---

2 The text of *Uji* begins with a quotation from Dharma Master Yaoshan Weiyan (745–827), who is called Yakusan Igen in Japanese: "Sometimes standing on the top of the highest peak, being time; sometimes going to the deepest ocean, being time; sometimes with three heads and eight arms; being time; sometimes eighteen or six foot high, being time; sometimes a staff or whisk, being time; sometimes a pillar or lantern, being time; sometimes Mr Ordinary, being time; sometimes the good earth and the vast firmament of the sky, being time" (my translation).

fine robe. A couple of hours later one is cleaning out the cesspit or turning the compost. Neither role is more in the Dao than the other and neither is less.

One day you will be Buddha. Yes! And when you are, you will find that sometimes you are on high and sometimes in the pit... and so on. The difference is not in having arrived at a final state, it is in taking *uji* for what it is. The secret of life is to be what you are when you are it. The reason that people do not progress is not because they do not have the means to get somewhere else, it is because they are *trying to be* somewhere else. The way to get to the promised 'somewhere' is really to be where you are while it lasts. When we totally exhaust *this*, something unexpected will mysteriously emerge from it. The cherry blossom is exquisite, and then it is gone.

Joy and sorrow both pass. Perhaps this morning I have to give the Dharma lecture to assembled guests. Perhaps this afternoon I have to go on a journey. Perhaps I am cutting grass. Perhaps I am meditating. Perhaps I am in hell. Perhaps I am in heaven. It is all just for the time being, and in every instance there is a way to be, and that way is always kōan, and when it is kōan, then genjō is happening and the rite or sacrifice of life is unfolding as it should.

INCIDENTAL GLORIES

In a previous section, we saw that the Buddha incidentally gets to see the nāga palace and the string of pearls because he is involved empathically with the nāga and the god. He also gets to see the pus and blood, because, at another time, he is engaged with the hungry ghost. However, he is not in the business of trying to see or collect these wondrous or terrible qualities for himself. They are purely incidental. This is because he is in the state of body and mind having fallen away; in other words, the neediness of the body and the neediness of the mind have ceased to be his first concern. Perhaps when Dōgen got back from China people asked him if he had seen all the tourist resorts or famous sights, but that is not why he went.

In the business of practice and realization, it is a fallacy to think that one has got to get somewhere before starting. If we think, "When I am enlightened, I shall be able to..." then we are like the fish that wanted to know the whole ocean before swimming, or wanted to use up every morsel or explore every single crevice. A bird that wanted to know the whole sky would be concerned only for his own body and mind. If we think of Buddhism as a path to enlightenment, and we also think that this is going to take a long time, then we have effectively decided to avoid most of our life. One day you are going to be an *arhat*; what are you going to do in the meantime?

THE UNKNOWABLE BOUNDARY

When each person plays his allotted part naturally, with fullness of heart, then he stays within his sphere and his side of the mirror is dark. He is not clamouring or agitating. Others, therefore, see the myriadfold Dharma reflected. He himself is unaware of the boundary – the mirror surface – as personal knowledge, even though it is happening. Others receive from him the benefit of the Dharma while he himself is just going about his business. It is precisely because he is not self-conscious that this is so. Therefore, this unknowable mirror face accompanies him everywhere he goes, yet is generally unknown to himself.

XIV

LINES 69–74: WHERE THERE'S DHARMA THERE'S PRACTICE

69. Zen Master Baoji was using a fan.
70. A passing monk came by and asked, "The nature of wind (*fū shō*) is that it is always abiding (*jō jū*). There is no place that the always abiding nature of wind does not encompass. What is the priest still holding onto, that he needs to use a fan?"
71. The teacher answered, "Even though you just know that the nature of wind is to always abide (*fū shō jō jū*) and there is nowhere that it does not reach, you do not know the performance of the Way (Dao-Li)."
72. The monk said, "How is it that [knowing that] 'there being no place it does not reach' is not the performance of the Way (Dao-Li)?"
73. The master simply carried on using the fan.
74. The monk bowed.

XIV.1 COMMENTARY

In this bit of banter, there is a play on words. *Fū shō* (風性), the 'wind-nature', is a pun for *fū shō* (不生) meaning the 'unborn' and *jō jū* ('always abiding') is an allusion to *fu metsu*, the 'deathless' or 'undying'. We have already seen that *fū shō* and *fū metsu* appear both in the Heart Sūtra and in the chapter on eternal life of the Lotus Sūtra. So, in saying, "wind abides everywhere" (line 70) the monk is also saying "the unborn is the deathless", which means, "everything is already perfect", with the implication, "isn't it sufficient just to know this?"

The master replies: "Even though you know this, you do not understand its application." In other words, mere knowledge is sterile. Particularly, merely to know about such concepts as 'original enlightenment' leads only to quietism. One has to play one's part. The monk asks him what he means and he carries on using the fan. In other words, he carries on playing his part or, we could say, performing the appropriate rite. The monk then plays *his* part by bowing. At this point they are 'Buddha together with Buddha'. We could say, somewhat ironically, that it takes two to be non-dual. Such is the nature of transmission.

Things that depend upon conditions are subject to impermanence – to 'birth and death'. Buddha says in the *Udāna* that if there were nothing other than conditioned things, there would be no liberation. Not everything is impermanent,[1] but it is still necessary that the unborn penetrate and pervade and, when it does so, one will continue to 'use the fan'. Thus, Dōgen's Buddha Dao has a Li. The music asks us to dance. Li is to behave in a manner such as to play one's part in this great scheme, to perform one's duty and, therefore, to use the fan.

The monk's question is an analogue of Dōgen's own kōan: if the Dharma nature is already accomplished, eternal and omnipresent, why is there any need to practise? The master fanning himself is Dōgen's answer. The Buddha Dao may be perfect, beyond time and conditions, but it has a Li. We also have a duty to perform in order to play our proper part, otherwise there is no point in it. To know about dancing, but never dance, or to know about swimming yet never get in the water, is sterile knowledge, merely academic. We have this astonishing possibility of a human life – why waste it?

The Dharma nature penetrates everywhere in order that we may act in accordance with it, by fulfilling our allotted part, free from show and pretence, and thus be liberated from delusion ourselves and a service to all sentient beings. This is not a matter of doing a practice in order to get something to satisfy body or mind; that itself is delusion, just chasing after indulgence or

1 Brazier 2013.

after credentials in the hope that these will prove that one is a real person. To practise is to fulfil one's part in the scheme, to dance one's steps in the dance: then one is a real 'person without credentials'.[2]

The Buddha Dao is the dance, but for the dance to mean anything one has to get up and let one's partner lead one round the floor, not simply sit and watch. One's partner here is the myriadfold 'Dharma that is other than self'.

The monk's bow is not only a matter of acknowledging the strength of the master's argument. It is also itself an example of Dao Li. It is a natural expression of respect. The monk is, therefore, doing his duty (Li) in relation to the Buddha Dao and so playing his part (kōan).

XIV.2 DISCUSSION

WHAT IS THE PRIEST HOLDING ONTO?

When the monk asks what the master is holding onto, he is asking if he is still attached to things and, therefore, still in need of training, which is to say, not yet enlightened. The implication is that when one understands, one does not need to practise – the 'original enlightenment' question once again. The master, however, replies that it is not like that. When one understands then one knows what one has to do and the important thing is to do it. Simply knowing about universal Buddha nature or non-duality or natural enlightenment is like knowing about a journey, but never going on it.

THE MEANING OF THE FAN

The story does not tell us what the master was using the fan for. One might assume that he was cooling himself on a hot day. However, we should not mistake the code. Buddhist masters often carry and use a fan. The fan is not just used for cooling the skin. The fan is also a symbol of modesty. When the teacher

2 Master Linji (Rinzai) famously said: "Within the flesh body there is a true man of no status." See e.g. Chang, Chung-Yuan 1969. *Original Teachings of Ch'an Buddhism*, New York: Pantheon: 120.

gives a particularly potent teaching, such as when transmitting the precepts, he may cover his face with the fan. This is to indicate that this transmission is not coming from the human person of the master, but from the *sambhogakaya* of Buddha. A fan, therefore, symbolizes the occlusion of the personal ego.

The monk's question can, therefore, also be construed as "Is it the case that you still have an ego that needs to be occluded?" In other words, if one really understands that the Dao Li is everywhere and always, then is it not true that it is in oneself also and if that is the case, surely one does not need to hide one's nature? However, the master demonstrates that it is by both being human *and* using a fan that the Dharma *is* demonstrated in the world of conditions. The enactment of the Dharma is not merely the existence of the unconditioned, it is the fact that it penetrates and pervades and so has effect. Thus, it is not that the conditioned nature is evil and must be eliminated, nor is it that the ultimate must so prevail that no conditioned nature subsists. The Dharma is the unconditioned in the conditioned. It is the master using the fan.

The fan is a ritual object. So the question of the passing monk is like the assertion that Buddhism is not a religion because it is about non-duality and the reply of the master confirms that it is a religion – the ritual objects, such as the fan, must be used, and used in the right way – precisely because, just as yin and yang are non-dual, the non-dual manifests as yin and yang. Li, remember, fundamentally means the correct usage of ritual objects, which is religion. To reduce Buddhism to a philosophy is to lose the religious consciousness and thereby render it academic, not vital.

The fan, therefore, is a symbol of self-effacement. For the master, there is no conflict between acting naturally and acting dutifully or ritualistically. One does not have to be the composer of the music for it to be natural to join in the dance.

The fan covers the face and is equivalent to the 'darkening' of self. By putting the fan in front of the face, the master conveys a message of putting himself out, which is one of the meanings of nirodha in the four truths spoken by Buddha, as discussed earlier. It is *nirodha* that converts desire and passion (*duḥkha-*

samudaya) into the path of enlightenment (*mārga*). The Li of the Buddha Dao is the eightfold path and in Dōgen's scheme of things this is enacted in a pure form in the highly ritualized regime of the Zen monastic community.

CONSCIOUS OR UNCONSCIOUS

Does this mean that, before the monk came along, the master was conscious of fanning as a symbol of Dharma practice, or that he was himself reflecting the light of all the Buddhas? No and yes. Perhaps he was just fanning himself because it was a hot day, or, perhaps, he was using the fan in a ritual. He might have been consciously aware of the symbolic meaning at the time or not. It does not matter. Enlightenment is not a matter of being aware of everything all the time. It is enough that the symbolic meaning was there – one does not need to be constantly self-consciously aware. Sometimes the master might have used the fan as a conscious and deliberate teaching strategy and sometimes he might not have, yet either would have been a lesson, nonetheless. He would, certainly, have known about the meaning of a fan and the symbolism of wind and so on, so that when the monk spoke it was not like hearing a foreign language. They both knew the code.

Consciousness often goes hand in hand with affectation. The goal is to live the Dharma in an uncontrived way, in the bones rather than in the head. Consciousness may sometimes be a temporary means, a stage in learning, but it is not a goal in itself. In the realized state, self-consciousness falls away and consciousness is merely a component of experience. When one acts in a straightforward, pure-hearted way, it is not particularly conscious. When one is completely familiar with something, one does not have to keep thinking about it all the time. Thus what is transmitted is not self-conscious knowledge or self-conscious action. The master was not self-consciously fanning himself. What is transmitted is the natural, spontaneous behaviour of Buddhists that makes the universal radiance manifest. The Dharma is declared in the lived life.

RIGHT TRANSMISSION

This story has shown us an instance of 'transmission'. What does it consist of?

At the beginning of the exchange, the monk invites the master into an intellectual game, but by the end, this has been replaced by an enactment. When the monk understands, he bows to the ground. Like using the fan, prostrations are acts of self-effacement. They express the monk's love and respect for, and gratitude to the master, but here the master is only a channel for the eternal, another dewdrop reflecting. The monk is both bowing to the omnipresent Buddha and inspired to do so by the entry of the same love and Dharma light into himself. People say much about breaking down the barrier between self and other, but the useful meaning of this idea is that it is all reflecting Dharma. I am me, and you are you, and we are both dewdrops reflecting the same vast universe of eternal light. This is to awaken to faith in the Great Way.

The master demonstrates Li. The disciple bows, thereby also demonstrating Li. So in this meeting they become identical. They are not identical in height, weight, health or body. They are not identical in character, habits or mind. All that falls away. They are identical in enacting their parts in accordance with the Buddha Dao. This is kōan and, therefore, kōan, in Dōgen's sense, *is* transmission.

XV

LINES 75–7: ALL THE WAY TO HEAVEN

75. The proof of the Buddha Dharma, the living path of right transmission, is like this.
76. As for the idea of not using a fan since wind is 'always abiding', it does not comprehend 'always abiding' nor 'wind nature'.
77. 'Wind nature always abiding' (*fū shō jō jū*) means that the breeze blowing from the House of Buddha brings forth a golden age on earth and ripens the ambrosia in heaven.

xv.1 COMMENTARY

Buddha Dharma is not just an idea or philosophy, not just an intellectual pursuit; it is a living transmission, and simply knowing Buddhist principles will not enable one to participate in that transmission. In particular, the idea that the truth is everywhere is just a sterile idea unless it enters into one and gives one a part to play in the Buddha's great work of bringing to fruition the golden potential of earth and the silver riches of heaven.

xv.2 DISCUSSION

ALWAYS ABIDING

'Always abiding' refers to the eternal nature of the Buddha Dao. It is the unborn, undying. However, that does not separate it from the world of birth and death, the yin-yang world. Dao is yin-yang. It is the pathos of life. To live it is to experience that pathos fully. It is not a matter of cutting ourselves off from flowers falling and weeds proliferating. It is, on the contrary, such cutting-off that is delusion and that renders life half-hearted and hesitant.

Fu shō, the unborn, refers to the fact that enlightenment is not born out of delusion. Its past is the eternal existence of all the Buddhas. Similarly, *fu metsu*, the deathless, means that enlightenment does not turn back into delusion. This being so, enlightenment and delusion are two completely separate species of being. Although they are completely separate, the first can and does penetrate and completely pervade the second, and thus gives meaning, colour and bitter-sweet feeling to life.

The monk is asking: "Isn't knowing about Buddha Dao enough?", and the master answers: "Buddha Dao has its Li." So it is not that one has to practise in order to attain to the Buddha Dao; it is that the Buddha Dao inevitably expresses itself as practice. Practice is not a path to enlightenment, but the expression or celebration of enlightenment, a celebration that involves tears of sadness and joy.

GOLD AND SILVER

The text of line 77 is another play on words with a multiplicity of subtle allusions. It is impossible to translate completely as it mixes metaphors that are not fully present in English language and Western culture.

Firstly, there is a metaphor relating to the maturing of milk into a variety of wholesome products – various forms of yoghurt, cheeses and cream drinks, which I have rendered as 'ambrosia', because it is in heaven and ambrosia is the drink of the gods.

Secondly, there is the "breeze blowing from the house of Buddha". The 'house of Buddha' means Buddha's disciples and devotees. The image here probably draws upon the Shinto notion of the *kami kaze* – the divine wind – which is the influence of the gods here on earth. Here the 'Dharma wind' matures the trainees, just as milk matures into ambrosia.

Thirdly, the great band of stars across the night sky is, in Chinese, called the 'long river' or 'silver river'. Interestingly, in English, we refer to it as the Milky Way. There is an implicit mirroring of silver and gold, both of which are also metals that, when polished, do function as mirrors.

Fourthly, gold does have the same double meaning in English in phrases like 'a golden age'. So there is an implication here that those who practise the Dharma by playing their part in it contribute to the coming of such a golden age on earth.

Fifthly, in Chinese folklore, the Silver River (the Milky Way) contrasts with the earthly Yellow River (or Golden River), which is one of the great rivers of China. These two rivers – the silver one in the sky and the golden one on earth – are seen as the major dividers of their respective domains. So, here again, in the last lines, we have another of Dōgen's yin-yang images. The silver sky is yang and the golden earth is yin, again making a complete circle representing perfection.

In folklore, the place where the two rivers meet is more or less equivalent to 'the end of the rainbow' in Western folklore: a place of plenty, harmony and consummation. There are folk stories of people riding a raft or sailboat to such a place. So these two rivers encompass romance and dreams. The perfect circle manifests as the world of multitudinous passions.

Sixthly, the golden earth also echoes the golden ground of the Pure Land in the Amida-kyō, the Smaller Pure Land Sūtra, so that there is here again another answer to Hōnen, with Dōgen claiming that the satori of Zen is also a way to enter the Pure Land, which can also be equated to the place where the two rivers meet. In the Larger Pure Land Sūtra, the Buddha's disciple Ānanda has a vision of the Pure Land and in the Contemplation Sūtra, Queen Vaidehī does so, thus demonstrating that ordained, and lay, men and women were capable of such visions in the time of Buddha.

The gold and silver rivers play a significant role in Chinese romantic fiction. Generally the lovers have, at some point, to get to the other side of the golden river, whose waves are difficult to cross. Star-crossed lovers have their heavenly equivalent, or echo, who also have similar problems crossing the Silver

River. So, in a certain way, Dōgen's final references are a bit as though he were alluding to Romeo and Juliet.

These images of silver and gold are metaphors, but there is also a touch of literalness about them. Dōgen is talking about a change in how we actually perceive the world. When kōan occurs there is genjō, which is a real change of perception and appearance. After satori everything looks different. Psychologically, we can say that this is because of a change of preoccupation, or, rather, because of a falling away of our previous preoccupation with and projection of self. Metaphorically, we can say that we are now outside, or looking outside, rather than always indoors in the little rooms of self. We now perceive a vast vista and find it good. This is the actual experience of satori.

Dōgen is advocating that each person live according to Li, and thus play his or her part in such a vision of silver and gold – a world where we all benefit one another naturally by living in accordance with the Buddha Dao. Dōgen's mirror metaphor tells us that this benefitting of others is not a function of the power or personality of the person in question. The person does become a vehicle for the reflection of the Dharma light, but this is because he lets his own self become dark, so that his being becomes like the dewdrop reflecting the moon. Modesty, faith and non-artificiality constitute the requisite Li to generate what Dōgen calls kōan.

The behaviour of a truly religious person is naturally and spontaneously good. This natural spontaneity means that it flows directly from experience without artificial contrivance. Thus, to see a situation and then think, "I should do something compassionate here. What compassionate thing shall I do?" is not the way because it is artificial, self-conscious and contrived. The person who is in the Dao simply sees the situation and does something and what they do could be called a compassionate act if seen by an observer, but the wayfarer is probably not particularly conscious that what they have done is compassionate; he or she just did what seemed to be needed.

LIVING THE LIFE

For the person who has been penetrated by the Dharma, the Buddhas are always present – as present as the air – no matter what domain one is passing through at the time. The Dharma is always present. There is no place that Buddha and Dharma do not reach. This is the eternal life of the Tathāgata.

However, one can understand intellectually that the Buddhas and the Dharma are everywhere present and still think in a way that is about gaining things for the self. When one does so the doctrine is just a clever idea. It does not penetrate because one's appreciation of the ubiquitous and eternal presence is just conceptual. One is still caught up in creating and destroying – *shō* and *metsu* – and has not understood *fu shō, fu metsu*. In *Genjō Kōan, fu shō* and *fu metsu* manifest in *shō* and *metsu*.

The moon is always shining but we are too attached to our little sparkle of cleverness to create the conditions in which it can penetrate, pervade and reflect. It is not that there is anything wrong with thought as such – it is vitally useful – but it should not be a substitute for life. Having a supreme idea – even the idea of original enlightenment – is no substitute for living the life. Instead of allowing oneself to be bowled over by the glory of the presence of Buddha in every atom and moment of one's life, one is still just gathering ideas in a selfish spirit, motivated by a desire to make one's own mind and body stand out. By treating the Dharma as a commodity one keeps the knowledge at a distance. This is a reductive manoeuvre, in which abstract knowledge is substituted for real religious experience. Such intellection prevents the Dharma from penetrating. It keeps it as a commodity to be used by one's mind. The purpose of the Dharma reaching everywhere is to allow one to practise. There is no point in finding it if one is not going to participate in it.

When the wind arrives, it stirs. The Buddha wind transforms the earth. When it reaches you it makes you do things. The Dharma lacks for nothing yet needs something. It needs you.

PART FOUR

POSTSCRIPTS AND AFTERTHOUGHTS

I

WHAT *GENJŌ KŌAN* PROPOSES

The underlying message of *Genjō Kōan* is identical to that of Śākyamuni Buddha: take refuge and go forth. Taking refuge means living a life of faith in the world as it actually is. Thus, in a later talk, Dōgen echoed *Genjō Kōan*, saying "Enter the grass (weeds), and transmit the wind",[1] thus capturing the top and tail of *Genjō Kōan*. Further, refuge is the moon entering and pervading. It is not a function of the mirror except in that the reflecting medium – ourselves – is required to be still and receptive. In more common Western religious language we could say, stand in awe before the holy and let it do what it wilt. The holy – the Buddhadharma – is not created by oneself – no deluded thought could give rise to the unconditioned: "The host is there from the beginning while the guest is in *shashu*."[2] *Shashu* is the gesture that goes with the posture of attending. What it will do is send one forth to transmit the 'wind'. One will then live a vigorous life, doing the Buddha's bidding. Such a life will be both completely independent, in that one will not follow fashion, and completely submissive, since one will serve the Buddha Dao. However, the Buddha Dao can never be reduced to a fixed formula, dogma or protocol.

Therefore, one is to wait upon instruction. Things become clear though the self-revelation of the Dharma of all Dharmas

---

1 Leighton and Okumura 2004: 97.
2 Leighton and Okumura 2004: 96.

itself, which happens all the time through the miscellaneous circumstances of daily life, if we are willing to be open to them in that way. Such circumstances rouse us and make emotions flow.

> Even if awakened, the cold wind blows and chills me, and I don't know for whom the bright moon is white.[3]

It is easy for us to make the mistake of thinking that results flow from our own power and wisdom, but the light comes from the moon. "A white heron stands in the snow, but they are not the same colour".[4] This last is a reference also to a Chinese text, the Jewel Mirror Samadhi.[5] Even if, as a snowy egret, one were nearly as white as the moon, one can never take its place. The simple message here is "Don't play God."

In Dōgen, to do one's duty in relation to the Dharma and to be natural are essentially the same thing, since the Dharma is reality. Living in a vigorous, yet unpretentious manner is not a matter of being or becoming something, nor even of not becoming something, since all our efforts to make ourselves into something are bound to be based on delusion. So practice is simply a matter of doing one's natural duty without fuss. When one does so, things happen, and what does happen is the wondrous penetration of Dharma into the infinite diversity of conditioned existence. By being what one truly is one's being becomes a display of truth. This may seem tautologous, but it has manifold practical implications. Further, in Dōgen's schema, what one is cannot be extracted and isolated from the concrete situation that one is inhabiting for the time being. One's times are one's being and one has to act accordingly. This means that while broad principles can be enunciated, they are never final or absolute. It is not a matter of arriving at the right formulation, but of learning to enter into the rite of life and dance with the music.

Conditioned and unconditioned are as different as fish and fowl, and one cannot make itself into the other. Still, an amazing transformation can occur which is like the sudden appearance of

---

3 Leighton and Okumura 2004: 98.

4 Leighton and Okumura 2004: 98.

5 銀碗盛雪 明月藏鷺 類而不斉 混則知處: "A silver bowl full of snow / a white egret hidden in the moonlight / these are not the same / comparing them we can appreciate our own place" (my translation).

the moon reflected in a dewdrop. It is nonetheless quite possible for this transformation to go completely unnoticed because its result is that one simply lives one's life and does one's duty in a completely natural way, free from any kind of pretension.

In *Genjō Kōan*, Dōgen begins by making a distinction between, on the one hand, Buddhism as a practice in which people exercise their own will in order to create a salvation for themselves and, on the other, Buddhism as a mode of being in which one is everywhere confronted by Dharma that is 'other than self'. One might initially assume that he is going to declare one of these – probably the second – as superior and then describe how to attain it. However, he does not do that. Rather, he says that the Buddha Dao is big enough to encompass all such seeming opposites. In a way this gives a sense of non-duality, but it is a non-duality that encompasses and includes duality, so much so that every instance of either part of the yin-yang cycle comes to be seen as an instance of the Buddha Dao itself.

Buddhism is a teaching for those caught in the cycling of birth and death, and it offers not so much a way out into a domain of non-creation and non-destruction – the birthless and deathless state that is nirvāṇa – but rather a way of being in birth and death with all its joys and sorrows, yet still pervaded by Dharma.

Dōgen is impressed by the fact that if the birthless *is* birthless then it cannot possibly be a function or result of any conditions established in the realm of birth and death. If it were so, it would be just as much subject to conditions and ephemeral as they are. He, therefore, first shows us that the two domains of saṃsāra and nirvāṇa are as different as wood and ash. However, he then has to explain how one domain enters and pervades the other. At first sight, it appears that for a deluded being to become an enlightened one is as difficult as for a fish to become a bird.

Dōgen, therefore, has recourse to the well-established Buddhist image of the moon reflecting in water. He tells us that you can certainly work on yourself and make improvements in your character, but enlightenment will not come through any such accumulation of good characteristics. Dharma is the moon. We are the water. Enlightenment is the one shining on the other. We might be only the tiniest drop, but if we become still, the whole moon and sky will reflect in us. This glorious image has a considerable number of implications, some of which may appear startling.

1. The effort that one must make is not to enhance oneself, but to efface oneself.
2. The moon-light of Dharma can reflect in people of any character.
3. One will not necessarily know as personal knowledge that one is enlightened.
4. It is more important that others see the Dharma in one than that one see it oneself.
5. The Dharma is not obtained by trying to obtain it.
6. The Dharma that others see in a sage is not a characteristic of the sage.
7. The Dharma nature has neither beginning nor end, but is not static.
8. One participates in it when it penetrates one.

Thus, what is required of practitioners is not that they reform themselves into a particular type of person, nor that they get the right idea, but rather that they all simply play their allotted parts unassumingly. Thus, Dōgen, who was himself the master of the monastery, always wore the black kimono of a junior monk. This was his way of actualizing in his time the essential nature of the life of the *bhikṣu* from Buddha's time, who was expected to subsist upon whatever was put into his bowl. We can say that the prescription is to live to the full, but to live lightly and accept what comes.

True to his principle that there can be no causal relationship between saṃsāric effort and nirvāṇic arrival, Dōgen concludes that all developments are included within the Buddha Dao, and, therefore, the thing to do is to live completely the state that you are in for the time being. This includes emotional vicissitudes. You cannot possibly know how to transform from fish to fowl, but if the fish are truly and completely fish, totally free from affectation, then they may well, surprisingly, find themselves to have become birds, or may even have become birds without noticing.

Another way of thinking of this is to consider life to be a ritual or dance. Whatever station in life you find yourself in, it will have its own 'music', and there will be corresponding steps or ways of right performance. This is called Li. The important thing is to conform to Li. This is a fine metaphor because when a ritual is properly performed, the sacred appears. The people performing the ritual may be ordinary people of no great individual virtue, but when they act in harmony together, the sacred appears. Dōgen says that this is exactly like the moon appearing in water when the water is dark and the sky is bright.

In the matter of the moon appearing in water we can see:

1. The moon is never part of the water.
2. The moon does not get wet.
3. The appearance is sudden.
4. The water does not create the moon.
5. The moon was there before the water and will be there after the water.
6. It does not matter how big or small the body of water is.
7. The more humble the water, i.e. the further it places itself below the moon, the deeper the reflection will be.

Thus Dōgen shows how knowledge is not enough and one needs to practise; yet it is not the case that practice *causes* enlightenment. Enlightenment is caused by the light that is already there. However, practice brings one to a halt. This stopping is the sign of enlightenment. It makes one into a beacon for the world. In true dialectical form, however, this stopping does not hold us still, but sends us forth.

Genjō Kōan begins by asserting the Buddha Dao. Dōgen then establishes an orientation to practice in which it is the Buddhas who are enlightening us rather than we who are enlightening others. In *Yui Butsu Yo Butsu* Dōgen tells us that the experience of enlightenment is nothing like what we might expect, and that the thoughts that we have before enlightenment in no way contribute to enlightenment happening. His image of the mirror in *Genjō Kōan* makes clear how this is so. What one sees when looking into water that is clear to the bottom is quite different from what one sees when the water is dark and the sky is reflected. The person who is trying to contrive enlightenment for himself is like one trying to see all the way to the bottom or to see just the right combination of fish. However, when one sees to the bottom the sky is invisible. However, the sky, heaven, *kū*, is still there and, as a matter of fact, if it were not, one could not see anything at all.

When the self is known for what it is, it is forgotten. It no longer fascinates or troubles. It becomes the dark side of the water. The water becoming dark makes it into a mirror of the radiance. Such illumination occurs all at once, just as the reflection appears suddenly. It is not constructed and not piecemeal. Just as the reflection depends upon the stillness and darkness of the water, so enlightenment depends upon rigorous effort in the practice of deep stillness that Dōgen calls zazen.

Dōgen's central metaphor, of reflection that only occurs when one side is dark, is a brilliant modification of the already established Buddhist trope of the mirror mind. It provides a picture of the mechanism by which other-power – 'the moon', representing the Dharma nature, the Dharma of the myriad Buddhas, the Buddhas of the myriad Dharmas – combines with the Buddhist teaching of self-effacement. It unifies stillness and effort. It shows how enlightenment cuts through karma without destroying its inexorable hold upon us. The practitioner, by adopting the yin position in relation to the yang radiance of the ever-shining, but generally unseen, Dharma, sets up a situation where that radiance enters him and reflects upon the world, without the practitioner himself necessarily even being aware that it is happening. This is a wonderful resolution of the self-power/other-power problem as well as being a solution of Dōgen's own doubt about the function of practice in a universe in which the Dharma nature is already omnipresent. Omnipresent it may be, but mere knowledge of that fact does not suffice. The Dao functions everywhere, calling us to join the dance (Li). Performing this rite allows Dharma to appear. When lived, this practice makes us into 'Buddhas together with Buddhas', whether we have conscious knowledge of it or not, and this gracious condition is the fulfilment of perfect community.

Dōgen paints image after image of the totality of imperfection constituting perfection, yin and yang together constituting the Dao, the upper realm and the lower constituting the complete circle. He helps us to get a sense of this bigger picture, yet even more, he advocates that we play our part in it by accepting the lot that we have, whatever it may be, just as he himself had done in China, for it is only in doing so that we ourselves become instances of genjō kōan.

So it is not so much that one gets something as that one returns to being natural and less worried (or not at all worried) about self. Dōgen says in *Yui Butsu Yo Butsu*:

> whenever we feel that we are useless, there is something that we should know; namely, that we have been afraid of becoming small.[6]

In *Genjō Kōan*, he tells us that even the smallest dewdrop is a sufficient mirror. When we are proud, the light of self is shining and preventing us from becoming the dark side of the mirror, and that is our basic mistake.

The Chinese sense that the original nature of things is best shines through. However, here we do not see the original nature of the person asserted as original enlightenment. Even less do we see an advocacy of a Rousseauesque return to nature or of a living out of the inner child. Dōgen's work is an invitation to spiritual maturity.

Dōgen is acutely aware of the obtuse nature of human character. Nonetheless, the Dharma is all around us in myriad forms. To play one's original part is what is required for the Dharma nature to do its part. All this requires faith. Since "the self does not need to know All Buddhas" (line 10), a great deal has to be taken on trust. However, it is that trust, or faith, that makes all this possible.

Dōgen went to China wanting to get something for himself. There, however, he came to trust Rujing. That faith blossomed and when it did so everything fell into place. He had the kind

6 In Nishijima and Cross 1994, vol. 4: 213–20.

of turning point in his understanding and perception of things that occurs when one realizes that it is the boat that is moving and not the shore. Body is impermanent and unreliable. Mind is impermanent and unreliable. Yet all around us are the treasures of the Dharma. Dōgen then got on a real boat and sped back to Japan and tried to get his new understanding accepted. This was a long struggle in which he was successful only to a limited degree. In China he had had to accept demotion, and in Japan his hopes were also thwarted, yet, because he accepted his lot, he was able to establish a remarkable monastic tradition and produce some of the world's most wonderful spiritual writing that continues to fascinate us to this day. Now, 800 years later, he is suddenly becoming more widely studied at last.

II

A PERSONAL NOTE

I did not plan to write this book. It crept up on me. I was in the middle of revising some notes on *Genjō Kōan* when I was struck down by a severe pulmonary embolism. Without modern medical intervention I might well have died. After a period in hospital I had a year of convalescence. My work on the text gradually grew and became more and more fascinating and rewarding. Initially I undertook it solely for my own benefit and understanding, but gradually it became apparent that the resulting work might be publishable.

I have been practising and studying Buddhism for more than half a century. I began in my adolescence when I was in search of an explanation for religious experiences that I had had as a child. Spiritual light had certainly fallen upon me in unmistakeable ways, but this left me longing for understanding. My habit of being a copious reader of spiritual books thus started at a young age, and in Buddhism and other Eastern religions I seemed to find answers to some of my questions. In my early twenties I lived in Cambridge, and there studied *samatha* meditation with Nai Boonman, a teacher from Myanmar, sat at the feet of Chogyam Trungpa Rinpoche, the controversial, highly gifted Tibetan lama, and listened to weekly lectures by representatives of a wide variety of different schools of Buddhism. In due course I became chair of the Cambridge Buddhist Society and in that capacity heard that Jiyu Kennett Rōshi, an English Zen teacher who had trained in Japan, was returning to England and would be offering *sesshin* – 'heart searching' – retreats. I promptly signed up and had a never-to-be-forgotten two-week experience of undiluted Sōtō Zen in Gloucestershire. The rōshi's lectures were based on Dōgen and I have been fascinated by his work ever since.

Jiyu Kennett Rōshi was then in the full flush of the inspiration she had received in Japan. I think that there was nobody on that retreat in Gloucestershire who was not significantly changed by the experience. I became a disciple. From Rōshi Kennett I learnt the life of a Zen *unsui*. Rōshi Kennett was deeply respectful of the teachings of Dōgen, translated many of them, and among these teachings regarded *Genjō Kōan* as particularly important. Later I was to study with other teachers in other traditions, but Dōgen has always remained a singularly significant star in my firmament.

As I got older and more experienced I wrote books and started to be invited to teach. I have found myself making a substantial number of visits to the Far East, especially Japan and Korea. These visits have been eye-opening in many ways. It became apparent to me, going back and forth between East and West, that Buddhism in the West has evolved in a distinctive way that has, as all variations tend to do, some advantages and some drawbacks, some insights and some blind spots. Naturally enough, we have tended to take Buddhism and fit it into our established categories – a bit like trying to put a square peg into a round hole – and we have asked Buddhism to answer the perennial questions of our own culture and spirituality, many of which were not questions of any relevance in the cultures within which Buddhism originated and was formed. Sometimes this cross-fertilization has been fruitful. Sometimes it has led to considerable distortion of the original message. Perhaps we have too much expected Buddhism to change in order to suit us, rather than allowing ourselves to be changed by Buddhism, or perhaps this is a necessary phase that we must pass through.

As we have become more and more a consumerist society, we have come to expect that things will be shaped to suit us. Our self, our preferences and our identity become the measures of all things, and we tend to choose a religion, if we do, in much the same self-serving way as we might choose a car or a music system. Buddhism becomes another consumable item. This, however, is almost exactly the attitude that Dōgen wanted to eliminate. Buddhism is intended to bring about a change, an enlightenment, in those who practise. That awakening experience is the main subject of *Genjō Kōan*.

Working on this book has itself been an intense practice. Coming as it did in my period of illness, it was accompanied by many personal reflections upon impermanence and the deeper meaning of life. Pulmonary embolism means blood clots in the lungs. The clots, however, do not form in the lungs; they move there from the legs. They form in the legs due to restriction of circulation. My letter of discharge from hospital says that the likely cause is excessive practice of zazen!

There is no doubt that Dōgen was an extreme enthusiast for zazen practice. He wrote:

> After hearing [of the importance of meditation] from the instruction of my former teacher of T'ien-t'ung, I practised zazen day and night. When other monastics gave up zazen temporarily for fear that they might fall ill at the time of extreme heat or cold, I thought to myself: 'I should still devote myself to zazen even to the point of death from disease...' Thinking thus continually, I resolutely sat in zazen day and night, and no illness came at all.[1]

However, Dōgen died young at the age of 53, unexpectedly, of a mysterious illness that could not be cured by the medicine of his day. Given my own circumstance, I cannot help but wonder if it was his over-zealous pursuit of zazen that killed him in the same way that it nearly did me.

1 Etō Sokuō, Shūso to shite no Dōgen zenji: 162–3, quoted in Kim 2004: 51.

III

THE ZAZEN QUESTION

It is apparent that Dōgen was devoted to zazen. He advocates it strongly as a major element in the training and practice that he offers at his monastery. At times you get the impression that he thinks that zazen is the be-all-and-end-all of Zen and of Buddhism. However, those times are rare. In *Genjō Kōan* he does not mention it, nor does it occur in the vast majority of his major writings. Modern commentators are almost invariably keen to interpret these works as making reference to zazen, but sometimes this seems somewhat forced. Clearly there is a paradox here.

In *Fukanzazengi*, Dōgen reminds us that Śākyamuni meditated for six years. However, this must refer to his period of asceticism, a period which he, Śākyamuni, later renounced as having been vain and futile. Also, it is by no means clear that Śākyamuni did spend all of that time doing zazen as narrowly defined. It seems much more likely that he spent it doing a diversity of ascetic yogas. It seems unlikely that Dōgen wants us to identify the term zazen with self-starvation, walking on coals, or anything of the kind. However, it is possible that Dōgen did have a much broader definition of zazen than we generally imagine. The fact that he describes one method in *Fukanzazengi* need not imply that his understanding of the term was limited to that. When he says that all the spiritual ancestors did zazen, he may well be including all forms of religious contemplation. Only then could his statement be accurate.

He also reminds us of Bodhidharma's nine years spent facing a wall. This, however, must refer to Bodhidharma's period of retreat after arriving in China when he was, presumably, already enlightened. There is a mythology around this and it figures as a powerful symbol, but should not be taken too literally.

In Dōgen's descriptions of monastic life, zazen appears as one element, but the emphasis is upon an all-encompassing regulation of behaviour. The two major references to zazen in the body of his major texts are both, in a sense, negative. One is his repeated reference to the story of Baso and Nangaku, in which the punch line is that one cannot make a Buddha by meditating, and the other is his encounter with the cook from Ayuwang Mountain Monastery, to whom he suggests that doing zazen might be more important than buying mushrooms and is told that he is completely mistaken.

Again, we sometimes have the impression that he is telling us that all the Zen ancestors became enlightened by means of the practice of zazen. However, in the *Denkōroku*, written by his successor Keizan, there are few if any accounts of people becoming enlightened while meditating. Mostly they become so in the course of an interpersonal encounter, and it is not at all clear that in all cases the person being illuminated had been an ardent practitioner of meditation prior to the meeting. What appears as more important in most cases is the relation with the teacher. Dōgen also refers to this factor much more in his writings than he does to sitting meditation.

If we consider the case of Huineng, for instance, it is not at all clear whether he was a practitioner of meditation before he became enlightened by hearing a man reciting the Diamond Sūtra in the street. He rushed to the monastery and the abbot did not send him to the meditation hall, or even to the library. He set him to pound rice for a few months before transmitting the Dharma. Zazen there may have been, but it does not figure with any prominence.

In Dōgen's own case, it is apparent that he threw himself into the practice while at Tiantong monastery, but his actual awakening experience came when he heard Rujing reprimanding the monk sitting next to him. One can read a good deal into this incident and never be quite sure what is the correct interpretation. It seems to me that Rujing believed in the value of zazen, wanted his disciples to practise ardently, and showed his care for them by doing so himself and remonstrating with them so that they did likewise. It is certainly credible that what really impressed Dōgen was the old man's dedication and love in continuing thus at great cost to his own body and mind despite his advanced age. Rujing let body and mind fall away by exerting himself strenuously on behalf of others. This happened to be through the medium of doing and fostering zazen, but is there any reason to think that the practice being zazen specifically mattered that much? Could any other practice have been as effective?

If we consider another practice, such as calling the name of Buddha, which was and still is a highly popular practice in Japanese Buddhism, it is not that clear where Dōgen stood on the matter. On one occasion he derides it, likening it to the croaking of frogs.[1] However, nearer to the end of his life he recommends it and says that one should call out the refuge in Buddha so devotedly that one hopes to continue doing so in the bardo stage between lives. Did Dōgen change his mind? Or in his reference to frogs was he only criticizing those who did the practice in an empty-headed fashion?

It is evident that Dōgen practised zazen and encouraged others to do so. At the same time it is also evident that he wanted his disciples to understand Buddhist teaching in depth and in a manner that was not widely appreciated in his time. His voluminous writings would be completely unnecessary if all that was needed was to sit in zazen. What he is recommending is religious contemplation under a competent teacher in a Buddhist context. However, he also believes competent teachers to be exceedingly few and far between.

There is a tendency in our contemporary world to treat meditation as a kind of treatment of a quasi-medicinal nature. Doing a practice of mindfulness will, it is proposed, cure one of a wide range of maladies. From the perspective of Dōgen, this

---

1 In *Bendōwa*, though this text was only discovered in the seventeenth century.

is surely misguided on at least two counts. Firstly, for Dōgen, the purpose of religious contemplation is to set oneself in the right relation to the Buddha and that right relation is that one be still, receptive and humble. It has nothing to do with gaining something for the sake of body or of mind. Secondly, Dōgen does not present zazen as a remedy or technique that has an intrinsic effectiveness like taking a pill. He presents it as a way of enacting one's part vis-à-vis the Dharma. It is, essentially, a form of worship.

How, then, should one understand *Genjō Kōan*? In *Genjō Kōan*, zazen is not mentioned either directly or obliquely. What is described is a path of humility or 'darkening of self' that permits the light of the Dharma to so reflect within one that there is an illumination of the world. There is no reason to doubt that zazen could be a significant element in such a path. At the same time, there is plenty of reason to suppose that we are here talking about a whole way of life and not simply one activity within it. Again, if *Genjō Kōan* were taken on its own, one would not naturally assume that the practice of zazen was implied. Yet this is Dōgen's foundational text describing how satori happens.

These days, zazen is popular, and the interest in Dōgen is substantially sustained by this popularity. Dōgen is famous as the great advocate of zazen even though only a tiny proportion of his writings speak of it directly. There is, therefore, a strong tendency for interpreters to read zazen into everything that Dōgen wrote. For instance, if you look in the index of the four volumes of the Nishijima and Cross translation of *Shōbōgenzō*, you will find a great many references to zazen. However, if you look these up, you will find that almost all of them are references to the editors' notes, not to Dōgen's text.

The implicit assumption in the contemporary reading of Dōgen, therefore, is that zazen is at the unspoken heart of everything that he says. However, although there may be some truth in that, there would be even more truth in the assumption that implicit in all his work is the act of taking refuge in Buddha, Dharma and Sangha. Fundamentally, Dōgen's opus rests upon a faith commitment. Thus, while *Genjō Kōan* may obliquely give us some hints that may help our zazen practice, it certainly does advance ideas of direct relevance to understanding what taking refuge might mean. Indeed, the whole notion of darkening the self so that the Dharma light may enter can be read as a direct commentary upon taking refuge. If there really is one central practice that underlies the whole of his work, it is this.

No doubt we shall continue to assume that the practice of zazen lies in the background of everything that Dōgen said and wrote, but if one takes a text such as *Genjō Kōan* with an open mind, one finds a brilliant piece of generic spiritual writing whose central message goes well beyond any one religious practice. It would be a shame if this message were confined within a sectarian boundary or limited to proponents of a single practice when the content of the work as it stands speaks a universal spiritual language, relevant to all Buddhists certainly, and to followers of some other religious paths too.

There are few religious geniuses who have had such a wide scope to their thought yet who have just as much concerned themselves with the fine detail. It is fitting in some ways that Dōgen is regarded as the founder of Sōtō Zen, since so much of his energy and time went into training a cadre of successors and establishing a thorough monastic system. However, he himself regarded the notion of a Zen School as a foolish idea, and it is a shame that it tends to keep his thought within a sectarian frame. His mind encompassed something much grander than the establishment of a sect, or the propagation of a single yogic ritual practice.

Dōgen's religion was focussed on humility, learning, discipline and vigour. He was deep and thoughtful. His teaching was coherently organized around his understanding of the experience of satori, and it is that understanding that *Genjō Kōan* presents. However, this grounding, as much steeped in extensive learning as in personal experience, does not lead Dōgen to eschew the forms of the Buddhist religion; quite the opposite. For Dōgen it is ultimately a matter of taking refuge in the Three Treasures. When he did have his satori experience, his first act was to burn incense and worship Buddha. What he objects to in other forms of Buddhism is laxity and avoidance of practical application.

It would be wrong to assume that Dōgen was a doctrinal purist. His poetic style incorporates many influences and this is apparent in *Genjō Kōan*. Indeed, it is difficult to understand *Genjō Kōan* without an appreciation of Dōgen's capacity to unite diverse religious currents. This was not a purely theoretical integration so much as an expression of his own experience through the medium of different philosophical perspectives. It is the authority of experience that gives him the confidence to take such liberties with the source material.

IV

BIRTH, DEATH AND SATORI

Perhaps the biggest general shift in human consciousness in the past thousand years has been the change from looking backwards to looking forwards. The European Enlightenment and subsequent Modernism, including all our rational, socialist, capitalist, progressive, liberal, and even modern conservative social ideas, our attitude to technology, medicine, food, comfort, and all the things that impinge on ordinary life, all of this is permeated by the vague general idea of progress: a general, taken for granted, vague sense that things inevitably improve. There is, of course, quite a pile of evidence that points in the opposite direction, especially now in the domains of ecology and military technology, but this has at most only slightly dented the basic attitude that still prevails throughout our culture. The details of this matter are for other books and debates, but my concern with it here is as a window through which to look at how we interpret *Genjō Kōan*.

In the twelfth century it was natural for people to think that the past was better. For Buddhists this especially meant that the time when Buddha lived was better. For the Chinese it meant that the time of Confucius and even earlier times were better. Decay and degeneration were to be expected. Karma accumulates. "Good actions attract no retribution." When doing zazen one was not generating karma. Goodness did not contribute to the inevitable decay and so served, overall, to slow the process a little, but there was a sense that triumph is brief and death inevitable. Religion, therefore, was much concerned with the matter of death. Buddhism in Japan still is.

Most recently the belief in progress has started to waver. A sense of foreboding has crept into our consciousness as the heap of contrary evidence grows. We have not completely given up our belief in the future and, substantially, most of us still think and act as though progress is necessarily benign, but we are nowadays less certain than we were that our children will enjoy a richer and better world than we did ourselves. Increasingly, cut off from any sense of a golden age in either the past or the future, we try to live in the 'here and now'. Arguably, this is the most dangerous and least productive attitude, but it is understandable, and I do not here want to delve into a deeper assessment of whether these changes – firstly from past to future orientation, and secondly from future to present orientation – are fundamentally for the better or for the worse, merely to see how all this bears on our subject.

To many people these days, the Holy Grail is to live fully here and now. The leading apologists for Buddhism today commonly begin their submission by asserting that everybody is in search of happiness. The hope is that happiness will be found immediately or in the near future. Progress will contribute to this, so there is a confluence between material and psychological goals. We can say, perhaps, that the here and now mentality has not yet penetrated deeply and remains superimposed upon belief in progress. We believe that we can make the here and now better soon. Philosophically, this may be a contradiction of terms, but I think it represents the outlook of many people, including that of many people practising Buddhism today.

One direct result of this change in thinking has been a widespread denial of death. Dōgen thought that the most important question in Buddhism was to understand birth and death profoundly, whereas the modern attitude is, substantially, to forget about birth and death and to concentrate upon the present and the immediate future. Thus, Western teachers of Buddhism, skilfully adapting to the contemporary age, have closely identified it with living in the here and now. A quintessential example of this is what has become of 'mindfulness'. Mindfulness (*smṛti* in Sanskrit, *sati* in Pali) has come to mean 'being in the present on purpose'.[1] Mindfulness in the time of Buddha meant to keep in mind ancient wisdom. The words *smṛti* and *sati* are forms of the verb 'to remember'. Mindfulness taught by Buddha was oriented toward the past. Mindfulness as taught now is about "living in the present moment",[2] and this has become widespread and popular, indicating that this notion fits well with the spirit of our age.

So, the person who sits in zazen today probably has a very different attitude toward what he thinks he is doing than the person who sat in Dōgen's own *zendō*. The contemporary practitioner is likely to believe that what he or she is doing will aid his or her mindfulness in the modern sense, will make her happier, more effective in life and better able to manage the emotional vicissitudes that come along. These are essentially hopes for a strengthening of personal capacity. Modern people might read *Genjō Kōan* hoping to find support and advice useful for this personal project.

What were people thinking in Dōgen's own day? They will have been much more conscious of the imminence of death. They believed that the human lifespan was getting shorter. Dōgen himself died aged 53. They all had friends and relatives who had been affected by plague and by civil war. The mythology around death and the possibility of going to hell was little different in medieval Japan to medieval Europe. If people sought an increase in personal capacity at all it was not in order to live happily in the present moment, but to have the resilience to cope with what might afflict them in the nightmare conditions of the bardo between lives after this one ended. However, the general sense was that one could not hope to navigate this inter-life trial unaided: hence the value of being penetrated and pervaded by the grace of the Buddhas. What people oriented in this way would see in *Genjō Kōan* is quite different from what the modern reader is looking for.

In fact, the medieval person with a religious understanding, such as those following Dōgen, would have been likely to see the

---

1 Kabat-Zinn, Jon 1996. *Full Catastrophe Living*, London: Piatkus: 29.

2 Tart, Charles 1994. *Living the Mindful Life: A Handbook for Living in the Present Moment*, Boston, MA: Shambhala.

here and now and its attractions as a trap, sometimes terrible, sometimes honey-coated, but always dangerous. The state of being mesmerized by the here and now was what they sought release from. What is nowadays called living in the here and now would, to use one of Dōgen's images, have been seen as passing one's days watching the fish swimming in the pool and never seeing the reflection of the moon, never realizing that it was only by the light from the moon that even the fish were visible.

With this perspective we can get some idea of what satori meant and of how our modern ideas on the subject may be different. It is possible that contemporary Buddhism, while using similar forms and language, is actually a radically different religion from the one that Dōgen realized, taught and practised.

We also see a similar difference of perspective in Dōgen's handling of the issue of light and dark, or yin and yang. While it, perhaps, comes naturally to us to write 'light' first in this pairing, yin comes before yang. In medieval religion, the light came from elsewhere. In modern spirituality the emphasis is upon looking 'within'. Even 'emptiness' is to be found 'within'.[3] In Dōgen all these terms tend to point in a different direction. Darkness is not to be shunned. It is in the dark that the moon appears. It is the darkening of the glass that makes reflection possible. Disappearance is good. The inconspicuous is preferable. All of these are elements of death. Buddhist practice, here, is to practise dying. If one can die within life, then when life ends dying will not be a terror. The greatest compassion may be, therefore, to be, in a certain sense, dead, and to show that dark path to others. All of this is quite different to how we are taught to think nowadays.

Birth and death are a duality. We can say that, in a sense, in every moment, one is being born and also dying. This way of putting it seems to us to affirm a kind of dynamism that absorbs death into life. Even this is a kind of denial of death. In the classic Buddhist sense, a person is not something that is born and then dies, a person is something that *undergoes* birth and

3 E.g. Todres, L. 1999. "How Does Liberating Self-insight Become Tacit Understanding?", in *The Psychology of Awakening*, Watson, Gay, Stephen Batchelor and Guy Claxton (eds), 177–96, London: Rider.

death. We suffer birth and death, death and rebirth and death again, and so on. They happen to us. The Dao encompasses all this impermanence, and if we accept our lot as sufferers of birth and death we may become mirrors of that greater light. The notion of kōan as accepting one's lot, therefore, ultimately means accepting mortality.

V

NON-DUAL RELIGION?

Many contemporary Buddhists, and followers of other spiritualities too, think that what is needed is to go beyond duality and dwell in a non-dual state or attitude. Dōgen does not deny this, but he rejects the implicit exclusiveness of it. His non-duality manifests *as* duality, not in a separation from it.

Actual life goes on in the domains of yin and yang. The non-dual, in Dōgen's scheme, is the Buddha Dao. The term non-dual has a more static and exclusive ring to it than the notion of Dao. Dao is inclusive and actively functioning. Its functioning *is* yin and yang, dark and light, death and birth. So being in the non-dual Dao means being in the duality of being yin and being yang by turns. While many commentators emphasize that yin and yang are non-dual, Dōgen emphasizes that the non-dual is yin and yang. Whether you are enlightened or not, flowers still fall.

Thus, Dōgen's non-duality encompasses duality and does so in a robust and vigorous way. It is not a matter of excluding duality, but of recognizing that every occurrence of supposedly dualistic phenomena is an instance of the Dao functioning, just as every individual wave or current is an instance of the ocean functioning. In this way, Dōgen is at ease with separation, seeing it as part of a dialectical process. Indeed, separation, beginning with the death of his parents, and continuing with those of Myōzen and Rujing, was the indelible watermark of Dōgen's life experience.

However, life goes on. Whether it is leading a holy rite, or washing the steps to the temple, or going to the market to buy mushrooms, or talking to a foreigner on a boat, the principle is the same. The practitioner does not need more. Unpretentious conduct is, in principle, open to anybody, no matter what karmic history one may have. Playing one's proper part is the essential meaning of Dōgen's use of the term kōan. So it is not that Dōgen wants to abolish the mundane in favour of the sacred, or the dual in favour of the non-dual.

The mundane is yin-yang, but as yin or yang it has its rightful place within the sacred, which is the Dao. The oneness lies not in the one displacing multiplicity, not in yin-yang giving way to Dao, but in the recognition that there is no Dao without yin and yang, no oneness that is not a multiplicity.

In one sense, what Dōgen is advancing is a collective form of enlightenment, a utopian vision, yet for this to function, all individual elements need to play their separate parts. The wholeness is constituted by elements functioning together. If the sun is yang and the moon is yin, then Dao is the functioning universe within which sun and moon each has its allotted place. There is no point in the sun trying to be the whole, and the same goes for the moon. When one plays one's own allotted part, then one can appreciate the other and the whole in all their glory, whereas when one is blind to or in rebellion against one's allotment, one feels out of sorts no matter what.

V.1 BUDDHISM AS A RELIGION

All of this bears on the question of whether Buddhism is a religion or not and whether, as a Buddhist, one should perform religious acts and rituals. Does one need religious consciousness to be on the Buddhist path and, if so, what is the function of religious consciousness in Buddhism? If not, what sort of consciousness could one have and still be Buddhist? For Confucius, the rites were all-important. Many modern people have lost touch with what ritual is about. Where does Dōgen stand?

If you spend time in a Zen temple, whether in Kyoto or San Francisco, you will encounter a lot of ritual and a plethora of religious symbolism. There is no doubt that Dōgen not only performed such rituals but that he made ritual into a ruling element in the life of his community and thought it vitally important.

The most superficial acquaintance with Buddhism will reveal to any observer that Buddhism sets up a multitude of dualities based on religious consciousness, some of which are alluded to in the very first line of *Genjō Kōan*. These include saṃsāra and nirvāṇa, deluded and enlightened, the householder life and the homeless life, the world and the monastery, the laity and people in robes, disciples and gurus, and so on. Not only are there many such religious dichotomies, there are also many systems of gradations and steps between – stages on the path to enlightenment, stages of the bodhisattva life, levels of kōans and realizations, and so on. Quite clearly, Durkheim would have had classified Buddhism as a religion.

However, despite this compelling empirical evidence, there are many people who claim that Buddhism is not a religion and the philosophical basis for this claim is an assertion that Buddhism, despite all superficial appearance, is really about non-duality. The essence of the matter, it is claimed, is to realize non-duality, in one way or another. Whether this means the oneness of subject and object, the equality of beings and Buddhas, or the assertion that saṃsāra is nirvāṇa, does not affect the basic principle here.

The same issue comes up in one form or another in most religions. In Hinduism, the only ultimate reality is Brahma, within whom there is no duality. However, it would make something of a nonsense of language to say that Hinduism is not a religion. So if the argument from non-duality holds, then all religions are not religions and we shall have to reinvent our language.

Many people see the first two lines of *Genjō Kōan* as contrasting duality (line 1) with non-duality (line 2). Line 1 is then the deluded state and line 2 is the enlightened one. However, there are problems with this interpretation, one being that line 1 does represent the way that actual Buddhas do teach the Dharma, another being how Buddhism invariably manifests in the world.

In Dōgen the Buddha Dao is, in a sense, non-dual, but only in the sense that it accommodates, includes and manifests as all dualities and pluralities. It is not that twoness or multiplicity is to be discarded in favour of oneness, because from the one ceaselessly emerges the two, and from the two, multiplicity. So these three concepts, yin, yang and Dao, suggest a view in which duality and non-duality are simply two different ways of seeing the same thing. Non-duality is no more fundamental than duality or multiplicity. Just as every multiplicity can be part of a greater whole, so every supposedly singular whole breaks down into a set of plural elements. These elements then interact and interrelate and Dōgen is primarily occupied with the question of the right mode of such relating.

Furthermore, this is a form of religious consciousness in the Durkheimian sense because the Buddha Dao remains the holy supra-mundane element. Thus Dōgen's philosophy is religious, and beautifully encompasses both the sacred and the mundane.

There is a vast literature about Buddha Nature, and this is quite often interpreted as a kind of soul or self-actualizing function within the person. Dōgen does not understand it that way. Buddha Nature is other. It is not self. It resides in the myriad Dharmas that advert to the myriad Buddhas, but it is not, never was, and cannot be a personal attribute that one could possess in any sense. This otherness of Dōgen's is a religious orientation. The Buddha Dao may appear to us at the time of genjō, and we may revere it, but we cannot appropriate it or reduce it to a mundane category without losing it.

In a certain way the whole of Dōgen's writing is about Buddha Nature, but in Dōgen's view of the subject, Buddha Nature cannot be considered as a personal possession. It does not belong to one's body or to one's mind. It only appears when body and mind fall away. In Dōgen, Buddha Nature is closer to the Chinese idea of Dao than it is to the European idea of the soul. It belongs to the universe, rather than the individual. So the Buddha Dao is much more like God than like the soul, but, unlike most conceptions of God, the Dao is manifest as yin-yang functioning everywhere.

I think it is important for us to try to adopt the mentality of Dōgen and people of his time. What is at stake here is salvation, not simply getting the right answer to an intellectual puzzle. When we have the right eye and, thus, do the right thing, devils do not see us, karma is not created, and salvation is accomplished. One is no longer bound to the wheel of retribution for eternity. It is, perhaps, difficult for people educated in modern times to realize how strong the fear of hell or some equivalent destiny was for medieval people.

V.2 PROFOUND RELIGIOUS EXPERIENCE

The term non-duality seems to deny dichotomies, yet the very fact that the word is constituted as a rejection of another state – duality – means that it is inherently, itself, part of such a dichotomy. Non-duality is defined as not being duality. So this duality asserts that there are no dualities, and this non-duality is made of a duality. It is rather like the question of whether the assertion "This statement is untrue" is true or not – if it is, it is not, but if it is not, then it is. If it asserts anything, then it is the impossibility of flawless rationality.

The dualism between non-dualism and ordinary life comes out in a real and important aspect of religious life in the matter of profound religious experience. Buddhism gives considerable prominence to cathartic, life-changing, sudden experiences. These may be called *kensho* or satori, realization or enlightenment. Reflecting upon such experiences, those who have had them often describe them in what could be called non-dualistic language. They say such things as "I was one with the universe" or "There was a profound equality between things" or "I was immersed in a radiance that encompassed everything." These, then, are glimpses of the holy and the holy shows up as non-dual. However, Dōgen points out that even after satori we hate to see blossoms fall.

One may experience such mystical states, and if they are genuine they are apodictic, leaving an indelible mark upon the person, but one cannot stay in that state indefinitely. One has to return to the humdrum reality of 'cutting wood and fetching water' or, nowadays, even more stressful complications. So, in this case, experiencing the non-dual mystical state brings home very forcefully the duality between that state and the rest of life. Yet the holy life does not stop when the vision fades. It goes on. If, however, it goes on with this contrast (between the holy, as so powerfully experienced, and the mundane, as so evidently apparent in daily life) alive in the mind of the practitioner, then what has happened is that the experience of the non-dual has greatly strengthened the duality of religious consciousness. This paradox is inescapable.

When we think of this issue in linear terms – how to get from delusion to enlightenment – this problem seems insoluble, but with Dōgen's dialectical approach, it is just what one would expect. Opposites are not intended ever to eliminate one another. Rather, they stimulate one another and thus bring the mountains and seas to life.

This reciprocal relationship between duality and non-duality, where experience of one sets up the other, and vice versa, fits easily into Dōgen's idea of the Buddha Dao. It also explains many of the apparent contradictions that appear to the reader, who is implicitly trying to fit Dōgen into a linear model. For Dōgen, it is not that one state should supersede the other permanently, whether the two states in question be delusion and enlightenment, duality and non-duality, etc. The two states need each other and circulate endlessly, and that very combination of circulation and complementarity is itself the manifestation of the Buddha Dao.

For Dōgen, "delusion and enlightenment retain their places".[1] Call this duality if you like, or call it non-duality if you prefer, but do not fall into a facile conclusion. Here everything is in its place, has a part to play, and cannot play it on its own, yet must necessarily do so in order to join in. The danger of duality is that one wants to be the leader of the dance. The danger of non-duality is that one never takes one's partner's hand to walk out onto the floor. All people need to play their part and that is enough.

1 *Eihei Kōroku* 4. See Leighton and Okumura 2004: 286.

VI

DID DŌGEN CHANGE HIS MIND?

One of the hottest topics in Dōgen studies in recent years has been the question of whether or not he changed his mind about important issues in the last few years of his life. In 1247–8 Dōgen made an extended visit of some months to Kamakura, the effective centre of power in Japan at that time. After his return to Echizen he continued to write, but there is a distinct change in tone and content. Where previously he relied heavily upon Chinese Zen materials, he now starts to make much greater use of Indian Buddhist texts, and when he does use Chinese material it tends to be Tien Tai rather than Zen. Also, the message appears to be different. What he is now writing is much closer to orthodox traditional Buddhism. He writes about taking refuge, keeping precepts, about the thirty-seven doctrines and so on. Furthermore, there is also evidence in the form of a postscript to Dōgen's last piece of writing, added by his disciple and editor Koun Ejō, to the effect that it had been Dōgen's intention to revise all of his earlier writings and eventually publish the whole as a one hundred-chapter book. Dōgen died before this project could be accomplished. The question remains, however, of how and why he wanted to revise his earlier work.

The relevance of all this to *Genjō Kōan* is that *Genjō Kōan* was one of Dōgen's first writings and it is one that he did revise. However, it is believed that the revisions were slight. It therefore does appear that, at least as far as this text is concerned, Dōgen did not change his mind.

Some writers believe that the post-Kamakura writings represent Dōgen's final and most important statements and that all of the rest should be treated as provisional. Some think that the earlier writings are the definitive Dōgen and the later writings are an afterthought. Some think that the difference is major and revolutionary, and others that it is not that significant.

I have a view on the matter, but it is, necessarily, only my view and I cannot really claim more evidence for it than the various other scholars in this debate can for their respective positions. I am, however, persuaded, by the evidence of his consistent adherence to the ideas expressed in *Genjō Kōan* and of his continuing reference to the Lotus Sūtra as supreme among Buddha's teachings, that Dōgen did not fundamentally change his views. I agree that he changed his style and the content that he presented. Why the one and not the other?

It may be a matter of positioning his work. One writes in order to communicate, and what actually gets communicated depends almost as much upon the reader as on the writer. Going to Kamakura would have exposed Dōgen to current thinking, fashion and opinion. It will have given him important feedback not only about what other Buddhists were saying and doing, but also about how his own work was being received and interpreted. One aspect of this would have been the discovery that he was being classified as a 'one practice' teacher. The full scope of his vision was not generally appreciated.

It is my opinion, therefore, that Dōgen did not change his mind, but he realized that, given what he had presented, he could easily be misunderstood. He, therefore, decided to try to make it as clear as possible that what he was teaching was the fundamental meaning of Buddhadharma, indeed the Buddhadharma of all Dharmas. For this purpose, *Genjō Kōan* remained a good introduction and summary of his position. Now, however, he also needed to write about karma, about venerating the Buddha, about the bodhisattva vow, about the moral life, and about how the whole idea of discovering one's original nature is heretical. None of this, however, is inconsistent with what he said at the very beginning in *Genjō Kōan*. In this new presentation, zazen becomes simply one practice among many.

Now, of course, all of this has some relevance to our reception of Dōgen in modern times. Do we also tend to see him as the promoter of a single method, and overlook the importance that he attached to being grounded in Buddhist fundamentals? Is the appeal of Buddhism in our time substantially based upon a reading of him as a religious philosopher rather than a man of faith? And is this reading achieved by concentrating on a small selection of his works, ignoring his later writings, and misinterpretating *Genjō Kōan* in various ways? Sometimes I think it may be. Dōgen might have been quite right to be worried about how he was going to be understood by future generations.

VII

COMPARISONS

VII.1 DŌGEN AND HŌNEN

At the beginning of this study I suggested Saigyō and Hōnen as landmark figures by which to gain some perspective upon Dōgen, his times, and his mission. This subject is worth another book, but within the scope of this commentary upon a single essay of Dōgen, some brief comparison helps to throw light on the issues of the day at the time Dōgen was writing and also gives a perspective upon the spiritual meaning that the essay advances. We should now be in a position to make some assessment of their similarities and differences.

Dōgen and Hōnen are the two most seminal religious writers of their time. The religious orders that they brought into being still thrive. Hōnen instituted a religious revolution with his idea, drawn from the Chinese teacher Shandao, that even the most sinful person could be acceptable to Amitābha Buddha. Dōgen, in *Genjō Kōan*, asserts that even the smallest dewdrop can reflect the whole moon and firmament and, further, that the lower the dewdrop is in relation to the moon, the deeper the reflection can be.

It is not difficult to see a close similarity between these ideas. The schools of Buddhism that have derived from these two geniuses have some distinct differences, but, as is so often the case, the similarity between the two sages is much greater than that between their respective sets of disciples. In the modern world, many people prefer Dōgen because he is more intellectual in his mode of presentation and because the Sōtō approach attributed to him is presented as self-power, which can, at least initially, be accommodated within a secular mentality. In their own time, most preferred Hōnen because he had the common touch and, although vastly erudite, spoke the common language. Dōgen, as the monk who went to China, was, perhaps, seen as preaching from on high, whereas Hōnen, who never went to China, came across as quintessentially Japanese. Many of Dōgen's Dharma discourses take the form of stories about repartee between past masters, to which he adds what he himself would say if asked the same question. This can easily seem arrogant. However, beneath the superficial appearances and modes of presentation, both were deeply compassionate and genuinely humble men.

We can summarize some of the points of similarity and contrast. Dōgen and Hōnen were both Buddhist monks who lived their whole adult lives within the framework of the Buddhist precepts. Clearly each valued this moral framework highly, yet neither saw it as sufficient on its own as the ground of religious life. Each has a religious sense: an awareness of something beyond humdrum daily life that receives or enters the self and saves it from itself. Dōgen speaks of a transformation occurring when one is penetrated and pervaded by the Buddha light, and Hōnen speaks of the practitioner being seized by Amitābha, the Buddha of measureless light. For this to happen, in either case, there has to be humility on the part of the practitioner. In the systems of both, contrition plays a significant part in establishing the humility or darkening. Both Hōnen and Dōgen emphasize the importance of rigorous practice, yet each of them integrated practice with daily life. Mundane daily life excludes the Dharma, but when one fully plays one's part, it is precisely within daily life that the Dharma is then found. The practices that they recommended – zazen in the case of Dōgen and *nembutsu* in the case of Hōnen – are different at a practical level, but both are concerned essentially with self-diminution in relation to the Buddha light.

We can see from this comparison that although the language and metaphors used are very different, there is by no means as much difference in the understanding of the fundamentals between these two as appears on the surface.

VII.2 DŌGEN AND SAIGYŌ

We can obtain further useful perspective on Dōgen by making a similar comparison with the poet Saigyō. Dōgen was a religious innovator and, at the time he was active, Hōnen was the forebear best known in this respect. However, Dōgen was also a poet and, in this domain, the antecedent model was Hōnen's contemporary, Saigyō.

Saigyō and Dōgen were both independent Buddhist monks. Saigyō was, perhaps, even more independent than Dōgen in that he seems never to have been strongly identified with one sect, although he clearly did have a great respect for Kūkai and, therefore, a leaning toward Shingon. He spent a good deal of time in retreat on Mount Kōya, but never actually became a Shingon monk.

Saigyō seems to have kept abreast of current affairs more intently than Dōgen did. At least, we have little record that Dōgen did so, but, then, the times of Saigyō were more dramatic with major civil war overrunning the country. Dōgen may, in fact, have made more effort than Saigyō to curry favour with those who wielded power and influence, but such efforts were intermittent and brought scant fruit.

Saigyō had seen more worldly life than Dōgen, since he had been a samurai and part of the 'north-facing guard' of the retired emperor before his ordination. He had clearly had a love-life of some kind, but evidence is contradictory and the details have been lost. Many of his poems reveal him to be a sensitive man who sublimated his passions into a love of beauty. Nonetheless, he also spent much time engaged in challenging ascetic practices.

This mix of tenderness and harshness, appreciation of beauty and also of strict discipline, is characteristic of both men. Both came out of an aristocratic tradition, both rejected the worldly life and its hypocrisies, and both sought to find an answer to the seemingly contradictory currents of grief and delight that flowed through them as a result of their personal experiences of the Buddhist truth of impermanence. Dōgen eventually took his community to the mountains. Saigyō never had a community and went to the mountains alone. Both believed that this kind of *yamabushi* experience was, as we would say, 'good for the soul'.

Saigyō had opened doors for Dōgen, especially in the domain of the permissibility of feelings. Where many believed that the proper course for a Buddhist monk was to renounce all passion by repressing it, by the time Dōgen came along, Saigyō had demonstrated that a Buddhist monk could record his loneliness, grief, longing, sense of desolation, fear of shame, embarrassment, sentimentality, and many other emotions, and still come to be regarded as a saint.

Saigyō was a follower of the idea of *honji suijaku*, according to which Shinto deities were identified with celestial Buddhas. His sense of religion was, therefore, not at all narrow and could accommodate a wide range of influences, uniting them as much for their aesthetic qualities as for any doctrinal similarities. Dōgen is generally portrayed as the founder of a sect, but, as I have shown, this designation is rather misleading and, like Saigyō, he united within his approach to Dharma a much wider range of influences than many realize.

In the rather literal sense of sharing what I have in this book called a code, Saigyō and Dōgen spoke the same language, and the wide extension and currency given to this 'language' by Saigyō certainly helped to pave the way for Dōgen's masterpieces.

In my own view, if we are ever to deeply appreciate the true flower and fruit of Japanese Buddhism, rather than using ideas taken from it as ammunition in what are really Western religious controversies, then we would do well to consider these three sages in particular as representing vitally important perspectives upon a single religious truth.

FINAL WORDS

So, what is Buddhism? Ask the ordinary person in the West today and they are likely to say "meditation"; if, on the other hand, you ask the many people who are in the know, they may well mention the name of Dōgen as a support for this practice. Dōgen was a prime proponent of zazen. However, as we have seen, in *Genjō Kōan* zazen is not mentioned. Nor, indeed, is it mentioned in *Shushōgi*,[1] which, in many ways, now functions as the standard of faith for the Sōtō School of Buddhism of which he is the *de facto* founder. Instead, one finds references to contrition, the moral precepts, charity, tenderness, sympathy and gratitude.

In *Genjō Kōan* the central mirror metaphor brings all these qualities to a single point. The fundamental reference of this metaphor is encounter. In *Genjō Kōan*, it does not matter whether you find the light within yourself or not; it matters whether others find it in you, and they are likely to do so when you see the Dharma in others. Furthermore, genjō occurs in the context of meeting. Kōan here is a manner of meeting. In such a meeting there is a Buddha together with a Buddha.

Genjō Kōan is written for monks and laypeople alike. It tells us that when we put ourselves out we shall be of value to others, not just to the extent of our own skills or accomplishments, but well beyond these, and we shall create the condition in which

1 Kennett 1972: 129–35.

such kōan meeting can occur. This is why the transmission of the light is not a matter of individuals perfecting a practice, but of encounters between masters and disciples – mountains and clouds.

It is commonly thought that one cannot help another to go further than one has got oneself. This is not so. It is the virtue of the moon, not the virtue of the mirror, that matters.

Śākyamuni Buddha had his great enlightenment experience immediately after being cared for in a self-effacing way by the milkmaid Sujata. She too is a hero of the transmission of the Dharma. Learning and accomplishment are fine things, but they are not, in themselves, what are necessary.

What is necessary is that the firewood become ash. From the ash, innumerable new trees may grow, but the ash will probably never be aware of this. Ash becomes ash when firewood is destroyed, not when it is perfected. Ash is ash. Its continuity is with the ash of ages – all the enlightened bodhisattvas who have sprung up from the earth[2] when the conditions needed them to do the Buddha's work, yet who did so without self-conscious awareness that by extinguishing themselves they were doing anything extraordinary or beyond the call of natural duty.

At the end of *Genjō Kōan*, Dōgen hints that there is a kind of heaven or Pure Land for the Zen practitioner, but it is the Chinese Shangri-La where the two rivers meet, a fairy tale land of heaven on earth, but not only this. By a sparkling display of hints and allusions, Dōgen tells us how we may be in order that the ways of heaven and earth coalesce, that the many be one and the one many, the everywhere be here, and here be cosmic.

Genjō Kōan was to have been the first chapter of Dōgen's great work. That work was to have revealed the nature of satori as the realization of the Buddha Dao. While keen to assert the unique importance of the Buddhist experience of satori, and the superiority of the Buddha Dao over that of Confucius or Laozi, Dōgen expounds principles that in effect explain the underlying vision of many spiritual paths and reveals how deeply he had been affected by exposure to the Chinese synthesis of the three religions.

---

2 An image from the Lotus Sūtra.

Within Buddhism, Dōgen unites Hīnayāna and Mahāyāna thought, insisting on the importance of karma and, later in life, writing texts on the thirty-seven fundamental doctrines that bridge this divide. The imagery of *Genjō Kōan* presages this with an image of enlightenment that incorporates the overcoming of self. Dōgen unites self-power and other-power, showing how other-power, symbolized by the moon and the firmament, is reflected in even the tiniest dewdrop, but he still gives the dewdrop an important role. He unites original enlightenment and endless practice by showing how the wind of the Dharma is eternally present, yet how that eternal presence itself demands the rite of practice. He unites esoteric and exoteric by explaining how the sudden appearance of the Dharma light inevitably comes as a mystery while, at the same time, being ubiquitously and undisguisedly present – the moon was always there even before its reflection appeared in the water. He unites the ideas of sudden awakening and gradual cultivation by showing how the mirror effect occurs suddenly as a result of diligent darkening of the self by its unassuming conduct of "the same life, the same practice" (line 67).

Dōgen accepted his lot in China. He did so again in Japan. Along the way he wrote this short treatise and, like an old mirror found buried in a forgotten place, it now reflects the Dharma for us and reminds us to walk lightly upon the earth.

BIBLIOGRAPHY

Abe, Masao 1992. *A Study of Dōgen*, New York: State University of New York Press.

À Kempis, Thomas 1952. *The Imitation of Christ*, L. Sherley-Price (trsl.), Harmondsworth, Middlesex: Penguin Books.

Brazier, David 1997. *The Feeling Buddha*, London: Robinson.

– 2009. *Love and Its Disappointment: The Meaning of Life, Therapy and Art*, Ropley: O Books, J Hunt Publishing.

– 2013. *Not Everything is Impermanent*, Malvern: Woodsmoke Press.

Buber, Martin 1970. *I and Thou*, W. Kaufmann (trsl.), New York: Charles Scribner's Sons.

Chang, Chung-Yuan 1969. *Original Teachings of Ch'an Buddhism*, New York: Pantheon.

Cleary, Thomas 1992. *Rational Zen: The Mind of Dōgen Zenji*, Boston, MA: Shambhala.

De Bary, William Theodore, Donald Keene, George Tanabe, and Varley, Paul 2001. *Sources of Japanese Tradition*, New York: Columbia University Press.

Groner, Paul 2000. *Saichō: The Establishment of the Japanese Tendai School*, Honolulu: University of Hawaii Press.

Heine, Steven 2006. *Did Dōgen Go To China?* Oxford: Oxford University Press.

Hubbard, Jamie and Paul Swanson 1997. *Pruning the Bodhi Tree: The Storm over Critical Buddhism*, Honolulu: University of Hawaii Press.

Ireland, John (trsl.) 1990. *The Udāna: Inspired Utterances of the Buddha*, Kandy, Sri Lanka: Buddhist Publication Society.

Kabat-Zinn, Jon 1996. *Full Catastrophe Living*, London: Piatkus.

Katō, Bunnō, Yoshirō Tamura, and Kōjirō Miyasaki 1975. *The Threefold Lotus Sutra*, Tokyo: Kosei.

Kennett, Jiyu 1972. *Selling Water by the River: A Manual of Zen Training*, New York: Pantheon Books.

Kim, Hee-jin 2004. *Eihei Dōgen: Mystical Realist*. Boston, MA: Wisdom Books.

Kim, Young-ho 1990. *Tao-sheng's Commentary on the Lotus Sūtra*, Albany, NY: State University of New York Press.

LaFleur, William R. 2003. *Awesome Nightfall: The Life, Times and Poetry of Saigyō*, Boston, MA: Wisdom Books.

Leighton, Taigen Daniel and Shohaku Okumura 2004. *Dōgen's Extensive Record*, Somerville, MA: Wisdom Books.

Murdoch, Iris 1963. *The Unicorn*, Harmondsworth: Penguin Books.

Ñāṇamoli and Bodhi 1995. *The Middle Length Discourses of the Buddha*, Boston, MA: Wisdom Books.

Nearman, Hubert and Daizui MacPhillamy 1996. *The Shōbōgenzō or The Treasure House of the Eye of the True Teaching by Great Master Dōgen*, Mount Shasta, CA: Shasta Abbey.

Nishijima, Gudo and Choto Cross 1994. *Master Dogen's Shobogenzo*, 4 vols, Woking: Windbell.

Okumura, Shohaku 2010. *Realizing Genjokoan: The Key to Dogen's Shobogenzo*, Somerville, MA: Wisdom Books.

Payne, Richard Karl (ed.) 1998. *Re-Visioning "Kamakura" Buddhism*, Honolulu: Kuroda.

Reynolds, David 1989. *Flowing Bridges, Quiet Waters: Japanese Psychotherapies, Morita and Naikan*, New York: State University Press.

Shimano, Eido and Charles Vacher 1997. *Dōgen Shōbōgenzō Uji*, Fougères: Encre Marine.

Tanahashi, Kazuaki 2000. *Enlightenment Unfolds: The Essential Teachings of Zen Master Dogen*, Boston, MA: Shambhala.

Tart, Charles 1994. *Living the Mindful Life: A Handbook for Living in the Present Moment*, Boston, MA: Shambhala.

Trungpa, Chogyam 1974. *Cutting Through Spiritual Materialism*, Boston MA: Shambhala.

Watson, Burton 1991. *Saigyō: Poems of a Mountain Home*, New York: Columbia University Press.

Watson, Gay, Stephen Batchelor, and Guy Claxton (eds) 1999. *The Psychology of Awakening*, London: Rider.

GLOSSARY

Abbreviations

*	Indicates word present in glossary
C	Chinese
GK	*Genjō Kōan*
J	Japanese
P	Pali
S	Sanskrit
T	Tibetan

Amaterasu (J): The sun goddess of Shinto* religion.

Amida (J): Another name for Amitābha*.

Amitābha (S): The Buddha of infinite light. Object of devotion for Pure Land* Buddhists.

Ānanda (S): Disciple and younger cousin of Śākyamuni*, who was the Buddha's close assistant, yet who did not become enlightened until after the Buddha's death. Ānanda's awakening occurred during an encounter with Kāśyapa*.

anātma (S): No self, selfless.

an ri (J): Daily life, daily practice. Also baggage.

ash: In GK, symbolizes the person who is not prone to become inflamed by passion. Ash is immune to fire, but is fertile. See also firewood*.

bardo (T): Literally 'gap'. The period between lives. In a system of belief in rebirth or reincarnation, existence passes through or undergoes lifetimes with gaps between these. Each of these lifetime or gap periods is a bardo. What one experiences during each bardo determines the form of the next one.

birds: In GK, symbolize those who live in emptiness, the sky, *kū**. See also fish*.

Bodhidharma (sixth century): Regarded as the first Zen patriarch in China. Youngest son of the king of southern India and disciple of Buddhist teacher Prajñātārā.

bodhisattva (S): Originally indicated a person on the way to Buddhahood. Later came to mean one who embodies the qualities of spiritual awakening, such as compassion.

Chan (C): Zen*.

chū (J): Middle, middle way.

clouds: In Japanese and Chinese Buddhist imagery, these represent (a) delusions and obscurations, and (b) Buddhist practitioners. See *yuan**.

Confuciansim: One of the three religions* of China following the teachings of Confucius emphasizing social order and propriety.

Critical Buddhism: A group of commentators in Japan in the post-war period, critical of *hongaku** and of social malpractice by Buddhist schools, especially Zen*.

Dao (C): Way. The ultimate 'way' that is prior to the Way of Heaven and the ways of the world. See yin* and yang*.

Daoism: One of the three religions* of China, deriving from the teachings of Laozi*, and emphasizing naturalness and spontaneity.

Dao De Jing (C): Ancient book attributed to Laozi*, foundational to Daoism*.

Daosheng (*c*.360–434): Buddhist monk who wrote an influential commentary upon the Lotus* Sūtra in Neo-Daoist* style.

Daruma Shū: Buddhist school of followers of Nōnin*.

dewdrop: In GK symbolizes the person in whom the moonlight (Dharma) can be reflected. The dewdrop is fragile and transitory but has the capacity to reflect.

Dharma (S): Reality, the true teaching, real things.

Dharmakāya (S): The 'body' of Buddha manifesting as ultimate truth. See Trikāya*.

Dharmarakṣa (*c*.240–*c*.300): Monk who first translated the Lotus* Sūtra into Chinese.

dhātu (S): An underlying reality, essence.

dhātuvāda (S): A doctrine that asserts the existence and importance of an underlying, unifying essence. The Critical Buddhists* regard *hongaku** as a *dhātuvāda*.

duḥkha (S): Affliction.

Echizen (J): Rural area to which Dōgen moved his community in 1243, where he established Eihei-ji*.

eightfold path: Right view, right thought, right speech, right action, right livelihood, right effort, right mindfulness, and right samādhi*. The fourth of the four truths*.

Eihei-ji (J): Head temple of Sōtō* Shū. The monastery established by Dōgen in Echizen.

Eihei Kōroko: A collection of Dōgen's Dharma talks, and major resource for studying his teachings.

Eisai (1141–1215): Founder of Kennin-ji*. Teacher who brought the Rinzai* Zen method to Japan.

Ejō: See Koun Ejō*.
Enryaku-ji (J): The temple on Mount Hiei where Dōgen was ordained. Head temple of Tendai* Buddhism.
fan: A Buddhist teacher often carries a fan that can be used to cover the face, signifying self-effacement.
firewood: In GK, symbolizes the ordinary person who is prone to become inflamed by the passions of life in saṃsāra*. See also ash*.
fish: In GK symbolize ordinary beings immersed in their element, saṃsāra*. See also birds*.
Fo (C): Buddha.
Four truths. Also four noble truths, four truths for noble ones. *Duḥkha**, *Samudaya**, *Nirodha** and *Mārga**. Teaching set out in the first major sermon given by Śākyamuni* after his enlightenment.
fu metsu (J): No death, the deathless, no destruction. See *metsu**.
fu shō (J): No birth, the unborn, no creation. See *shō**.
genjō (J): Appearance, in the sense of what suddenly becomes apparent.
going forth: Buddha practised and advocated leaving the conventional life and 'going forth' into the spiritual life.
grandmotherly mind: The attitude of tender care required of a Buddhist teacher.
Guanyin (C): Bodhisattva* of compassion.
guru (S): Teacher.
Hanshan (C): Hermit, poet, Chan* master of the eighth or ninth century. The name means 'cold mountain'.
Hiei (J): Mountain near to Kyoto. Site of Enryaku-ji* and many other temples.
Hōnen (1133–1212): Founder of Jōdo* Shū. Pure Land* Buddhist teacher who broke the mould of traditional Buddhism by establishing an independent school. Taught other-power* and the practice of *nembutsu**.
hongaku (J): The doctrine of 'original enlightenment', according to which all sentient beings are already enlightened and what is needed is for them to realize this.
honji suijaku (J): The equating of Shinto* deities with Buddhist celestial Buddhas and bodhisattvas*.
Huineng (638–713): Sixth Zen patriarch in China.
Huiyuan (334–417): Buddhist teacher at Mount Lu in China, who established a society for devotion to Amitābha*.
jiriki (J): Self-power*.
Jōdoshin Shū (J): School of Pure Land* Buddhism established on the basis of the teachings of Shinran*.
Jōdo Shū (J): School of Pure Land* Buddhism established by Hōnen*.
Jukai (J): Ten precepts.
Kamakura (J): Period of Japanese history, 1185–1333.
Kāśyapa (S): Disciple of Śākyamuni*, regarded by the Zen* Shū as his immediate successor.
ke (J): Provisional truth.

Keizan Jokin (1268–1325): Successor to Dōgen, often regarded as the second founder of Sōtō* Shū.
Kennin-ji (J): Rinzai Zen temple established by Eisai* as a sub-temple of Enryaku-ji*. Dōgen studied there before going to China and stayed there initially when he returned.
kōan (J). As explained in Part One, we can distinguish the normal use of the term kōan and Dōgen's usage. Normally, kōan refers to a spiritual problem used as a subject for religious reflection, often based on the story of a spiritual ancestor. In Dōgen's use the term means 'keeping to one's lot or part'.
Kōin: The Buddhist teacher at Enryaku-ji* who advised Dōgen to study Zen.
Kōshō-ji (J): A temple established by Dōgen near to Kyoto after he left Kennin-ji*. This is where he wrote GK.
Koun Ejō (1198–1280): Dōgen's leading disciple and editor.
Kōya (J): Mountain in south of Honshu, site of the head temple of Shingon*.
kū (J): Emptiness. A key term in Buddhist metaphysics. The word also means 'sky'.
Kūkai (774–835): Founder of Shingon* Shū.
Kumārajīva (344–413): Monk who translated many Buddhist texts, including the Lotus* Sūtra, into Chinese.
lakṣaṇā (S): A sign that indicates something other than itself, an indicator.
Laozi: Supposed author of the *Dao De Jing*, a book of short verses setting out a philosophy of humility and naturalness that has become the foundation of Daoism*.
Li (C): Originally referred to the sacrificial rites and their proper performance. Later it came to refer to proper performance of life generally, imparting a sense of life as a great ritual in which each plays a part.
Lotus Sūtra: A Mahāyāna Buddhist sūtra often thought to be the most important of all sūtras, and which had a major influence upon Dōgen.
Mahāyāna (S): The Buddhism prevalent in north and east Asia that emphasizes the bodhisattva* ideal.
mappō (J): The Dharma Ending Age. The idea that one lives in an age so remote from the time of Śākyamuni* Buddha that it is impossible to practise Buddhism in the full way indicated in the sūtras*.
mārga (S): Track, especially the 'eightfold path'*.
metsu (J): Death, destruction.
moon: In Japanese poetic symbolism, represents the source of spiritual light, the Dharma.
Myōzen (1184–1225): Successor to Eisai*. Dōgen's teacher at Kennin-ji*. Dōgen accompanied him to China.
nāga (S): Underwater dragon.
Nāgārjuna (first/second century): Eminent Buddhist philosopher and teacher in India.

naikan (J): Inward inspection. A form of self-study, often leading to contrition.
nembutsu (J): The verbal invocation of Amitābha* Buddha. See also refuge*.
Neo-Daoism: A religious philosophy that is an amalgam of Daoism* and Confucianism*.
Nichiren (1222–82): Founder of a school of Buddhism based upon the Lotus* Sūtra.
nirodha (S): Containment, damping down, going out (as a fire).
Nōnin (d.1196): Buddhist teacher who taught natural enlightenment, based on the idea of *hongaku**.
Original Enlightenment: See *hongaku**.
other-power (*tariki*): The idea that we do not have the power to become enlightened by ourselves (either inherently, or because we live in *mappō**) and need the helping grace of a Buddha to save us. See also self-power*.
pāramitā (S): Literally 'other shore'. From the perspective of enlightenment. *Pāramitās* are unconditional qualities.
prajñā (S): Wisdom. Diagnosis.
Pure Land: The paradise land of a Buddha. A domain where the intention of a Buddha prevails. The desired destination of rebirth for many Buddhists.
Pure Land Buddhism. A style of Buddhism focussed upon the invocation of Amitābha* Buddha. See also *nembutsu**, Jōdo*, Jōdoshin*.
refuge: The primary religious act for a Buddhist is to take refuge in the Three Jewels*, especially in the, or a, Buddha.
religious consciousness: The frame of mind in which people recognize some things as holy and others as profane, holy things being those worthy of reverence or worship.
Rinzai Zen (J): a form of Zen Buddhism that emphasizes the use of formal kōan study. See Zen*, kōan*, Sōtō*.
rōshi (J): A Buddhist teacher, especially in Zen*. Literally 'old teacher'. See *shi**.
Rujing: Dōgen's master at Tiantong* Monastery in China.
rūpa (S): Form, appearance, icon.
Saichō (767–822): Founder of Tendai* Shū.
Saigyō (1118–90): independent monk and poet, widely regarded as one of the greatest Japanese poets.
Śākyamuni (S): A name for the historical Buddha who was the sage (*muni*) from the Śākya people.
samādhi (S): Rapture, meditation, concentration. The consummate vision induced by deep religious contemplation.
samatha (S): Calm meditation. Tranquil abiding.
sambhogakāya (S): In the Trikāya* doctrine, the 'body' of Buddha enjoying liberation and appearing in spiritual form. Celestial bodhisattvas*, such as Guanyin*, are *sambhogakāya* Buddhas.

saṃsāra (S): The unending cycle of birth, death and ordinary deluded life.
saṃskāra (S): Mental confection. Elaboration of mental notions.
samudaya (S): Arising, especially passion surging up.
sarva Dharma anātma (S): All Dharma(s) is/are not self. See *anātma**, Dharma*.
satori (J): The experience of enlightenment.
self-power (*jiriki*): The idea that one can attain enlightenment by one's own effort and the realization of one's own potential. See also other-power*.
shaku (J): Trace, especially the enduring sign of enlightenment.
shi (J): Teacher, as in rōshi*.
Shin (J): Jōdoshin* Shū.
Shingon Shū: The tantric school of Buddhism in Japan founded by Kūkai*.
shinjin (J): Faith.
Shinran (1173–1263): Disciple of Hōnen*. Author of works on Pure Land* Buddhism, now regarded as the founding figure of Shin* Buddhism.
Shinto: The Japanese indigenous religion centred upon the sun goddess and other deities.
shō (J): Birth, creation, making.
Shōbōgenzō: Dōgen's master work in which GK was intended to be the first chapter.
Shotoku (574–622): Prince regent who oversaw and encouraged the establishment of Buddhism in Japan. Regarded as a Buddhist saint.
Shū (J): A 'school' of Buddhism, e.g. Sōtō Shū*, Jōdo Shū*.
Sōtō Shū (J): The Sōtō* Zen sect.
Sōtō Zen (J): form of Zen Buddhism that emphasizes silent contemplation. See Zen*, Rinzai*.
spiritual materialism: A term coined by Chogyam Trungpa signifying the tendency to retain worldly modes of thinking and attitudes within spiritual practice.
śraddhā (S): Faith, wholeheartedness.
sui (J): Water*.
sūtra (S): Buddhist scripture.
tariki (J): Other-power*.
Tathāgata (S): Buddha, especially in the sense of one who comes as saviour.
Tendai (J): A school of Buddhism centred upon the Lotus* Sūtra.
Tiantong Monastery: The temple in China where Dōgen practised and was enlightened under the abbot Rujing*.
Three Jewels: Buddha, Dharma and Sangha. The objects of refuge in Buddhism.
three religions of China: Buddhism, Daoism and Confucianism.
transmission: The passing of the Dharma from master to disciple.
Trikāya (S): Buddhist doctrine of the Three Bodies of Buddha: *nirmāṇakāya*, *sambhogakāya** and *Dharmakāya**.
un (J): Cloud*.

unsui (J): Literally 'cloud and water'. A Zen monk.
upāya (S): Skilful means.
Vairocana (S): The primordial Buddha, especially in Shingon* identified with the *Dharmakāya**.
vipassanā (S): Insight meditation.
water: Symbol in Daoism* and in Zen* for the flowing quality of Dao and also the domain of ordinary beings. See *unsui**.
Way: In Chinese thought, the ideas of the Way of Heaven, the Way of the Ancestors, and so on, have great importance. The word for way is Dao*.
wei wu wei (C): Acting without acting. Naturalness.
wind: In GK, symbolizes the influence of the Dharma or the light of the Buddhas, which penetrate everywhere and pervade the world.
wood: See firewood*.
wu wei (C): Unconditioned.
Yakou (J): Friend of Yō Kōshū*, who also showed interest in Dōgen's approach.
yamabushi (J): Mountain ascetics.
yang (C): The masculine, light, creative principle that forms part of the functioning of the Dao*. See yin*.
Yijing (C): Book of divination and wisdom. One of the great Chinese classics.
yin (C): The feminine, dark, receptive principle that forms part of the functioning of the Dao*. See yang*.
Yō Kōshū (J): The layperson to whom Dōgen gave GK.
yuan (C): Flat-topped mountain, head. The second syllable of Dōgen's name in Chinese.
zazen (J): Sitting meditation.
Zen (J): A style of Buddhism. The two main forms in Japan are Sōtō* and Rinzai*.
zendō (J): Meditation hall.

INDEX

INTRODUCTORY NOTE

References such as '178–9' indicate (not necessarily continuous) discussion of a topic across a range of pages. Wherever possible in the case of topics with many references, these have either been divided into sub-topics or only the most significant discussions of the topic are listed. Because the entire work is about 'Zen Buddhism', 'Dōgen', and the '*Genjō Kōan*' the use of these terms and certain others which occur constantly throughout the book as entry points has been minimized. Information will be found under the corresponding detailed topics.

WINDHORSE PUBLICATIONS

Windhorse Publications is a Buddhist charitable company based in the UK. We place great emphasis on producing books of high quality that are accessible and relevant to those interested in Buddhism at whatever level. We are the main publisher of the works of Sangharakshita, the founder of the Triratna Buddhist Order and Community. Our books draw on the whole range of the Buddhist tradition, including translations of traditional texts, commentaries, books that make links with contemporary culture and ways of life, biographies of Buddhists, and works on meditation.

As a not-for-profit enterprise, we ensure that all surplus income is invested in new books and improved production methods, to better communicate Buddhism in the 21st century. We welcome donations to help us continue our work – to find out more, go to windhorsepublications.com.

The Windhorse is a mythical animal that flies over the earth carrying on its back three precious jewels, bringing these invaluable gifts to all humanity: the Buddha (the 'awakened one'), his teaching, and the community of all his followers.

Windhorse Publications
17e Sturton Street
Cambridge
CB1 2SN
UK
info@windhorsepublications.com

Perseus Distribution
210 American Drive
Jackson
TN 38301
USA

Windhorse Books
PO Box 574
Newtown
NSW 2042
Australia

THE TRIRATNA BUDDHIST COMMUNITY

Windhorse Publications is a part of the Triratna Buddhist Community, an international movement with centres in Europe, India, North and South America and Australasia. At these centres, members of the Triratna Buddhist Order offer classes in meditation and Buddhism. Activities of the Triratna Community also include retreat centres, residential spiritual communities, ethical Right Livelihood businesses, and the Karuna Trust, a UK fundraising charity that supports social welfare projects in the slums and villages of India.

Through these and other activities, Triratna is developing a unique approach to Buddhism, not simply as a philosophy and a set of techniques, but as a creatively directed way of life for all people living in the conditions of the modern world.

If you would like more information about Triratna please visit thebuddhistcentre.com or write to:

London Buddhist Centre
51 Roman Road
London E2 0HU
UK

Aryaloka
14 Heartwood Circle
Newmarket
NH 03857
USA

Sydney Buddhist Centre
24 Enmore Road
Sydney
NSW 2042
Australia